Local Heroes in the Global Village

INTERNATIONAL STUDIES IN ENTREPRENEURSHIP

Series Editors:
Zoltan J. Acs
University of Baltimore
Baltimore, Maryland USA

David B. Audretsch
Indiana University
Bloomington, Indiana USA

Other books in the series:
Black, G.
 The Geography of Small Firm Innovation
Tubke, A.
 Success Factors of Corporate Spin-Offs
Corbetta, G., Huse, M., Ravasi, D.
 Crossroads of Entrepreneurship
Hansen, T., Solgaard, H.S.
 New Perspectives in Retailing and Store Patronage Behavior
Davidsson, P.
 Researching Entrepreneurship
Fornahl, D., Audretsch D., Zellner, C.
 The Role of Labour Mobility and Informal Networks for Knowledge Transfer

Local Heroes in the Global Village
Globalization and the New Entrepreneurship Policies

David Audretsch
*Max Planck Institute for Research into Economic Systems, Jena, Germany
and Indiana University, Indiana, USA*

Heike Grimm
*Max Planck Institute for Research into Economic Systems, Jena,
and University of Erfurt, Germany*

Charles W. Wessner
National Academies of Science, Washington D.C., USA

 Springer

Library of Congress Cataloging-in-Publication Data

A C.I.P. Catalogue record for this book is available
from the Library of Congress.

ISBN 0-387-23463-2   e-ISBN 0-387-23475-6   Printed on acid-free paper.

© 2005 Springer Science+Business Media, Inc.
All rights reserved. This work may not be translated or copied in whole or in part without the written permission of the publisher (Springer Science+Business Media, Inc., 233 Spring Street, New York, NY 10013, USA), except for brief excerpts in connection with reviews or scholarly analysis. Use in connection with any form of information storage and retrieval, electronic adaptation, computer software, or by similar or dissimilar methodology now know or hereafter developed is forbidden.
The use in this publication of trade names, trademarks, service marks and similar terms, even if the are not identified as such, is not to be taken as an expression of opinion as to whether or not they are subject to proprietary rights.

Printed in the United States of America.

9 8 7 6 5 4 3 2 1   SPIN 11327851

springeronline.com

TABLE OF CONTENTS

List of Figures	*Page*	vii
List of Tables		ix
List of Contributors		xi
Acknowledgements		xiii

Part One: Globalization and New Entrepreneurship Policies

Chapter 1 Entrepreneurship Policy in Comparative-Historical Perspectives
Heike Grimm and David B. Audretsch — 3

Chapter 2 The Emergence of Entrepreneurship Policy
David B. Audretsch — 21

Part Two: Entrepreneurship Policies in Germany and the U.S.A.

Chapter 3 European Integration and the Challenges for Economic and Research Policy
Dagmar Schipanski — 47

Chapter 4 U.S. Federal Policies for Innovative Start-ups: Lessons in Social Capital Formation and the Role of the Research University
James Turner — 57

Chapter 5 Entrepreneurship and the Innovation Ecosystem Policy Lessons from the United States
Charles W. Wessner — 67

Part Three: Assessment of Entrepreneurship Policies

Chapter 6 Entrepreneurial Behavior in Differing Environments
Friederike Welter — 93

Chapter 7 Entrepreneurship in German Regions and the Policy Dimension - Empirical Evidence from the Regional Entrepreneurship Monitor (REM)
Rolf Sternberg — 113

Chapter 8 Assessment of Entrepreneurship Policies   145
         across Nations and Regions
         Heike Grimm

Part Four: Implications and Recommendations

Chapter 9 The Global Entrepreneurship Monitor: 173
         Implications for Europe
         Paul Reynolds

Index   189

LIST OF FIGURES

2.1	Employment in large firms	Page 28
2.2	Employees in manufacturing in the Stuttgart region	29
5.1	The myth of the linear model of innovation	70
5.2	A non-linear model of innovation	71
5.3	*The valley of death*	75
5.4	Total equity investments into venture backed Companies	76
5.5	Estimated distribution of funding sources for early-stage technology development	78
5.6	How ideas are commercialized: transferring university technology to firms	82
7.1	The REM case study areas	120
7.2	Total Entrepreneurial Activity (TEA) by region, 2003	121
7.3	Perception of start-up opportunities by REM region, 2003	123
7.4	Fear of failure by REM Region, 2003	124
7.5	Assessment of eight entrepreneurial framework conditions by REM Region, 2003	125
7.6	High priority for start-ups among state government and share of nascent entrepreneurs, 2003	130
7.7	High priority for start-ups among local government and share of nascent entrepreneurs, 2003	132
7.8	Regulations/bureaucratic rules and share of nascent entrepreneurs, 2003	133
7.9	Range of public policy programs and share of nascent entrepreneurs, 2003	134
7.10	Quick contacts within consulting services and share of nascent entrepreneurs, 2003	136
9.1	GEM conceptual model	175
9.2	Total Entrepreneurial Activity (TEA) per country	177
9.3	Opportunity-based entrepreneurial activity by country	179
9.4	Necessity-based entrepreneurial activity by country	180

9.5	TEA entities-replication versus market expansion by global type	182
9.6	TEA overall and national economic growth: 2 yr lag	183
9.7	TEA overall and national economic growth: 2 yr lag	184

LIST OF TABLES

2.1	Change in employment figures in Western Germany and at foreign subsidiaries (1991-1995, in thousands)	Page 28
2.2	Illustrations of entrepreneurship policies	36
5.1	Precedents for public role in commercialization of science in the U.S.	69
5.2	Policy incentives for local heroes	77
5.3	Contributions of SBIR concept	80
7.1	Correlations between the single statements of political framework conditions and entrepreneurial activity, 2003	137
7.2	Correlations between eight entrepreneurial framework conditions (indices) and entrepreneurial activity, 2003	139
8.1	GEM ranking "entrepreneurial framework conditions" (2001)	151
8.2	What kind of information do you offer? We provide information about...	155
8.3	What kind of counseling do you offer?	155
8.4	Are federal programs of high importance to entrepreneurs?	156
8.5	Are state programs of high importance to entrepreneurs?	157
8.6	Are regional programs of high importance to entrepreneurs?	157
8.7	Are municipal programs of high importance to entrepreneurs (a)?	158
8.8	Are municipal programs of high importance to entrepreneurs (b)?	158
8.9	Diversity of public financial assistance programs for start-ups across regions	162
8.10	Is the number of public assistance programs for start-ups adequate with regard to the demand in your region?	164
8.11	Do public assistance programs play an important role for start-ups within your regions?	165

LIST OF CONTRIBUTORS

David B. Audretsch, *Max Planck Institute for Research into Economic Systems, Jena, Centre for Economic Policy Research (CEPR), and Indiana University, U.S.A.*

Heike Grimm, *Max Planck Institute for Research into Economic Systems, Jena, and The University of Erfurt, Germany*

Paul Reynolds, *Florida International University, U.S.A.*

Dagmar Schipanski, *President of the Parliament of the Free State of Thuringia, Germany*

Rolf Sternberg, *University of Cologne, Germany*

James Turner, *House Committee on Science, U.S. Congress, U.S.A.*

Friederike Welter, *Rheinisch-Westfälisches Institut für Wirtschaftsforschung (RWI), Essen, and Jönköping International Business School (JIBS), Sweden*

Charles W. Wessner, *The National Academies, U.S.A.*

ACKNOWLEDGMENTS

This project originated in a conference sponsored by the Federal German Ministry of Economics and Labor and the Federal German Ministry of Education and Research, which was held in Erfurt on September 4, 2003. The volume brings together the conference contributions of leading academics and policy advisors from the United States of America and Europe. While the transatlantic conference on new entrepreneurship policies was held in Germany and was organized by The University of Erfurt, the program benefited from the co-operation with the Indiana University and the presence of U.S. Congressional and National Academies' staff familiar with policy-making at the senior levels of the U.S. government. We are grateful for the support provided by The U.S. National Academies, as well as the funding bodies.

PART ONE

GLOBALIZATION AND NEW ENTREPRENEURSHIP POLICIES

Chapter 1:

ENTREPRENEURSHIP POLICY IN COMPARATIVE-HISTORICAL TRANSATLANTIC PERSPECTIVES

Heike Grimm
Max Planck Institute for Research into Economic Systems, Jena, and The University of Erfurt

David B. Audretsch
Max Planck Institute for Research into Economic Systems, Jena, Centre for Economic Policy Research (CEPR), and Indiana University

1. INTRODUCTION

Public policies continue to be important determinants of economic growth so long as institutions and policy-makers interfere in order to shape the market economy. But what are "smart policies" designed for the promotion of an "entrepreneurial economy"?

While traditional econometric theories and models assert that economic growth originated from companies, labor, capital, technology or natural resources, the key resource today is said to be people; above all, "creative" people (Florida 2003; Audretsch and Thurik 2001). Economic growth and the competitiveness of regions and nations are strongly interrelated with the ability of policy-makers to attract, cultivate and mobilize "creative people".[1] Therefore, new policies need to be developed and traditional policy approaches need to be re-defined for the "strategic management of places" (Audretsch 2003: 20). The focus of public policy for the promotion of regions and nations has changed. The key dimension for policy-makers is now to understand how to attract a substantial mass of creative, entrepreneurial people. The role of "smart policies" for attracting people with entrepreneurial and innovative potential cannot be underestimated, particularly in highly developed, knowledge-based countries, such as the United States of America and Germany.

Furthermore, the locus of policies for the promotion of regions and nations has changed. The federal government traditionally designed and implemented policy instruments. However, during the last few decades all levels of government at the federal, regional and municipal level have become key players in the promotion of the "entrepreneurial economy" (Gilbert, Audretsch and McDougall 2004). In Chapter 2 of this volume, Audretsch demonstrates that the re-emergence of entrepreneurship and the shift from a market economy to an entrepreneurial economy accelerated due to an increased globalization and has lead to the development of new entrepreneurship policies implemented at all levels of government. Change and innovation became the drivers of the so-called entrepreneurial economy (in contrast to the traditional "market economy") which is, among others, characterized as having a high degree of turbulence and diversity (Audretsch and Thurik 2004). This change from the market to the entrepreneurial economy had a deep impact on the policymaking process: Policy-makers in developed countries face the challenge of having to develop new entrepreneurship policies to ensure economic growth within their regions and nations.

Nonetheless, there seems to be a vacuum of innovative policies which successfully promote an "entrepreneurial society" in the early years of the 21st century. More importantly, there is no comprehensive approach yet for how to define and measure policies which contribute to the attractiveness of places. The objectives of entrepreneurship policies implemented by policy-makers are multifaceted and for the most part, unspecified. They therefore cannot be evaluated (Storey 2003). This deficit is important because locations do not just become attractive *per se*; rather, public policies greatly contribute to turn them into attractive ones. The question is which ones are really appropriate for facing the challenges of an "entrepreneurial" society?

Despite great tribute having been paid to the role of human capital in economic growth (for example, Mathur 1999; Putnam 2000; Simon 1999), sufficient attention has not yet been given to the entrepreneurship policies implemented by people and institutions in order to attract entrepreneurial, and "creative" people. As Wennekers and Thurik point out "…both culture and the institutional framework are important conditions which co-determine the amount of entrepreneurship in an economy and the way in which entrepreneurs operate in practice" (Wennekers and Thurik 1999). Both researchers take into consideration the cultural and institutional bases of entrepreneurship which can not as easily be transferred into new entrepreneurship policy strategies by policy-makers and researchers alike as the economic bases, mainly due to a lack of measurability.

In the following chapter, we aim to clarify why a U.S.-German comparison of new entrepreneurship policies is of special interest to researchers and policy-makers alike. In a nutshell, the deep and enduring changes of the last decades are not technological but social and cultural. A U.S.-German comparison is, therefore, of special interest because both countries may, on the one hand, be described as developed, highly industrialized, and relatively wealthy. On the other hand, different cultural and ethical values exist, as do different institutional roots. If entrepreneurial people require a positive and inspiring social and economic environment, and if "smart", new entrepreneurship policies are needed to generate economic growth it is important to re-consider which cultural, institutional and ethical values are existent in both countries and whether they have a strong influence on the entrepreneurial environment. Furthermore, the roots and characteristics of the German and American political economies need to be reviewed in order to provide a better understanding of opportunities and problems to enable the development and implementation of new entrepreneurship policies in both nations.

2. CONTENTS OF THIS VOLUME

With a better understanding of the complexity and variety of existing entrepreneurship policies in the U.S.A. and Germany, the reader of this book will be able to formulate best practice, hands-on strategies, which aim to promote nations and regions in an "entrepreneurial economy".

The purpose of this book is to introduce public policies for the promotion of entrepreneurship on a comparative, primarily German-American level. It contributes to the debate on what role public policies play in stimulating national and regional economic growth. For several years now, scientific research has provided us with empirical data worldwide about the significant relationship between entrepreneurship and regional and national economic development. Moreover, the process of globalization continues and challenges us to assess and evaluate, on a global scale, existing public and economic policies for start-ups, in order to develop and re-design innovative policies to enable entrepreneurs to succeed at a local level.

This project started with a conference on September 4, 2003, organized by its editors in Erfurt, the capital of the Free State of Thuringia, in Germany. The conference aimed to strengthen networks and contacts between German and American enterprises, professionals and researchers, and to provide a platform for initiating future projects and cooperation. This publication represents the results of the conference's proceedings and brings together the views and findings of policy-makers and researchers alike. It aims to provide, not only scientific evidence of how to optimally promote regions and nations in two highly developed countries, but also insights from policy-makers who are responsible for developing and implementing "smart" entrepreneurship policies. One of the major goals of the transatlantic conference (organized in order to achieve a better understanding of what has been and what needs to be done from a policymaking perspective to improve the conditions for "local heroes" (i.e. entrepreneurial and innovative people) in a "global village"), was to facilitate a vivid and fruitful exchange of thoughts, results and findings from practitioners as well as researchers.

With this book, the editors provide both a cross-national and cross-regional comparison which is specifically focused on entrepreneurship policies. It is not our aim to compare the advantages and disadvantages of the policy schemes "made in Germany" and "made in the U.S.A" in some kind of black and white pattern, but rather to identify differences and similarities and to discover new and innovative ideas and entrepreneurship policies on both sides of the Atlantic. We do not believe that there is a one-size-fits-all strategy, which policy-makers may apply universally. Each place has to assess which policies, programs and ideas developed in this book contribute in an optimal way to innovative economic growth. As Richard Florida points out, "...we still lack a good working model of the economic and social system that is carrying us into the Creative Age" (Florida 2002:23). The aim of this book is to contribute to the development of just such a comprehensive working model.

In this first chapter, Heike Grimm and David B. Audretsch provide an introduction to the book by reviewing the cultural and institutional roots of the political economies of Germany and the U.S.A. They discuss how cultural and institutional differences may influence the entrepreneurial environment. In the second chapter, David Audretsch refers to globalization and the development of new entrepreneurship policies. In this first part of the edition, we introduce the cross-national approach and the importance of local-global perspectives in assessing new entrepreneurship policies.

In the second part of this book, we introduce the comparison of European versus American policies for the promotion of entrepreneurship and innovative research. In the Chapter 3, Dagmar Schipanski shows that the European integration process has a major influence on future European research and economic policies. She underlines the significance of a joint-European research policy by referring to two specific areas – nanotechnology, as well as aeronautics and space technology. In Chapters 4 and 5, James Turner and Charles Wessner provide an overview of the development of new entrepreneurship policies in the U.S.A. James Turner refers to the importance of federal government support for the entrepreneurial environment. He concentrates on four policy changes that have led to an increase in entrepreneurial activity in the U.S.A. (patent policy, policies related to access to federal laboratories, antitrust policy, and immigration policy) and discusses the changes in, as well as the consequences for, the competitiveness of the U.S.A. over the last 30 years. In Chapter 5, Charles Wessner discusses the innovation-ecosystem-policy lessons from the United States.

The third part of this book provides the reader with the evaluation of entrepreneurship policies in the U.S.A. and Europe with a special focus on Germany. In Chapter 6, Friederike Welter discusses entrepreneurial patterns in differing environments by providing an East vs. West European comparison. Rolf Sternberg presents empirical evidence from the Regional

Entrepreneurship Monitor, in Chapter 7, and discusses the role and importance of entrepreneurship policies in Germany and within different German regions. In Chapter 8, Heike Grimm provides results from a transatlantic qualitative-exploratory study of entrepreneurship policies.

After these assessments of entrepreneurship policies across two nations and several regions, the fourth and final part of this volume discusses future challenges for local heroes and policy-makers with regard to the importance of new entrepreneurship policy. In Chapter 9, Paul Reynolds summarizes the findings from the Global Entrepreneurship Monitor and discusses its implications for Europe.

3. POLITICAL ECONOMIES IN THE U.S.A. AND GERMANY

The similarities between Germany and the United States of America are fairly apparent: both may be described as developed, highly industrialized, relatively wealthy countries with similar but not identical political as well as economic systems, and similar but not identical ethical values (National Academies 2001).

Nevertheless, some striking differences between the U.S.A. and Germany exist with regard to political, social, and economic differences. In particular, economic realities in the U.S.A. differ widely from those in Germany. In the U.S.A., classic economic liberalism, theoretically discussed by its most prominent proponent, Adam Smith, plays a crucial role in American everyday life. The economic policy of the U.S.A. is characterized by the principle of classic economic liberalism which applies a simple regulatory scheme: it requires responsibility and initiative from the individual, market freedom and voluntary restraint by the state. Statutory regulations must not hinder the individual in improving his financial situation. Social welfare may not paralyse his motivation and business activities. The tasks of the government are restricted to taking care of law and order and protecting the society from outside enemies. There is hardly any other country in the world where this message fell on such fertile ground as in the United States of America, although such restrictions on the state in social and economic affairs have diminished in the 20th century.

In Germany, on the other hand, the so-called "*Ordnungspolitik*" (not yet translated into English) promotes the active involvement of the state in economic and market affairs. The "ordoliberal" foundations of the Social Market Economy which characterized Germany's economy in the second half of the 20th century to-date, were developed by the economist Alfred Müller-Armack in 1947 (Müller-Armack 1948). His economic plan refers to an economic and political order which is designed on the basis of the rules of a market economy which is, however, enriched with institutionalized and assured social complements (aimed to limit the negative consequences of a free market economy), and with legislative instruments (aimed to fight economic concentration and the misuse of power (Broyer 1996). This plan is to a great extent based on thoughts and considerations developed at the "Freiburg School" (Eucken 1989; Rieter and Schmolz 1993).

By comparing the different approaches to political economies in the U.S.A. and Germany, a stress ratio is set up in the following between a liberal political economy and an ordoliberal political economy, and the public policies implemented in both countries. On the one hand, this article aims to add to the discussion the extent to which a liberal approach in the political economy bears fruit in a country's entrepreneurial environment. On the other hand, it analyses and questions to what extent *Ordnungspolitik* is useful for a political economy at both federal and regional levels.

This analysis is crucial (while facing disputation, in Germany) in the argument, of whether and (if so) why we face a lack of innovative and entrepreneurial "personal assets" throughout the country? This relates to people with exceptional abilities and skills, and specialized know-how, acquired through training, further education and experience, who are aiming to start up a business. Germans are reluctant to accept the notion that a country, rich in Nobel Prize winners and inventors, can suddenly no longer produce innovative individuals. It is a matter of fact that there is no dearth of innovative "Germans", but there is a shortage of creative minds that actually work in Germany. Recent Nobel Prize winners live and work in the United States. Wolfgang Ketterle, for example, who won the Nobel Prize for Physics in 2001, and Günther Blobel, the 1999 Nobel Prize winner for Medicine: Would they have won the prize, had they had actually worked in Germany?

4. WHERE DOES "INNOVATION" COME FROM?

A great number of theories and empirical evidence points to the positive effects of innovativeness on economic growth, and employment rates. In these times of rapid technological advancement, investing in people is not only a decisive factor in terms of economic growth, but also a pivotal tool for strengthening the social fabric of our society. State and privately-owned businesses which "invest in people" increase their ability to face future challenges. At the same time, this correlation is underestimated with respect to the significance it has for the promotion of technological advancement and the bolstering of societal ties by both, the business and public sectors.

Workers and employees who are well equipped with inventiveness prove to be an immediate source of productivity and innovation. But what exactly is "innovation" and where precisely does it come from? Joseph Schumpeter formulated a classic definition, which still serves today as a basic definition of the word: Innovation is the planning, generation and realization of new products, product quality, manufacturing processes, new methods of organization and management, as well as the development of new markets to buy and sell goods. In addition, Schumpeter stresses that innovation is generated by people.

Schumpeter's concept of the word "innovation" is embedded in a theory of economic development that defines "economic change" as an evolutionary and irreversible change and perpetual "process of creative deconstruction" initiated by creative people (Schumpeter 1952: 121). In this context, the entrepreneur functions as the conveyor and promoter of the processes of change. He replaces the old-fashioned, obsolete manufacturing structures through "dynamic and new combinations". In this manner he pushes development forward. The so affected "creative deconstruction" is an essential part of the innovative process. The "economic revolutionary" performs a pioneering act and overcomes the period of stagnation (Schumpeter 1952: 130). According to Schumpeter, entrepreneurs are not only "pioneers" on a professionally independent basis, but are also leading managers or "vehicles for the reorganization of economic structures" (Schumpeter 1952: 28; see also Schumpeter 1946: 136/137). These people will try to stand out from the existing and established system in order to develop markets for new ideas, structures and processes.

Schumpeter considers the entrepreneurial personality to be an exceptional phenomenon, full of pioneering spirit, and that he/she is a key player in the "entrepreneurial economy" who does not weigh costs against benefits. The urge for creative and innovative development is not only determined by the individual's personal goals such as the motivation to achieve and to improve one's reputation, but also through the micro- and macro-social environment. The social and political drive to acquiring professionally independent thinkers, and society's ability to adapt to defeat and failure from entrepreneurial endeavors, belong to the entrepreneurial environment which positively influences innovative pursuits. Whoever thinks economically and entrepreneurially, is taking a large risk. He or she may fail. But, whoever thinks economically and entrepreneurially is also contributing to a "destructive", yet innovative developmental process, which is crucial for the country's economical growth – otherwise, socio-political infrastructure and educational policies would stagnate.

While Schumpeter emphasized innovativeness as a driving force for entrepreneurial, and "destructive" processes, Romer (1986) – another Nobel prize winner – and Lucas (1988 and 1993) and Krugman (1991) emphasize that knowledge has become the vital factor for endogenous economic growth; typically being measured in terms of R&D, human capital and patented inventions. The emergence of knowledge as a key driver for the growth and competitiveness in global markets has fueled the discussion regarding whether large versus small companies would better succeed in a global economy. Large companies do, without any doubt, benefit from globalization in many ways. In the "borderless" world (Ohmae 1995, 1990) the mobility of trade, capital and people has accelerated considerably, and especially large companies profit significantly from having better financial and managerial resources than small and medium-sized enterprises (SMEs). They are better equipped to change location and to set up or close down branches on a global scale. Such flexibility allows larger companies to save labor and manufacturing costs and to break into new markets. But multinationals and large companies do not hold all the advantages in a knowledge-based, global world: Local start-ups and SMEs can profit from globalization if they make maximum use of already existing location factors and, above all, occupy innovative and costly niches. As a matter of fact, SMEs have shown specifically that they can successfully engage in and generate entrepreneurial activity by occupying innovative niches. With the re-emergence of entrepreneurship, small firms, in particular, had good successes due to their flexibility and specialization in a global entrepreneurial economy.

Nonetheless, the discussion "small versus large" turned out to be misleading because neither large nor small firms turned out to be at a disadvantage in a knowledge-based global world. Despite the competition, new (as opposed to old) firms became vital due to the fact that entrepreneurship emerged as the engine of economic and social development. Besides knowledge, as a production factor, entrepreneurial capital turned out to be a key prerequisite for competitive advantage whereas the mere existence of knowledge itself did not guarantee this advantage - but rather, the spill-over of knowledge and R&D (Audretsch and Keilbach 2003).

5. HISTORICAL REASONS FOR THE "BRAIN DRAIN" TO AMERICA

America's attraction for entrepreneurs is based on the extraordinary micro- and macro-social conditions for entrepreneurial activity. American society is, therefore, very proud of its "short" history. The country's heritage speaks mainly of exceptional people with a pioneering, expansionistic and innovative drive.

The authors are aware of the problem that only one aspect (and a positive aspect at that) of the American economy can be looked at in this article. The existing problems of the American economic and social system have, of course, not eluded our attention, but we believe that by tracing the history of the innovative elite in America, we can help Germany orient itself in its own search for creative and entrepreneurial minds.

The early American republic had already legitimized itself through its uniqueness and singularity. The founding of the United States of America was truly original. For the founding fathers of the U.S.A, this was the physical embodiment of enlightened thinking. This spiritual notion of life forms the basis of the "American Way of Life" and Will Herberg has described this as "America's Civil Religion". He writes: "I should include under this head, first, belief in a Supreme Being, in which Americans are virtually unanimous, proportionately far ahead of any other nation in the Western world. Then I should mention idealism and moralism: for Americans, every serious national effort is a "crusade" and every serious national position a high moral issue. ... The basic ethos of America's civil religion is quite familiar: the American way is dynamic; optimistic; pragmatic; individualistic; egalitarian, in the sense of feeling uneasy at any overtly manifested mark of the inequalities endemic in our society as in every other society ...." (Herberg 1990: 78/79).

The discussion surrounding America's allure to innovative, freedom-loving people is as old as the United States of America itself. In the beginning, the search was primarily for religious freedom. Strongly pious individuals seeking freedom of worship left Europe at the beginning of the 17th century in order to try their luck in the "New World". One may identify this as the first European "brain drain" in favor of America's – a pattern which would repeat itself over the course of centuries to come. The causes for this "brain drain" and the emigration of creative, intelligent minds have changed, but the attractiveness of the United States of America and the American myth has remained constant.

In the 17th century, the search for religious freedom and prosperity led the first European immigrants, mainly Puritans, to America. The Puritans who sailed to America in 1620 aboard the *Mayflower* and landed at Cape Cod (in present day, Massachusetts) were among the founding fathers of American society and left a strong and unique impression on the American identity in terms of religion and economics. While still in England, these "pilgrims" insisted on radical reforms within the Anglican faith, and denounced the High Church of England. Having come into conflict with the English church, the Puritans also quarreled with the English monarchy, as the Anglican Church was a major part of the English state. Beginning in 1604, the majority of Puritans allied themselves with parliamentary opposition against the king, although a minority of them actually emigrated.

America owes its earliest economic development to these emigrants. Piousness, diligence, thrift, commercial judiciousness and a love for independence affected the lives of the Puritans and drove them towards economic success. Religious-based asceticism combined with hard work prepared the fertile ground for the America which exists today – ambitious, oriented towards success and full of pioneering spirit.

For a long time, the Christian faith of the highly religious European immigrants proved to be the decisive factor in the rapid economic development of America. Max Weber (1864 – 1940) attracted attention with his essays on the "Protestant Ethic" which appeared between 1904 and 1905. He claims that a close connection exists between confession (referring mainly to the Protestant denomination), capitalist spirit and economic growth and expansion. The "capitalist spirit" involves the "gaining of money upon money, purely for the purpose of self-advancement" (Weber 1905). The "pleasure" the individual receives when enriching himself, according to Weber, is fed mainly by religious fervor. Weber argues that within the world view of the Protestant denominations, devotion to God is reflected through one's economic and personal success over their lifetime and that hard work during one's life will be rewarded in the after-life.

Max Weber places the Calvinist belief, that the fate of humans is predestined, at the heart of his argument. God's mercy reveals itself in the economic success of people during their lifetime. Poverty was, therefore, a sign that God's mercy was wanting. Poverty was a consequence of either lack of earthly enthusiasm or material squandering.

As a result, the Calvinist lifestyle took on certain expectations and customs: hard work, modesty in everyday life and abstinence from worldly pleasures. In his day, the Puritan demonstrated that through his individual economic capacity, he is God's chosen creature.

6. THE CHILDREN OF THE "OLD ECONOMY" AND THE "NEW ECONOMY"

The economic prosperity of America is still a matter of great importance at the beginning of the 21st century. According to the latest surveys, economic prosperity is a vital issue and is regarded as being as important as foreign policy and military success. It is not only Bill Clinton who knew: "It's the economy, stupid!" The American voters greatly value long-lasting, personal prosperity and economic growth. In order to achieve this long-lasting prosperity, innovative and creative people who contribute to the technological advancement of the country are needed. The "American ideology" says that the dream of personal success, paired with economic prosperity, can become a reality. The land of the pioneering spirit offers many promising opportunities for "self-made men" and "self-made women". These opportunities have their roots in modern American history; particularly in the diffusion of religious and economic values, and also in the freedom to strive for these values without being hindered by authorities. Due to the oppression of craftsmen and the tormenting nobility, the old European innovative elite set out for the New World and the promise of freedom and prosperity.

Since the first immigrants from the "Old Europe" landed in the "New World", the lure of the U.S.A for German pioneers, independent workers and entrepreneurs began to take effect. History repeated itself time and time again. The example of Levi Strauss serves to illustrate this point. "Levi Strauss was born in the kingdom of Bavaria in 1829 and came as an adolescent to America in order to try his luck, requiring good sense and lots of energy," wrote the San Francisco newspaper *The Call* in Levi Strauss's obituary in a Sunday edition from September 1902. At the age of 17, young "Loeb" Strauss from Buttenheim, Bavaria, migrated after his father's death to the United States of America. Loeb Strauss belonged to the group of approximately 300.000 Germans who migrated to the United States of America before the First World War. Such an irreversible decision would appear today as a daring undertaking. Leaving everything behind in one's homeland and saying goodbye to family and friends to set out on a week long, trans-Atlantic cruise filled with hardship would certainly bring clear and drastic change in one's life.

The path to success was a rocky one for "Levi" Strauss (he received that name from the American immigration authority). He at first wandered through the streets of New York as a traveling salesman, selling ironware and clothes. With his little and hard-earned money he could only afford very simple accommodations - at a peddler's flophouse for three dollars a month. In his obituary in the newspaper *The Call*, it written: "With an inherent instinct for business opportunities and his early experience in New York where he learned what is important to Americans and lived the American way of life, he saw a broad opportunity for the supply of goods from near and afar in a rapidly growing land."

When Levi Strauss became aware of the gold rush on the west coast, he moved to San Francisco in order to start his own business there. He then undertook his second large journey by ship, sailing around Cape Horn, and reached the "Legendary Street of Gold" in 1852. He designed hard-wearing workpants, "the Pants of Levi's", for the gold prospectors in the area. News about the practical hip-high workpants spread through the goldmines like wildfire. The orders poured in. *The Call* reminds us that, "As a young man with little capital but a good head, determination and optimism, he opened the firm "Levi Strauss & Company", textiles and haberdashery, of which he remained head and primary owner for almost forty-nine years until his death." He made a considerable fortune and established a company with worldwide operations.

Levi was, without doubt, one of the grand pioneers of the "Golden West". In the goldmines of California he had designed an article of clothing that was sold in unbelievably large quantities and one which we could not live without today—the legendary "Jeans". Jeans are an article of clothing which we originally believed could only be an American invention. The designer, however, was actually German.

While the necessity of earning a living for himself was Levi's "mother of invention", necessity alone seldom leads to inventiveness in today's world. In order to be creative one needs to operate in an environment which guarantees freedom and acceptance. For creative minds, Germany appears to offer too little freedom and acceptance. As in past centuries innovative people cannot work unhindered by government authority either in university laboratories or in private businesses. The opportunities for them to become rich, creative and famous are limited (Frankfurter Allgemeine Sonntagszeitung 2004; Germis 2004). Although an appropriate and steady income may seem attractive, it is not a deciding factor in the realization of creative ideas. And it is exactly here where America, mainly due to its unique historical and cultural experiences, has for centuries shown itself to be flexible. If the "American Dream" formerly meant going from "dishwasher to millionaire", it today means going from "garage tinker to billionaire". While the "American Dream" gave the people living in the "Old Economy" the inspiration and power to work hard to be able to nourish their family, people today dream of jobs which are creative and (at the same time) put food on the table. This sort of work may be intellectually less challenging, and it requires different conditions. The freedom to work and think inventively helps the creative spirit to achieve wealth, and the state and society to make technological advances and to grow economically.

There are good reasons for observing more closely the conditions in which creative people start out in the United States of America. There are numerous characteristics inherent in the American economic model which determine its success and allow for a high proportion of new and innovative companies to be founded. These characteristics are economically assessable variables such as low tax rates, low work costs, and little regulation. In addition, American people are willing to realize visions, dreams and ideas and to strive for the apparently unattainable. The courage to take risks and a high degree of personal responsibility is held in high esteem by the American public. One of the most famous pioneers of recent times is the man who founded a multibillion dollar software company in his garage – Bill Gates. Often taken as an example, Bill Gates is the quintessential American phenomenon who would certainly have failed to get started in Germany because of the numerous regulations and bureaucratic obstacles (Siegele 2004). Who could start a business in a German garage without emergency exits or windows, and without coming into conflict with the supervisory board? And even if someone did try, how would his neighbors and colleagues react?

Regulations and ordinances are not merely recent problems with which Germany has suddenly been confronted. These controls may actually represent an aspect of the German "identity" (Leipold 2000: 32). This trait may discourage Germans from setting up businesses with the same engaging attitude as Americans; or from shutting them down, only to open another business up the next day under a different name. In America, this art of doing business carries no real stigma. The entrepreneur is not shackled with enormous debt if he or she fails as though he or she must suffer a "lifesentence" for taking the initial step to run his or her own independent enterprise. It is no wonder that German and European pioneers set out for America to try their luck. Previously, they were inspired by dish-washers who became jeans-designers – today they can be inspired by the freedoms provided for the innovative elite.

The children of the "New Economy" felt especially attracted by these freedoms and the opportunity to embrace them towards the end of the 20th century. Attracted by the soaring "New Economy", many particularly well-trained and highly educated young people migrated from Germany to America. Liliana Nordbakk can be counted as one such pioneer. She founded the company NorCom in 1989 in Palo Alto, Silicon Valley, and serves as a good example. Liliana Nordbakk started an e-business company on the west coast about the time the "New Economy" was at its zenith. Nordbakk recognized early, the potential in founding an e-business company. After the setback in the "New Economy," Liliana Nordbakk experienced the same as most of her competitors—stock rates fell drastically and the future became uncertain. But NorCom—which went public in October 1999 and has been registered as NorCom Information Technology AG since then—knew from the outset that the path would be rocky: "Nothing over here works as it does in Europe. And especially here on the west coast, we are living in a completely different culture", Liliana Nordbakk repeatedly emphasizes.[2] Time will show if the "American Dream" will come true for Liliana Nordbakk. But it really is not that important, since new business fields and opportunities open up to the pioneer almost daily.

7. ECONOMIC CULTURE: "MADE IN EUROPE" AND "MADE IN THE U.S."

The significance of historic and cultural influences comes to the forefront for pioneers and entrepreneurs as soon as they are required to decide where to start-up a business. The peculiarities of the German culture do not seem very attractive under these circumstances: These eccentricities include a tightly woven system of federal regulations and standards, as well as many institutions that control and uphold those standards. The German "*Bundesländer*"[3] are nowadays an inflexible and convenient group of welfare states in stark contrast to the American states. The average citizen in the U.S.A. carries a great deal of responsibility for himself.   America's allure lies in the economic and personal freedom which the country has to offer.

Alexis de Tocqueville identified America's vitality as stemming from the melding of Christian belief and freedom of thought (Tocqueville 1835). The economic policy of the USA was, and still is, influenced by the principles of classic liberalism. The nation's political order is simple. It demands self-responsibility and initiative from the individual, freedom for the market and a self-restricting state. Governmental regulations should not hinder the individual from bettering his material situation. The state's care of the individual should not diminish his entrepreneurial motivation or hinder his entrepreneurial spirit.

The liberal economic order in the U.S.A stems from these historical beginnings. Entrepreneurial initiative has found a great deal of room to develop in the U.S.A. "Think Big" is the motto that inspires people there. Phil Night, also a recent example for entrepreneurial success, stuck a piece of rubber tread onto a tennis shoe, named his company after the Greek goddess of victory, Nike, and summed up the most simple and efficacious business strategy of all in his catchy slogan: "Just do it!"

The U.S.A.'s excitement over product and technological innovation demonstrates an ambition that can be classified as "American". New products are thrown into the market and the quickly replaced by better ones. Research and development is quickly pushed forward. Sixty-five out of the 100 brand articles specified as being the most "valuable" come from America. Forty-one of the 100 companies with the greatest turnover, as ranked by the economic magazine *Fortune*, have their headquarters in the USA.[4]

8. LOCATION BENEFITS OF THE FUTURE

The United States of America has demonstrated proof of its exceptional productivity, in the last decade of the 20th century. After a short period of recession, the American economy recovered surprisingly quickly, beginning with an economic upturn in 1992. Between 1992 and 2000, approximately 5.9 million new small and medium sized businesses were founded. 20 million new jobs were created in America during this period. Locations such as California's Silicon Valley, at one point the hot spot of the computer industry and the "New Economy", experienced competition from other hot spots such as Silicon Alley, a new mainstay of suppliers and producers of information technologies just south of New York City, or from other firms in Austin, Texas, or Atlanta, Georgia. Many Southern states traditionally thought of as the backwaters of the USA, took part in the new race for innovation.

For Richard Florida (Carnegie Mellon University), the secret recipe responsible for the creation of these American hot spots is not today's low costs of doing business or low real-estate prices. "Technology, talent, and tolerance" are, according to his research findings, the magic words which attract the innovative elite to these places (Florida 2003: 249). Creative minds are attracted to technologically innovative places where a great deal of tolerance and acceptance exists for innovative and creative ideas, for different and likeminded people, and for the innovative elite from both America and abroad. The Clinton administration made significant contributions in order to provide the innovative elite with freedom and opportunities. As a result, egalitarian access to the internet was made available, more money was spent on research, development and higher education, and a braver immigration policy was instituted.

Have new entrepreneurship policies been developed much faster in the U.S.A. than in Germany in order to cope with the challenges of a global entrepreneurial society, and if so, why? Among others, this book aims to answer this question.

NOTES

[1] A comprehensive definition and discussion of the term "creativity" with special reference to "creative people" is provided by Florida 2003: 21-43.
[2] Access to this interview online via InformationWeek News, May 2001 (10).
[3] Germany is a federation of 16 states called *"Länder"* (singular *"Land"*) or *"Bundesländer"* (singular *"Bundesland"*, German *federal state*). Each *Land* is represented at the federal level in the *"Bundesrat"*. In the following, we will use the term *federal states* when referring to the German *Bundesländer*.
[4] See www.finfacts.ie/brands2003.htm.

REFERENCES

Audretsch, D. and Keilbach, M. (2003). *Entrepreneurship Capital and Economic Performance*. Center for Economic Policy Research Discussion Paper DP3678, London: CEPR.

Audretsch, D. and Thurik, R. (2001). "Sources of Growth: The Entrepreneurial Versus the Managed Economy." *Industrial and Corporate Change* 10: 267-315.

Audretsch, D. and Thurik, R. (2004). *A Model of the Entrepreneurial Economy, Discussion Papers on Entrepreneurship, Growth and Public Policy*. #1204, Jena: Max Planck Institute for Research into Economic Systems.

Broyer, S. (1996). *The Social Market Economy: Birth of an Economic Style*. Discussion Paper FS I 96 – 318, Berlin: Wissenschaftszentrum Berlin für Sozialforschung.

Eucken, W. (1940). *Grundlagen der Nationalökonomie (1940)*. Springer Verlag: Berlin, 1989 reprint, 9th ed.

Florida, R. (2002). *The Rise of the Creative Class: And how it's Transforming Work, Leisure, Community and Everyday Life*. Cambridge: Basic Books.

Frankfurter Allgemeine Sonntagszeitung (2004). "Brain Drain stoppen – Brain Gain forcieren." *Frankfurter Allgemeine Sonntagszeitung* 15.08.2004 (33): 33.

Germis, C. (2004). "Kampf um Köpfe." *Frankfurter Allgemeine Sonntagszeitung* 15.08.2004 (33): 33.

Gilbert, B.A., Audretsch, D.B. and McDougall, P.P. (2004). "The Emergence of Entrepreneurship Policy." *Small Business Economics* 22: 313-323.

Hart, D. (2003). *The Emergence of Entrepreneurship Policy. Governance, Start-ups, and Growth in the U.S. Knowledge Economy*. Cambridge: Cambridge University Press.

Herberg, W. (1990). "America's Civil Religion: What It Is and Whence It Comes." In D. Jones and R.E. Richey. *American Civil Religion*, San Francisco: Mellen Research University Press, 1990 reprint: 70-84.

Krugman, P. (1991). *Geography and Trade*, Cambridge, MA: MIT Press.

Leipold, H. (2000). "Die kulturelle Einbettung der Wirtschaftsordnungen." In B. Wentzel and D. Wentzel (eds.). *Wirtschaftlicher Systemvergleich Deutschland/USA*, Stuttgart: Lucius und Lucius, 1-52.

Lucas, R.E. (1993). "Making a miracle." Econometrica 61 (2): 251-271.

Lucas, R.E. Jr. (1988). "On the mechanics of economic development". *Journal of Monetary Economics* 22: 3-39.

Mathur, V.K. (1999). "Human Capital-Based Strategy for Regional Economic Development." *Economic Development Quarterly* 13 (3): 203-216.

Müller-Armack, A. (1948). „Die Wirtschaftspolitik sozial gesehen." In W. Eucken and F. Böhm (eds), F. *Ordo Jahrbuch für die Ordnung der Wirtschaft und Gesellschaft* 1: 125-154.

Ohmae, K. (1990). *The Borderless World. Power and Strategy in the Interlinked Economy*. London: Collins.

Ohmae, K. (1995). *The End of the Nation State: The Rise of Regional Economies*. New York: Free Press.

Putnam, R. (2000). *Bowling Alone: The Collapse and Revival of American Community.* New York: Simon and Schuster.

Rieter, H. and Schmolz, M. (1993). „The Ideas of German Ordoliberalism 1938-45: Pointing the Way to a New Economic Order." *The European Journal of the History of the Economic Thought* Autumn 1 (1): 87-114.

Romer, P.M. (1986). „Increasing returns and long-run growth." *Journal of Political Economy* 94 (5): 1002-1037.

Schumpeter, J.A. (1946). *Kapitalismus, Sozialismus und Demokratie.* Tübingen: Francke, 1993 reprint, 7th ed.

Schumpeter, J.A. (1952). *Theorie der wirtschaftlichen Entwicklung: eine Untersuchung über Unternehmergewinn, Kapital, Kredit, Zins und den Konjunkturzyklus.* Berlin: Duncker & Humblot, 1997 reprint, 9th ed.

Siegele, L. (2004). "Bill Gates – Der größte praktische Ökonom." In U.J. Heuser and J.F. Jungclaussen (eds.). *Schöpfer und Zerstörer. Große Unternehmer und ihre Momente der Entscheidung,* Reinbek bei Hamburg: Rowohlt Taschenbuch Verlag, 264-268.

Simon, C. (1998). "Human Capital and Metropolitan Employment Growth." *Journal of Urban Economics* 43: 223-243.

Storey, D.J. (2003). "Entrepreneurship, Small and Medium Sized Enterprises and Public Policy." In Z.J. Acs. and D.B. Audretsch (eds.). *International Handbook of Entrepreneurship Research,* Dordrecht: Kluwer Academic.

The National Academies (ed.) (2001). *Global Networks and Local Values. A Comparative Look at Germany and the United States.* National Academy Press: Washington, D.C.

Tocqueville, A. de (1990). *Über die Demokratie in Amerika.* Stuttgart: Reclam.

Weber, M. (1905). „Die protestantische Ethik und der Geist des Kapitalismus." *Archiv für Sozialwissenschaft und Sozialpolitik* XX/XXI: 1-110.

Wennekers, S. and Thurik, R.A. (1999). "Linking Entrepreneurship and Economic Growth." *Small Business Economics* 13: 27-55.

Chapter 2:

THE EMERGENCE OF ENTREPRENEURSHIP POLICY

David B. Audretsch
Max Planck Institute for Research into Economic Systems, Jena, Centre for Economic Policy Research (CEPR), and Indiana University

1. INTRODUCTION

Perhaps one of the less understood phenomena accompanying the increased globalization at the beginning of the 21st century has been a shift in the comparative advantage of high-wage countries towards knowledge-based economic activity. An important implication of this shift in this comparative advantage is that much of the production and commercialization of new economic knowledge is less associated with large traditional corporations and more associated with high-tech entrepreneurial firms found in innovative regional clusters, such as Silicon Valley, Research Triangle and Route 122. Only a few years ago the conventional wisdom predicted that globalization would render the demise of small firms and the importance of geographic location. Yet the obsession of policy-makers around the globe to "create the next Silicon Valley" reveals the increased importance of entrepreneurial firms taking advantage of geographic proximity and regional agglomerations. The purpose of this paper is to explain why and how a new type of public policy has emerged–the strategic management of places–and the central role that entrepreneurship plays in this new policy.

2. WHAT IS ENTREPRENEURSHIP?

While it has become widely acknowledged that entrepreneurship is a vital force in the economies of developed countries, there is little consensus about what actually constitutes entrepreneurial activity. Scholars have proposed a broad array of definitions, which when operationalize, have generated a number of different measures (Hebert and Link, 1989). Herbert and Link (1989) have identified three distinct intellectual traditions in the development of the entrepreneurship literature. These three traditions can be characterized as the German Tradition, based on von Thuenen and

Schumpeter, the Chicago Tradition, based on Knight and Schultz, and the Austrian Tradition, based on von Mises, Kirzner and Shackle. The Schumpeterian tradition has had the greatest impact on the contemporary entrepreneurship literature. The distinguishing feature from Schumpeter is that entrepreneurship is viewed as a disequilibrating phenomenon rather than an equilibrating force. In his 1911 classic treatise, *Theorie der wirtschaftlichen Entwicklungen* (Theory of Economic Development), Schumpeter proposed a theory of *creative destruction*, where new firms with the entrepreneurial spirit displace less innovative incumbents, ultimately leading to a higher degree of economic growth. Even in his 1942 classic, Capitalism and Democracy, Schumpeter (p. 13) still argued that entrenched large corporations tend to resist change, forcing entrepreneurs to start new firms in order to pursue innovative activity: "The function of entrepreneurs is to reform or revolutionize the pattern of production by exploiting an invention, or more generally, an untried technological possibility for producing a new commodity or producing an old one in a new way...To undertake such new things is difficult and constitutes a distinct economic function, first because they lie outside of the routine tasks which everybody understand, and secondly, because the environment resists in many ways."

Despite the Schumpeterian emphasis on the process of starting a new enterprise as the defining entrepreneurial activity, there is no generally accepted definition of entrepreneurship for the developed countries of the OECD (OECD 1998). The failure of a single definition of entrepreneurship to emerge undoubtedly reflects the fact that it is a multidimensional concept. The actual definition used to study or classify entrepreneurial activities reflects a particular perspective or emphasis. For example, definitions of entrepreneurship typically vary between the economic and management perspectives. From the economic perspective, Hebert and Link (1989) distinguish between the supply of financial capital, innovation, allocation of resources among alternative uses and decision-making. Thus, an entrepreneur is someone encompassing the entire spectrum of these functions: "The entrepreneur is someone who specializes in taking responsibility for and making judgemental decisions that affect the location, form, and the use of goods, resources or institutions" (Hebert and Link, 1989: 213).

By contrast, from the management perspective, Sahlman and Stevenson (1991: 1) differentiate between entrepreneurs and managers in that, "entrepreneurship is a way of managing that involves pursuing opportunity without regard to the resources currently controlled. Entrepreneurs identify opportunities, assemble required resources, implement a practical action plan, and harvest the reward in a timely, flexible way."

The most prevalent and compelling views of entrepreneurship focus on the perception of new economic opportunities and the subsequent introduction of new ideas in the market. As Audretsch (1995) argues, entrepreneurship is about change, just as entrepreneurs are agents of change; entrepreneurship is thus about the process of change. This corresponds to the definition of entrepreneurship proposed by the OECD, "Entrepreneurs are agents of change and growth in a market economy and they can act to accelerate the generation, dissemination and application of innovative ideas....Entrepreneurs not only seek out and identify potentially profitable economic opportunities but are also willing to take risks to see if their hunches are right" (OECD 1998: 11).

While the simplicity of defining entrepreneurship as activities fostering innovative change have its attraction, such simplicity also masks considerable complexity. Entrepreneurship is shrouded with complexity for at least two reasons. The first reason emerges because entrepreneurship is an activity crossing multiple organizational forms. Does entrepreneurship refer to the change inducing activities of individuals, groups of individuals such as networks, projects, lines of business, firms, and even entire industries, or even for geographic units of observation, such as agglomerations, clusters, and regions?

Part of the complexity involved with entrepreneurship is that it involves all of these types of organizational forms. No single organizational form can claim a monopoly on entrepreneurship.

The second source of complexity is that the concept of change is relative to some benchmark. What may be perceived as change to an individual or enterprise may not involve any new practice for the industry. Or, it may represent change for the domestic industry, but not for the global industry. Thus, the concept of entrepreneurship is embedded in the local context. At the same time, the value of entrepreneurship is likely to be shaped by the relevant benchmark. Entrepreneurial activity that is new to the individual but not the firm or industry may be of limited value. Entrepreneurial activity that is new to the region or country may be significant but ultimately limited. By contrast, it is entrepreneurial activity that is new across all organizational forms, all the way up to the global, that carries the greatest potential value.

Thus, one of the most striking features of entrepreneurship is that it crosses a number of key units of analysis. At one level, entrepreneurship involves the decisions and actions of individuals. These individuals may act alone or within the context of a group. At another level, entrepreneurship involves units of analysis at the levels of the industry, as well as at spatial levels, such as cities, regions and countries.

3. GLOBALIZATION AND THE STRATEGIC MANAGEMENT OF PLACES

The role of entrepreneurship in society and has changed drastically over the last half century. During the post-World War II era, the importance of entrepreneurship and business seemed to be fading away. While alarm was expressed that small business needed to be preserved and protected for social and political reasons, few made the case on the grounds of economic efficiency. This position was drastically reversed in recent years. Entrepreneurship has become the engine of economic and social development throughout the world. The role of entrepreneurship has changed dramatically between the traditional and new economies.

During the post-war period a generation of scholars spanning a broad spectrum of academic fields and disciplines devoted their research to identifying the issues involving this perceived trade-off between economic efficiency on the one hand and political and economic decentralization on the other. Scholars responded by producing a massive literature focusing on essentially three issues: (i) What are the gains to size and large-scale production? (ii) What are the economic welfare implications of having an oligopolistic market structure i.e. is economic performance promoted or reduced in an industry with just a handful of large-scale firms? and (iii) Given the overwhelming evidence that large-scale production resulting in economic concentration is associated with increased efficiency, what are the public policy implications?

This literature produced a series of stylized facts about the role of SMEs during the post-war economies in North America and Western Europe:

(1) *SMEs were generally less efficient than their larger counterparts.* Studies from the U.S. in the 1960s and 1970 revealed that SMEs produced at lower levels of efficiency, leading Weiss (1976: 259) to conclude that, "On the average, about half of total shipments in the industries covered are from suboptimal plants. The majority of plants in most industries are suboptimal in scale, and a very large percentage of output is from suboptimal plants." Pratten (1971) found similar evidence for the United Kingdom, where suboptimal scale establishments accounted for 47.9 percent of industry shipments.

(2) *SMEs provided lower levels of employee compensation.* Empirical evidence from both North America and Europe found a systematic and positive relationship between employee compensation and firm size (Brown, Hamilton and Medoff 1990, and Brown and Medoff 1989).

(3) *SMEs were only marginally involved in innovative activity.* Based on R&D measures, SMEs accounted for only a small amount of innovative activity.

(4) *The relative importance of SMEs was declining over time in both North America and Europe.*

In the post-war era, small firms and entrepreneurship were viewed as a luxury, perhaps needed by the west to ensure a decentralization of decision making, but in any case obtained only at a cost to efficiency. Certainly the systematic empirical evidence, gathered from both Europe and North

America documented a sharp trend towards a decreased role of SMEs during the post-war period.

Thus, it was particularly startling and a seeming paradox, when scholars first began to document that what had seemed like the inevitable demise of SMEs actually began to reverse itself starting in the 1970s. Loveman and Sengenberger (1991) and Acs and Audretsch (1993) carried out systematic international studies examining the re-emergence of SMEs and entrepreneurship in North America and Europe. Two major findings emerged from these studies – first, the relative role of SMEs varies systematically across countries, and secondly, in most European countries and in North America, SMEs began increasing their relative importance starting in the mid-1970s. In the U.S. the average real GDP per firm increased by nearly two-thirds between 1947 and 1980, from $150.000 to $245.000, reflecting a trend towards larger enterprises and a decreasing importance of SMEs. However, within the subsequent seven years, by 1987, it had fallen by about 14 percent to $210.000, reflecting a sharp reversal of this trend and the re-emergence of SMEs (Brock and Evans 1989). Similarly, SMEs accounted for one-fifth of manufacturing sales in the U.S. in 1976, but by 1986 the small-firm share of sales had risen to over one-quarter (Acs and Audretsch 1990).

The reversal of the trend towards large enterprises towards the re-emergence of SMEs was not limited to North America. In fact, a similar trend was found to take in Europe as well. For example, in the Netherlands the business ownership rate fell during the post-war period, until it reached a trough of 0.085 in 1982. But this downward trend was subsequently reversed, rising to a business ownership rate of 0.10 by 1998 (Audretsch et al. 2002). Similarly, the small-firm employment share in manufacturing in the Netherlands increased from 68.3 percent in 1978 to 71.8 percent in 1986; in the United Kingdom from 30.1 percent in 1979 to 39.9 percent by 1986; in (West) Germany from 54.8 percent in 1970 to 57.9 percent by 1987; in Portugal from 68.3 percent in 1982 to 71.8 percent in 1986; in the North of Italy from 44.3 percent in 1981 to 55.2 percent by 1987, and in the South of Italy from 61.4 percent in 1981 to 68.4 percent by 1987 (Acs and Audretsch 1993). An EIM documents how the relative importance of SMEs in Europe (19 countries), measured in terms of employment shares has continued to increase between 1988 and 2001 (EIM 2002).

As the empirical evidence mounted documenting the re-emergence of entrepreneurship as a vital factor, scholars began to look for explanations and to develop a theoretical basis. The early explanations (Brock and Evans 1989) revolved around six hypotheses:

1. That technological change had reduced the extent of scale economies in manufacturing.
2. Increased globalization had rendered markets more volatile as a result of competition from a greater number of foreign rivals.

3. The changing composition of the labor force, towards a greater participation of females, immigrants, and young and old workers may be more conducive to smaller rather than larger enterprises, due to the greater premium placed on work flexibility.
4. A proliferation of consumer tastes away from standardized mass-produced goods towards stylized and personalized products facilitates niche small producers.
5. Deregulation and privatization facilitate the entry of new and small firms into markets that were previously protected and inaccessible.
6. The increased importance of innovation in high-wage countries has reduced the relative importance of large-scale production and instead fostered the importance of entrepreneurial activity.

More recently, Audretsch and Thurik (2001) have developed the explanation for the re-emergence of entrepreneurship in Europe and North America based on increased globalization, which has shifted the comparative advantage towards knowledge-based economic activity. Conventional wisdom would have predicted that increased globalization would present a more hostile environment to small business (Vernon 1970). Caves (1982) argued that the additional costs of globalization that would be incurred by small business "constitute an important reason for expecting that foreign investment will be mainly an activity of large firms".

Certainly the empirical evidence by Horst (1972) showed that even after controlling for industry effects, the only factor significantly influencing the propensity to engage in foreign direct investment was firm size. As Chandler (1990) concluded, "to compete globally you have to be big." Gomes-Casseres (1997: 33) further observed that, "[s]tudents of international business have traditionally believed that success in foreign markets required large size. Small firms were thought to be at a disadvantage compared to larger firms, because of the fixed costs of learning about foreign environments, communicating at long distances, and negotiating with national governments."

According to Audretsch and Thurik (2001), SMEs did not become obsolete as a result of globalization, but rather their role changed as the comparative advantage has shifted towards knowledge-based economic activity. This has occurred for two reasons. First, large enterprises in traditional manufacturing industries have lost their competitiveness in producing in the high-cost domestic countries. Second, small entrepreneurial enterprises take on a new importance and value in a knowledge-based economy.

The loss of competitiveness by large-scale producers in high-cost locations is manifested by the fact that, confronted with lower cost competition in foreign locations, producers in the high-cost countries have three options apart from doing nothing and losing global market share: (1)

reduce wages and other production costs sufficiently to compete with the low-cost foreign producers, (2) substitute equipment and technology for labor to increase productivity, and (3) shift production out of the high-cost location and into the low-cost location.

Many of the European and American firms that have successfully restructured resorted to the last two alternatives. Substituting capital and technology for labor, along with shifting production to lower-cost locations has resulted in waves of *Corporate Downsizing* throughout Europe and North America. At the same time, it has generally preserved the viability of many of the large corporations.

The experience has not been different in Europe. Pressed to maintain competitiveness in traditional industries, where economic activity can be easily transferred across geographic space to access lower production costs, the largest and most prominent German companies have deployed two strategic responses. The first is to offset greater wage differentials between Germany and low-cost locations by increasing productivity through the substitution of technology and capital for labor. The second is to locate new plants and establishments outside of Germany. What both strategic responses have in common is that the German flagship companies have been downsizing the amount of employment in the domestic economy. For example, Siemens increased the amount of employment outside Germany by 50 percent, from 108.000 in 1984/85 to 162.000 in 1994/95. Over the same time period it decreased the amount of employment in Germany by 12 percent, from 240.000 to 211.000. Volkswagen increased the amount of employment in foreign countries by 24 percent, from 78.000 in 1984 to 97.000 in 1994. Over the same time period, it decreased employment in Germany by 10 percent, from 156.000 to 141.000. Similarly, Hoechst increased the number of jobs outside of Germany by 9 percent, from 78.925 in 1984 to 92.333 in 1994. The number of Hoechst employees in Germany fell over that same period by 26 percent, from 99.015 to 73.338. And BASF increased employment in foreign countries by 34 percent, from 29.966 in 1984 to 40.297 in 1994. Domestic employment by BASF fell by 17 percent over that same time period, from 85.850 to 65.969.

These examples are not isolated but rather typical of the wave of downsizing in Germany in the 1990s that has resulted in levels of unemployment–four million–not seen since the Second World War. As table 2.1 shows, between 1991 and 1995 manufacturing employment in German plants decreased by 1.307.000 while it increased in foreign subsidiaries by 189.000 (BMWi 2000). In the chemical sector, the decrease of domestic employment was 80.000, while 14.000 jobs were added by German chemical companies in plants located outside of Germany. In electrical engineering employment in German, plants decreased by 198.000. In automobiles employment in Germany decreased by 161.000, while 30.000 jobs were added outside of Germany.

Fig. 2.1: Employment in large firms

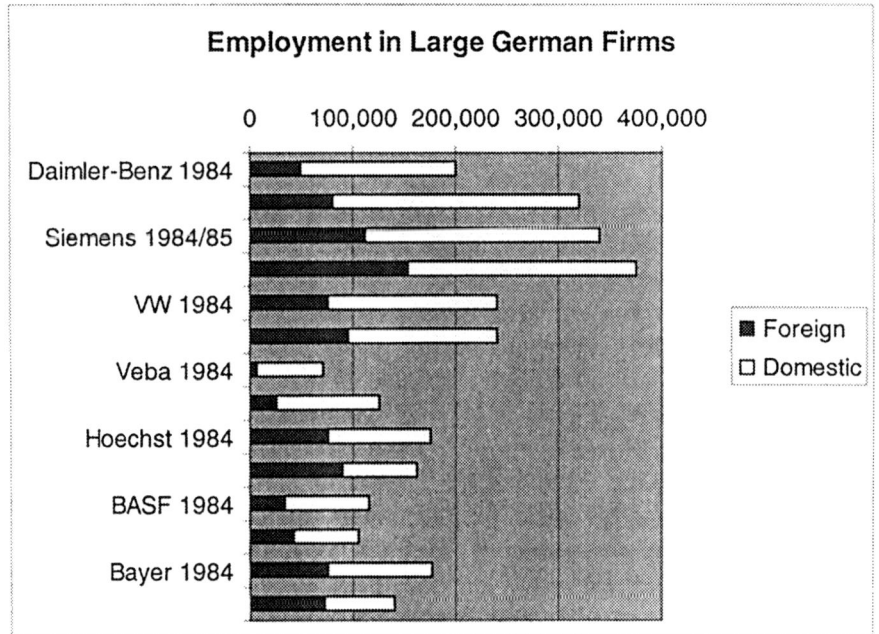

The German impact of corporate downsizing in Germany, in the 1990s, was registered not just by individual firms and industries but also by particular regions. For example, Stuttgart, which is home to Daimler-Chrysler (at the time Daimler-Benz), experienced an increase in manufacturing employment throughout the 1970s, 1980s, and into the 1990s. After reaching a peak of around 480.000 in 1991, manufacturing employment fell by more than one-third, to around 350.000 by the mid-1990s.

Tab. 2.1: Change in employment figures in Western Germany and at foreign subsidiaries (1991-1995, in thousands)

Employment Trend	Manufacturing	Chemicals	Electrical Engineering	Automotive	Mechanical Engineering	Textiles	Banking and Insurance
Foreign	+ 189	+ 14	- 17	+ 30	+ 16	- 6	+ 21
Domestic (West)	- 1.307	- 80	- 198	- 161	- 217	-68	+ 28

Source: BMWi 2000

Fig. 2.2 Employees in manufacturing in the Stuttgart region

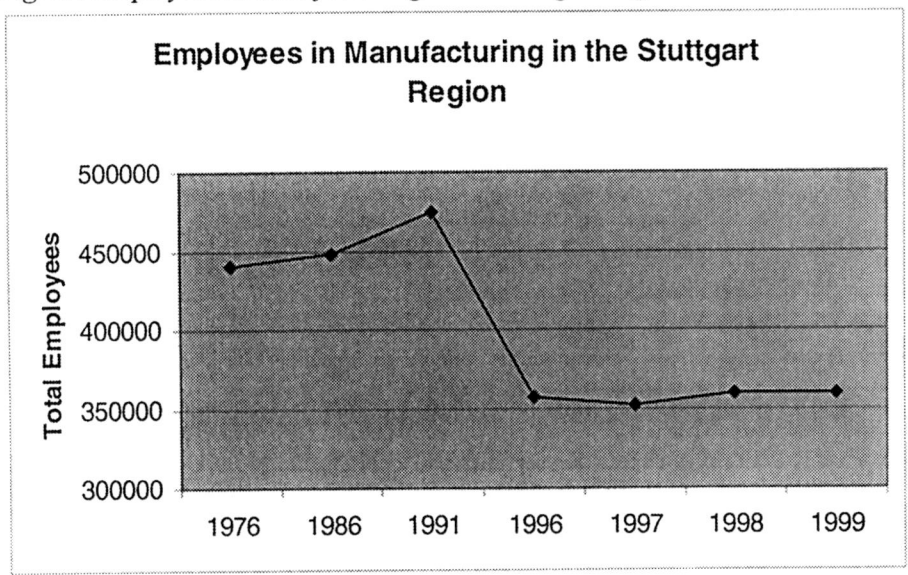

This wave of corporate downsizing triggered cries of betrayal and lack of social conscience on the part of the large corporations. But it was a mistake to blame the corporations for this wave of downsizing that has triggered massive job losses and rising unemployment in so many countries. These corporations were simply trying to survive in an economy of global competitors who have access to lower cost inputs.

Much of the policy debate responding to the twin forces of the telecommunications revolution and increased globalization revolved around a perceived trade-off between maintaining higher wages but suffering greater unemployment versus higher levels of employment but at the cost of lower wage rates. There is, however, an alternative. It does not require sacrificing wages to create new jobs, nor does it require fewer jobs to maintain wage levels and the social safety net. This alternative involves shifting economic activity out of the traditional industries where the high-cost countries of Europe and North America have lost the comparative advantage and into those industries where the comparative advantage is compatible with both high wages and high levels of employment – knowledge based economic activity.

Globalization has rendered the comparative advantage in traditional moderate technology industries incompatible with high wage levels. At the same time, the emerging comparative advantage that is compatible with high wage levels is based on innovative activity. Thus, the regional response to globalization has been the emergence of strategic management policy – not for firms, but for places. As long as corporations were inextricably linked to their regional location by substantial sunk costs, such as capital investment, the competitiveness of a region was identical to the competitiveness of the corporations located in that region. A quarter century ago, while the proclamation, "What is good for General Motors is good for America" may have been controversial, few would have disagreed that "What is good for General Motors is good for Detroit." And so it was with U.S. Steel in Pittsburgh and Volkswagen in Wolfsburg. As long as the corporation thrived, so would the region.

As globalization has rendered not only the degree to which the traditional economic factors of capital and labor are sunk, but also shifted the comparative advantage in the high-wage countries of North America and Europe towards knowledge-based economic activity, corporations in traditional industries have been forced to shift production to lower-cost locations. This has led to a de-linking between the competitiveness of firms and regions. The advent of the strategic management of regions has been a response to the realization that the strategic management of corporations includes a policy option not available to regions – changing the production location.

4. THE EMERGENCE OF ENTREPRENEURSHIP POLICY

During the Post World War II era, there was considerable concern about what to do about the existing firms and industrial structure, but little attention was paid to where they came from and where they were going (Audretsch and Thurik 2001). Oliver Williamson's classic 1968 article "Economies as an Antitrust Defense: The Welfare Tradeoffs," became something of a final statement demonstrating what appeared to be an inevitable trade-off between the gains in productive efficiency that could be obtained through increased concentration and gains in terms of competition, and implicitly democracy, that could be achieved through decentralizing policies. But it did not seem possible to have both, certainly not in Williamson's completely static model.

The fundamental policy issue confronting Western Europe and North America during the post-war era was how to live with this apparent trade-off between concentration and efficiency on the one hand, and decentralization and democracy on the other. The public policy question of the day was, *How can society reap the benefits of the large corporation in an oligopolistic setting while avoiding or at least minimizing the costs imposed by a concentration of economic power?* The policy response was to constrain the freedom of firms to contract. Such policy restraints typically took the form of public ownership, regulation and competition policy or antitrust. At the time, considerable attention was devoted to what seemed like glaring differences in policy approaches to this apparent trade-off by different countries. France and Sweden resorted to government ownership of private business. Other countries, such as the Netherlands and Germany, tended to emphasize regulation. Still other countries, such as the Untied States, had a greater emphasis on antitrust. In fact, most countries relied upon elements of all three policy instruments. While the particular instrument may have varied across countries, they were, in fact, manifestations of a singular policy approach – how to restrict and restrain the power of the large corporation. What may have been perceived as a disparate set of policies at the time appears in retrospect to comprise a remarkably singular policy approach (Audretsch and Thurik 2001).

In Europe Servan-Schreiber warned of the "American Challenge" in the form of the "dynamism, organization, innovation, and boldness that characterize the giant American corporations" (1968: 153). Because giant corporations were considered to be the engine of growth and innovation, Servan-Schreiber advocated the "creation of large industrial units which are able both in size and management to compete with the American giants" (1968: 159). According to Servan-Schreiber (1968: 159), "The first problem of an industrial policy for Europe consists in choosing 50 to 100 firms which, once they are large enough, would be the most likely to become world leaders of modern technology in their fields. At the moment we are simply letting industry be gradually destroyed by the superior power of American corporations." Ironically, the 1988 Cecchini Report identified the gains from European integration as largely accruing from increases in scale economies.

Public policy towards SMEs was oriented towards preserving what was considered to be inefficient enterprises, which, if left unprotected, might otherwise become extinct. Preservationist policies were clearly at work in the creation of the U.S. Small Business Administration. In the Small Business Act of July 10, 1953, Congress authorized the creation of the Small Business Administration, with an explicit mandate to "aid, counsel, assist and protect...the interests of small business concerns."[2] The Small Business Act was clearly an attempt by the Congress to halt the continued disappearance of small businesses and to preserve their role in the U.S. economy

By contrast, entrepreneurship policy is a relatively new phenomenon. An important distinction should be made between the traditional SME (small business) policies and entrepreneurship policies. SME policy typically refers to policies implemented by a ministry or government agency charged with the mandate to promote SMEs. The actual definition of SMEs varies considerably across countries, ranging from enterprises with fewer than 500 employees in some of the most developed countries, such as the United States and Canada, to fewer than 250 employees in the European Union, to 50 employees in many developing countries. The actual SME policy takes the existing enterprises within the appropriate size class as exogenous, or given, and then develops instruments to promote the viability of those enterprises. Thus, SME policy is almost exclusively targeted towards the existing stock of enterprises and virtually all of the instruments included in the policy portfolio are designed to promote the viability of the SMEs.

By contrast, entrepreneurship policy has a much broader focus. The definition introduced by Lundstrom and Stevenson (2001: 19) for OECD countries is certainly applicable in the context of the European Union, "Entrepreneurship policy consists of measures taken to stimulate more entrepreneurial behavior in a region or country...We define entrepreneurship policy as those measures intended to directly influence the level of entrepreneurial vitality in a country or a region."

There are at least two important ways that distinguish entrepreneurship policy from SME policy (Lundstrom and Stevenson 2002). The first is the breadth of policy orientation and instruments. While SME policy has a focus on the existing stock of SMEs, entrepreneurship policy is more encompassing in that it includes potential entrepreneurs as well as the existing stock of SMEs. This suggests that entrepreneurship policy is more focused on the process of change, regardless of the organizational unit, whereas SME policy is focused exclusively on the enterprise level. Entrepreneurship policy also has a greater sensitivity to framework or environmental conditions that shape the decision-making process of entrepreneurs. While SME policy is primarily concerned with one organizational level – the enterprise, entrepreneurship policy encompasses multiple units of organization and analysis. These range from the individual to the enterprise, and to the cluster or network, which might involve an industry or sectoral dimension, or a spatial dimension, such as a district, city, region, or even an entire country. Just as each of these levels is an important target for policy, the interactions and linkages across these disparate levels are also important. In this sense, entrepreneurship policy tends to be more systemic than SME policy. However, it is important to emphasize that SME policy still remains at the core of entrepreneurship policy.

The second way distinguishing entrepreneurship policy from traditional SME policy is that virtually every country has a ministry or governmental agency charged with promoting the viability of the SME sector. These ministries and agencies have by now developed a well established arsenal of policy instruments to promote SMEs. However, no such agencies exist to promote entrepreneurship. Part of the challenge of implementing entrepreneurship policy is that no country has yet to introduce an agency mandated with the charge of promoting entrepreneurship. Rather, aspects relevant to entrepreneurship policy can be found across a broad spectrum of ministries and agencies, ranging from education to trade and immigration. Thus, while SMEs have agencies and ministries that champion their issues, no analogous agency exists for entrepreneurship policy.

Just because entrepreneurship is positively linked to performance does not automatically justify public policy intervention. Rather, the mandate for public policy intervention is the result of three fundamental sources of market failure – network externalities, knowledge externalities, and learning externalities.

Network externalities result from the value of an individual's or firm's capabilities being conditional upon the geographic proximity of complementary firms and individuals. As Porter (2000) pointed out, local proximity is essential for accessing these knowledge spillovers. This makes the value of an entrepreneurial firm greater in the (local) presence of other entrepreneurial firms. The value of any individuals or firms capabilities is therefore conditional upon the existence of partners in a network Firms and workers place a greater value on locations within clusters which contain complementary workers and firms than on those outside of clusters. Such market failure can occur where there is a potential for geographic clustering, sectoral linkages, or networks.

The second source of market failure involves knowledge externalities. As Arrow (1962) documented, knowledge, which involves new ideas, is inherently a public good, so that its production generates externalities. However, as Porter (2000) pointed out, local proximity is essential for accessing these knowledge spillovers.

The second source of market failure emanating from entrepreneurship is that positive economic value for third-party firms and individuals is created even in entrepreneurial firms that fail. The high failure rate of new-firm startups has been widely documented and described above in this paper, and the failure rates in knowledge-based activities are especially great. This is not surprising since knowledge activities are associated with a greater degree of uncertainty. However, the failure of a knowledge-based firm does not imply no value was created by the firm; evidence suggests that ideas created by failed firms and projects often become integral parts of successful products and projects in successful firms.

The externalities sometimes associated with failed firms, also creates a market failure in the valuation of (potential) new enterprises by private investors and policy makers. Whereas the private investor can only appropriate her investment if the particular firm succeeds, a failed firm that generates positive externalities contributes to the success of other third-party firms. The private investor, however, does not appropriate anything from the original investment. Likewise, individual firms and workers would have no incentive to invest in the development of a cluster, which is the creation of other entrepreneurial firms, due to their inability to appropriate returns from such a cluster.

From the public policy perspective, on the other hand, it does not matter which firm succeeds, as long as some firm(s) do, and growth, along with the other benefits accruing from entrepreneurship, is generated for the locale.

The third source of market failure involves the learning or demonstration effect emanating from entrepreneurial activity. This is particularly valuable in regions where entrepreneurship has been noticeably absent and no strong entrepreneurial traditions exist. Entrepreneurial activity involves not just the firm or individual responsible. Rather, others will observe this activity and the results of entrepreneurship. Other people will learn that entrepreneurship is a viable alternative to the status quo. As a result of this demonstration effect, others will be induced to also develop entrepreneurial strategies. Thus, there is a strong and compelling positive externality associated with entrepreneurship, particularly in areas with no strong entrepreneurial traditions.

Thus, the market failures inherent in entrepreneurship – network externalities, knowledge externalities and demonstration or learning externalities – result in a gap in the valuation of entrepreneurial activities between private parties and the local public policy makers. Entrepreneurial activity, combined with the propensity for knowledge to remain localized, results in a new policy mandate for cities, regions, provinces and countries. It also results in a fundamental mandate for the role to serve as a partner to business, enabling and fostering the development of new and small entrepreneurial firms. By filling these gaps left by market failure, public policy can create a virtuous entrepreneurial circle, where entrepreneurs become networked and linked to each other, and strong role models of entrepreneurship exist for others to emulate.

As the comparative advantage has become increasingly based on new knowledge, public policy has responded in two fundamental ways. The first has been to shift the policy focus away from the traditional triad of policy instruments essentially constraining the freedom of firms to contract – regulation, competition policy or antitrust in the U.S., and public ownership of business. The policy approach of constraint was sensible as long as the major issue was how to restrain large corporations in possession of considerable market power. That this policy is less relevant in a global economy is reflected by the waves of deregulation and privatization throughout Europe and North America. Instead, a new policy approach is emerging which focuses on enabling the creation and commercialization of knowledge. Examples of such policies include encouraging R&D, venture capital and new-firm startups.

While the different types of entrepreneurship policies being implemented in the EU and US are two numerous to be identified and listed here, David Storey (2003) has identified examples of different types of entrepreneurship policies being undertaken in the EU and the U.S. In addition, he provides an assessment of the efficacy of the various types of policies undertaken. Illustrations of these policies are provided in table 2.2.

The policy shift to enabling the creation and viability of knowledge-based entrepreneurial firms is evidenced by passage by the United States Congress of the Small Business Innovation Research (SBIR) program in the early 1980s. Enactment of the SBIR was a response to the loss of American competitiveness in global markets. Congress mandated each federal agency with allocating around four percent of its annual budget to funding innovative small firms as a mechanism for restoring American international competitiveness (Wessner 2000). The SBIR provides a mandate to the major R&D agencies in the United States to allocate a share of the research budget to innovative small firms. In 2001 the SBIR program amounted to around $1.4 billion. The SBIR consists of three phases. Phase I is oriented towards determining the scientific and technical merit along with the feasibility of a proposed research idea. A Phase I award provides an opportunity for a small business to establish the feasibility and technical merit of a proposed innovation. The duration of the award is six months and can not exceed $70.000. Phase II extends the technological idea and emphasizes commercialization. A Phase II Award is granted to only the most promising of the Phase I projects based on scientific/technical merit, the expected value to the funding agency, company capability and commercial potential. The duration of the award is a maximum of 24 months and generally does not exceed $600.000. Approximately 40 percent of the Phase I Awards continue on to Phase II. Phase III involves additional private funding for the commercial application of a technology. A Phase III Award is for the infusion and use of a product into the commercial market. Private sector investment, in various forms, is typically present in Phase III. Under the Small Business Research and Development Enhancement Act of 1992, funding in Phase I was increased to $100.000, and in Phase II to $750.000.

The SBIR represents about 60 percent of all public entrepreneurial finance programs. Taken together, the public small-business finance is about two-thirds as large as private venture capital. In 1995, the sum of equity financing provided through and guaranteed by public programs financing SMEs was $2.4 billion, which amounted to more than 60 percent of the total funding disbursed by traditional venture funds in that year. Equally as important, the emphasis on SBIR and most public funds is on early stage finance, which is generally ignored by private venture capital. Some of the most innovative American companies received early stage finance from SBIR, including Apple Computer, Chiron, Compaq and Intel.

There is compelling evidence that the SBIR program has had a positive impact on economic performance in the U.S. (Wessner 2000; Lerner 1999). The benefits have been documented as:

- The survival and growth rates of SBIR recipients have exceeded those of firms not receiving SBIR funding
- The SBIR induces scientists involved in biomedical research to change their career path. By applying the scientific knowledge to commercialization, these scientists shift their career trajectories away from basic research towards entrepreneurship.

Tab. 2. 2: Illustrations of entrepreneurship policies

Problem	Programme	Description	Country	Success
Access to Loan Finance	Loan Guarantee Scheme	SMEs without access to own collateral obtain access to bank loans by state acting as guarantor	UK, USA, Canada France Netherlands	Yes, generally viewed as helpful, but small scale impact on the overall financing of SMEs in most countries
Access to Equity Capital	Enterprise Investment Scheme	Tax breaks for wealthy individuals to become business angels	UK	Unknown
Access to Markets	Europartenariat	Organisation of Trade Fairs to encourage cross-border trade between SMEs	EU	General satisfaction amongst firms that participated
Administrative Burdens	Units established within government to seek to minimise administrative burdens on smaller firms	Sunsetting Legislation deregulation Units	Netherlands Portugal, UK	The view of small firms themselves is that bureaucratic burdens have increased markedly in recent years
Science Parks	Property based developments adjacent to Universities	Seek to promote clusters of new technology based firms	UK, France, Italy and Sweden	Conflicting findings on impact of SPs on performance of firms
Managed Workspace	Property provision to assist new and very small firms	Often called business incubators, these provide premises for new and small firms on "easy- terms"	World-wide	General recognition that such initiatives are of value
Stimulating Innovation and R&D in small firms	Small Business Innovation Research Program	$1 billion per year is allocated via a competition to small firms to stimulate additional R&D activity	USA	Lerner implies SBIR enhances small firm performance, but Wallsten is unable to show it leads to additional R&D
Stimulating Training in small firms	Japan Small Business Corporation (JSBC)	JSBC and local governments provide training for owners and managers of small firms. The training programme began in 1963	Japan	Unknown
Entrepreneurial Skills	Small Business Development Corporations (SBDCs)	Counselling is provided by SBDC mentors to small business clients who may be starting a business or be already trading	USA	This study finds SBDC clients have higher rates of survival and growth than might be expected. Reservations over these findings are found in the text
Entrepreneurial Awareness	Entrepreneurship Education	To develop an awareness of enterprise and/or an entrepreneurial spirit in society by incorporating enterprise into the school and college curriculum	Australia, Netherlands, but leading area was Atlantic Canada	Conventional assessments are particularly difficult here because of the long "lead times"
Special Groups	Law 44	Provides finance and mentoring advice to young people in Southern Italy, where enterprise creation rates were very low	Southern Italy	This is an expensive programme, but most studies show the survival rates of assisted firms to be well above those of "spontaneous" firms

Source: Table taken (modified) from Storey (2003)

- The SBIR awards provide a source of funding for scientists to launch start-up firms that otherwise would not have had access to alternative sources of funding.
- SBIR awards have a powerful demonstration effect. Scientists commercializing research results by starting companies induce colleagues to consider applications and the commercial potential of their own research.

Sternberg (1996) has shown that a number of government-sponsored technology policies in four countries – Great Britain, Germany, the U.S. and Japan – have triggered the startup of new firms. The majority of the startup programs are targeted towards eliminated particular bottlenecks in the development and financing of new firms. Sternberg (1990) examines the impact that 70 innovation centers have had on the development of technology-based small firms. He finds that the majority of the entrepreneurs find a number of advantages from locating at an innovation center.

The second fundamental shift involves the locus of such enabling policies, which are increasingly at the state, regional or even local level. The downsizing of federal agencies charged with the regulation of business in many of the OECD countries has been interpreted by many scholars as the eclipse of government intervention. But to interpret deregulation, privatization and the increased irrelevance of competition policies as the end of government intervention in business ignores an important shift in the locus and target of public policy. The last decade has seen the emergence of a broad spectrum of enabling policy initiatives that fall outside of the jurisdiction of the traditional regulatory agencies. Sternberg (1996) documents how the success of a number of different high-technology clusters spanning a number of developed countries is the direct result of enabling policies, such as the provision of venture capital or research support. For example, the Advanced Research Program in Texas has provided support for basic research and the strengthening of the infrastructure of the University of Texas, which has played a central role in developing a high-technology cluster around Austin (Feller 1997). The Thomas Edison Centers in Ohio, the Advanced Technology Centers in New Jersey, and the Centers for Advanced Technology at Case Western Reserve University, Rutgers University and the University of Rochester have supported generic, pre-competitive research. This support has generally provided diversified technology development involving a mix of activities encompassing a broad spectrum of industrial collaborators. The Edison Technology Program of Ohio was established by the State of Ohio, as a means of transferring technology from universities and government research institutes to new firm startups. Carlsson and Brunerhjelm (1999) explain how the Edison BioTechnology Center serves an important dual role as a "bridging institution" between academic research and industry and between new startups and potential sources of finance. The Edison Centers in particular, try to link the leading universities and medical institutions, businesses, foundations, to civic and state organizations in Ohio in order to create new business opportunities. Numerous centers exist across the state. Similarly, the Edison Program has established a bridging institution to support polymer research and technology in Ohio. Carlsson and Brunerhjelm (1999) credit the program for the startup of new high technology firms in Ohio.

Other examples of enabling policies are evidenced by the plethora of science, technology and research parks. Lugar and Goldstein (1991) conducted a review of research parks and concluded that such parks are created in order to promote the competitiveness of a particular region. Lugar (2001: 47) further noted that, "The most successful parks...have a profound impact on a region and its competitiveness." A distinct exemplar of this effect is found in the Research Triangle Park in North Carolina.

The traditional industries in North Carolina – furniture, textiles, and tobacco – had all lost international competitiveness, resulting in declines in employment and stagnated real incomes. In 1952, only Arkansas and Mississippi had lower per capita incomes. According to Link and Scott (forthcoming: 2), a movement emerged to use the rich knowledge base of the region, formed by the three major universities – Duke University, University of North Carolina-Chapel Hill and North Carolina State. This movement, though it initially consisted only of businessmen looking to improve industrial growth, ultimately fell into the hands of the Governor's office which supported the efforts through fruition (Link 1995). Empirical evidence provides strong support that the initiative creating Research Triangle has led to fundamental changes in the region. Link and Scott (forthcoming), document the growth in the number of research companies in the Research Triangle Park as increasing from none in 1958 to 50 by the mid-1980s and to over 100 by 1997. At the same time, employment in these research companies increased from zero in the late 1950s to over 40.000 by 1997. Lugar (2001) attributes the Research Triangle Park with directly and indirectly generating one-quarter of all jobs in the region between 1959 and 1990, and shifting the nature of those jobs towards high value-add knowledge activities.

Such enabling policies are not restricted to the U.S. One of the most interesting examples of the new enabling entrepreneurship policy involves the establishment of five EXIST regions in Germany, where startups from universities and government research laboratories are encouraged (BMBF 2000). The program has the explicit goals of (1) creating an entrepreneurial culture, (2) the commercialization of scientific knowledge, and (3) increasing the number of innovative start-ups and SMEs. Five regions were selected among many applicants for START funding. These are the (1)

Rhein-Ruhr region (bizeps program), (2) Dresden (Dresden exists), (3) *Thüringen* (GET UP), (4) Karlsruhe (KEIM), and (5) Stuttgart (PUSH!).

These programs promoting entrepreneurship in a regional context are typical of the new enabling policies to promote entrepreneurial activity. While these entrepreneurial policies are clearly evolving, they are clearly gaining in importance and impact in the overall portfolio of economic policy instruments.

5. CONCLUSIONS

Globalization has shifted the comparative advantage in the OECD countries away from being based on traditional inputs of production, such as land, labor and capital, towards knowledge. This has triggered a divergence between the competitiveness of firms and the competitiveness of locations. As the strategic management of firms dictated a response to globalization of outward foreign direct investment combined with employment downsizing at high cost locations, public policy has responded by developing the strategic management of places. Policy to promote entrepreneurship has emerged as playing a central role in the strategic management of places, because entrepreneurial activity is the conduit between investments in knowledge and economic growth at the particular location. However, due to the two sources of market failure associated with investments in knowledge and entrepreneurial activity identified in this paper, private agents will tend to under invest in entrepreneurial activity. A major goal of the strategic management of places is to pursue policies that will compensate for this market failure by promoting knowledge-based entrepreneurship as a vehicle for the employment growth and global competitiveness.

NOTES

[1] As the German newspaper, *Die Zeit* (2 February 1996: 1) pointed out in a front page article, "When Profits Lead to Ruin – More Profits and More Unemployment: Where is the Social Responsibility of the Firms?" the German public has responded to the recent waves of corporate downsizing with accusations that corporate Germany is no longer fulfilling its share of the social contract.

[2] http://www.sba.gov/aboutsba/sbahistory.html.

REFERENCES

Acs, Z.J. and Audretsch, D.B. (1990). *Innovation and Small Firms*, Cambridge: MIT Press.

Acs, Z.J. and Audretsch, D.B. (eds.) (1993). *Small Firms and Entrepreneurship: An East-West Perspective.* Cambridge: Cambridge University Press.

Almeida, P. and Kogut, B. (1997). "The Exploration of Technological Diversity and the Geographic Localization of Innovation." *Small Business Economics* 9: 21-31.

Arrow, K. (1962). "Economic Welfare and the Allocation of Resources for Invention". In R. Nelson (ed.). *The Rate and Direction of Inventive Activity.* Princeton: Princeton University Press.

Audretsch, D.B. (1995). *Innovation and Industry Evolution.* Cambridge, MA: MIT Press.

Audretsch, D.B. (1998). "Agglomeration and the Location of Innovative Activity." *Oxford Review of Economic Policy* 14 (2): 18-29.

Audretsch, D.B and Thurik, A. (1999). *Innovation, Industry Evolution and Employment.* Cambridge: Cambridge University Press.

Audretsch, D.B. and Feldman, M. (1996). "R&D Spillovers and the Geography of Innovation and Production." *American Economic Review* 86 (4): 253-273.

Audretsch, D.B. and Stephan, P. (1996). "Company-Scientist Locational Links: The Case of Biotechnology." *American Economic Review* 86 (4): 641-652.

Audretsch, D.B. and Thurik, R. (2001). "What's New about the New Economy? Sources of Growth in the Managed and Entrepreneurial Economies." *Industrial and Corporate Change* 10 (1): 267-315.

Audretsch, D.B., Thurik, R., Verheul, I. and Wennekers, S. (2002). *Entrepreneurship: Determinants and Policy in a European-U.S. Comparison.* Boston: Kluwer Academic Publishers.

Berman, E., Bound, J. and Machin, S. (1997). *Implications of Skill-Biased Technological Change: International Evidence.* Working paper 6166, National Bureau of Economic Research (NBER), Cambridge, MA.

Braunerhjelm, P. and Carlsson, B. (1999). "Industry Clusters in Ohio and Sweden, 1975-1995." *Small Business Economics* 12 (4): 279-293.

Brock, W.A. and Evans, D.S. (1989). "Small Business Economics." *Small Business Economics* 1 (1): 7-20.

Brown, C. and Medoff, J. (1989). "The Employer Size Wage Effect." *Journal of Political Economy* 97 (4): 1027-1059.

Brown, C., Hamilton, J. and Medoff, J. (1990). *Employers Large and Small.* Cambridge, Mass.: Harvard University Press.

Brüderl, J., Preisendörfer. P. and Ziegler, R. (1992). "Survival chances of newly founded business organizations." *American Sociological Review*, 57: 227-242.

Bundesministerium für Bildung und Forschung (2000). *Zur technologischen Leistungsfähigkeit Deutschlands.* Bonn: Bundesministerium für Bildung und Forschung.

Carlsson, B. and Brunerhjelm, P. (1999). " Industry clusters: biotechnology/biomedicine and polymers in Ohio and Sweden". In D.B. Audretsch and R. Thurik (Eds.). *Innovation, Industry Evolution, and Employment*, Cambridge: Cambridge University Press, 182-215.

Carree, M.A., Stel, A. van, Thurik, A.R. and Wennekers, S. (2000). *Economic development and business ownership: An analysis using data of 23 OECD countries in the period 1976-1996*. Discussion Paper 00-6, Institute for Development Strategies, Indiana University.

Carree. M.A. and Thurik, A.R. (1999). "Industrial Structure and Economic Growth." In D.B. Audretsch and Thurik, A.R. (Eds.). *Innovation, Industry Evolution and Employment*, Cambridge: Cambridge University Press, 86-110.

Chandler, A. (1990). *Scale and scope: The dynamics of industrial capitalism*. Cambridge: Harvard University Press.

Cohen, W. and Levinthal, D. (1989). "Innovation and Learning: The Two Faces of R&D." *Economic Journal* 99 (3): 569-596.

Cooke, P. and Wills, D. (1999). "Small Firms, Social Capital and the Enhancement of Business Performance through Innovation Programmes." *Small Business Economics* 13 (3): 219-234.

Cooper, R.S. (forthcoming). "Purpose and performance of the small business innovation research (SBIR) program." *Small Business Economics*.

EIM (2002). *SMEs in Europe*. Report submitted to the Enterprise Directorate General by KPMG Special Services, EIM Business & Policy Research

Feldman, M. (1994). "Knowledge Complementarity and Innovation," *Small Business Economics*, 6 (3): 363-372.

Feldman, M., and Audretsch, D. (1999). "Science-Based Diversity, Specialization, Localized Competition and Innovation." *European Economic Review* 43: 409-429.

Feller, I. (1997). "Federal and State Government Roles in Science and Technology." *Economic Development Quarterly* 11 (4): 283-296.

Fritsch, M. (1997). "New Firms and Regional Employment Change." *Small Business Economics* 9: 437-448.

Gläser, E., Kallal, H., Scheinkman, J. and Shleifer, A. (1992). "Growth of Cities." *Journal of Political Economy* 100: 1126-1152.

Glasmeier, Amy (1991). "Technological Discontinuities and Flexible Production Networks" *Research Policy*: 469-485.

Gomez-Casseres, B. (1997). "Alliance strategies of small firms." *Small Business Economics* 9: 33-44.

Griliches, Z , (1979). "Issues in Assessing the Contribution of R&D to Productivity Growth." *Bell Journal of Economics* 10: 92-116.

Griliches, Z. (1992). "The Search for R&D Spill-Overs." *Scandinavian Journal of Economics* 94: 29-47.

Hannan, M. T. and Freeman, J.H. (1989). *Organizational Ecology*, Cambridge, MA: Harvard University Press.

Hebert, R.F. and Link, A.N. (1989). "In Search of the Meaning of Entrepreneurship." *Small Business Economics* 1 (1): 39-49.

Henderson, V., Kuncoro, A. and Turner, M. (1995). "Industrial Development in Cities." *Journal of Political Economy* 103 (5): 1067-1090.

Horst, T. (1972). "Firm and industry determinants of the decision to invest abroad: an empirical study." *Review of Economic Statistics*: 258-266.

Jacobs, J. (1969). *The Economy of Cities*, New York: Random House.

Jaffe, A. (1989). "Real Effects of Academic Research." *American Economic Review* 79: 957-970.

Jaffe, A., Trajtenberg, M. and Henderson, R. (1993). "Geographic Localization of Knowledge Spillovers as Evidenced by Patent Citations." *Quarterly Journal of Economics* 63: 577-598.

Kindleberger, C.P. and Audretsch, D.B. (1983). *The Multinational Corporation in the 1980s*, Cambridge: MIT Press.

Klepper, S. (1996). "Entry, Exit, Growth, and Innovation over the Product Life Cycle" *American Economic Review* 86 (4): 562-583.

Kortum, S. and Lerner, J. (1997). "Stronger Protection or Technological Revolution: What is Behind the Recent Surge in Patenting?" Working paper 6204, National Bureau of Economic Research (NBER), Cambridge: MA.

Krugman, P. (1991). *Geography and Trade*, Cambridge, MA: MIT Press.

Lerner, J. (1999). "The government as venture capitalist: The long-run effects of the SBIR program." *Journal of Business* 72: 285-297.

Link, A.N. & Scott, J.T. (forthcoming). "The growth of Research Triangle Park." *Small Business Economics*.

Link, A.N. (1995). *A generosity of spirit: The early history of Research Triangle Park.* Durham: Duke University Press.

Loveman, G. and Sengenberger, W. (1991). "The Re-emergence of Small-Scale Production: An International Perspective." *Small Business Economics* 3 (1): 1-38.

Lugar, M. and Goldstein, H. (1991). *Technology in the garden: Research parks and regional economic development*, Chapel Hill, N.C.: The University of North Carolina Press.

Lugar, M., 2001. The Research Triangle Experience. In C. Wessner (ed.). *Industry-laboratory partnerships: A review of the Sandia Science and Technology Park Initiative*, Washington, D.C.: National Academy Press, 35-38.

Lundstrom, A. and Stevenson, L. (2001). *Entrepreneurship Policy for the Future*, Stockholm: Swedish Foundation for Small Business Research.

Lundstrom, A. and Stevenson, L. (2002). *On the Road to Entrepreneurship Policy*, Stockholm: Swedish Foundation for Small Business Research.

Markusen, A. (1996). "Sticky Places in Slippery Space: A Typology of Industrial Districts." *Economic Geography* 72 (3): 293-313.

Organisation for Economic Co-Operation and Development (OECD) (1998). *Fostering Entrepreneurship*, Paris: OECD.

Porter, M. E. (2000). "Locations, Clusters, and Company Strategy." In G.L. Clark, M.P. Feldman and M.S. Gertler (Eds.). *The Oxford Handbook of Economic Geography*, Oxford: Oxford University Press, 253-274

Porter, M.E. (1990). *The Comparative Advantage of Nations*, New York: Free Press.

Porter, M.E., (2000). "Clusters and Government Policy." *Wirtschaftspolitische Blätter*, 47 (2): 144-154.

Pratten, C.F. (1971). *Economies of Scale in Manufacturing Industry*. Cambridge: Cambridge University Press.

Prevenzer, M. (1997). '"The Dynamics of Industrial Clustering in Biotechnology." *Small Business Economics* 9 (3): 255-271.

Reynolds, P.D., Miller, B. and Maki, W.R. (1995). "Explaining Regional Variation in Business Births and Deaths: U.S. 1976-1988." *Small Business Economics* 7: 389-407.

Reynolds, P.D., Hay, M., Bygrave, W.D., Camp, S.M. and Autio, E. (2000). *Global Entrepreneurship Monitor*. Kansas City: Kauffman Center for Entrepreneurial Leadership.

Saxenian, A. (1990). "Regional Networks and the Resurgence of Silicon Valley." *California Management Review* 33: 89-111.

Schumpeter, Joseph A. (1911). *Theorie der wirtschaftlichen Entwicklung. Eine Untersuchung über Unternehmergewinn, Kapital, Kredit, Zins und den Konjunkturzyklus*. Berlin: Duncker und Humblot.

Servan-Schreiber, J.-J. (1968). *The American Challenge*, London: Hamisch Hamilton.

Sternberg, R. (1996). "Technology Policies and the Growth of Regions." *Small Business Economics* 8 (2): 75-86.

Storey, D.J. (2003). "Entrepreneurship, Small and Medium Sized Enterprises and Public Policy." In Z.J. Acs and D.B. Audretsch (eds.). *International Handbook of Entrepreneurship Research*, Dordrecht: Kluwer Academic.

Stough, R.R., Haynes, K.E. and Campbell, H.S. Jr. (1998). "Small Business Entrepreneurship in the High Technology Services Sector: An Assessment for the Edge Cities of the U.S. National Capital Region." *Small Business Economics* 10 (1): 61-74.

Weiss, L.W. (1976). "Optimal Plant Scale and the Extent of Suboptimal Capacity." In R.T. Masson and P.S. Qualls (eds.). *Essays on Industrial Organization in Honor of Joe S. Bain*. Cambridge, Mass.: Ballinger.

Wessner, C. (ed.). (2000). *The Small Business Innovation Research Program (SBIR)*. Washington D.C.: National Academy Press.

Williamson, O.E. (1968). "Economies as an Antitrust Defense: The Welfare Tradeoffs." *American Economic Review* 58 (1): 18-36.

PART TWO

ENTRPRENEURSHIP POLICIES IN GERMANY AND THE U.S.A.

Chapter 3:

EUROPEAN INTEGRATION AND THE CHALLENGES FOR ECONOMIC AND RESEARCH POLICY

Dagmar Schipanski
President of the Parliament of the Free State of Thuringia, Germany

The following contribution is an excerpt of Professor Dagmar Schipanski's speech held at the Workshop "Where Is Europe Going? – And What Has America To Do With It" jointly organized by the Erfurt School of Public Policy, The University of Erfurt, and the School of Public and Environmental Affairs Board on Science, University of Indiana, in Erfurt, 11 June 2004.

1. INTRODUCTION

"I would like to welcome you to Erfurt, the capital of the Free State of Thuringia. It is a great pleasure to be here with you today and to be able to welcome you – not only as the Minister for Science, Research and Arts, but also as a citizen of Thuringia who has spent an important part of my scientific career at a Thurinigian university.

I am glad that students and scientists from the Indiana University have come to Erfurt University. It is a pleasure to have you here! When we signed the cooperation agreement between the Erfurt and Indiana universities in Bloomington last November, I really hoped that scientific exchange would be one of the results. So now I am very pleased to see that the cooperation is starting to be beneficial for both universities.

I suppose that for many of you it is your first time in Thuringia. You may well be surprised by the rich cultural heritage that you will no doubt experience during your stay. Thuringia, although a small area in the center of Europe, is essential to German cultural history. It has repeatedly been a source of creativity since the Middle Ages.

Many currents, events and epochs are intimately connected to places in Thuringia and Thuringian people. Please permit me to name just a few: One of the world's best known musicians and composers, John Sebastian Bach, was born in Thuringia and spent the first half of his life here. Bach is considered by many to be the greatest composer in the history of western music. Well, I am no expert in this field, but he certainly is the most famous composer from a large group of Thuringian musicians.

German Protestantism also has roots in Thuringia. The reformation started here with new ideas espoused by of Martin Luther, who lived as a student and monk in Erfurt from 1501 to 1511. Because of the power of his ideas and the enormous influence of his writings Martin Luther is regarded as the initiator of the Protestant Reformation. His disagreement with many of the doctrines of the Roman Catholic Church set off a chain of events that resulted in the establishment of the protestant church in Germany.

I hope you will take time to visit the monastery where Luther lived and worked during his decisive years.

Thuringia has not only been a center of religious reformation. Our Land also has strong traditions in classical German Literature. Weimar in particular, a beautiful town only 20 kilometers from Erfurt, attracted the cultural German elite like a magnet. In the 18th century it was the Court of Weimar, whose liberal inclinations and readiness to sponsor attracted great German poets such as Goethe, Schiller and Herder, which has contributed to the international fame of the town today.

Modern art has been very strong in Weimar, since famous architects and artists such as Henry van de Velde, Walter Gropius, Paul Klee, Oskar Schlemmer and Lyonel Feininger founded the Bauhaus tradition in Weimar. The Bauhaus University Weimar has taken up this tradition and still teaches its basic philosophy: the union of form and function, and of artistic design and industrial production.

When speaking of Weimar it is impossible to omit the unbearable proximity of classical culture and modern barbarism. Only a few kilometres from Weimar stands the memorial of the Buchenwald Concentration Camp. Between 1937 and 1945, a total of 250.000 people from all over Europe were imprisoned in Buchenwald. The number of victims who died there is approximately 56.000. On April 11, the Sixth Armoured Division of the Third U.S. Army reached Buchenwald Concentration Camp. Twenty-one thousand inmates experienced liberation upon arrival of the U.S. Army. We remember the liberation of Buchenwald and of Thuringia by American troupes with great thankfulness and deep respect.

One thing should not be forgotten when speaking about Thuringia: Our Land also has strong academic traditions. Jena University, in particular, is a famous place for both the study of philosophy and the natural sciences.

2. INNOVATIVE RESEARCH POLICY FOR THURINGIA AND EUROPE

The international fame the city enjoys today also has its roots in the days of Carl Zeiss, Ernst Abbe and Otto Schott, who laid the foundation stone for precision optical engineering. Their pioneering inventions – astronomical instruments and microscopes – spread from Jena to the far corners of the world and thus contributed hugely to the development of the natural sciences.

As was the case in Zeiss' time, science and the economy are again forming alliances in Jena. In just a short time the "boomtown" of Thuringia registered more listed start-ups than the West German financial metropolis of Frankfurt. According to McKinsey, consulting companies regard Jena as the second most important center for innovation in Germany, with Munich taking first place and Dresden third.

Jena is also crucial to the relationship between France and Germany, since the town experienced one of the cruelest battles in Europe's history for many centuries. It was occurred near Jena in October 1806 – during the Napoleonic Wars – when 120.000 French troops fought 110.000 Prussians and Saxons. In the battle, Napoleon smashed the Prussian army thereby removing a significant obstacle on his way to conquer Eastern Europe.

For centuries European history has been a chronology of such cruel battles between the peoples on our continent. Only the 20th century with two world wars has brought about real change: a clear understanding that only close cooperation between the European countries can avoid military conflict. The Hungarian author György Konrád summed up the necessity of European unification in the following sentences: "Geographical circumstances make us dependent upon each other; a separation is impossible. Unification, however, is essential if we wish to disrupt the tradition of bloody struggles that have lasted for many thousands of years".

The process of European integration has indeed generated more than almost 50 years of peace, democracy, stability, and prosperity. Never before in our history have such a large number of Europeans enjoyed so much peace and democracy.

European unification has thus far proved to be the most successful political project in the history of our continent, particularly since the fall of the Iron Curtain. It has brought about reconciliation among people, and has undeniably prepared the ground for economic prosperity. The first step to make war materially impossible was to place the coal and steel industries under common control.

The initial project "Never again war between Germany and France – never again war between the peoples of Europe" has since evolved. Gradually, the governments and peoples of Europe realized that together they could achieve much more. This also applies to the Eastern Enlargement of the EU. I am optimistic about the synergies this process will bring.

This brings us to the topic that I wish to discuss with you today: research policy and European integration. For most people the word "Europe" suggests farm subsidies, regional aid, and occasionally too, student exchange. There is probably only a very small scientific community in existence for which it would suggest European research policy.

Today's event is therefore a good opportunity to advocate the general significance of research policy, and its particular significance in a European context. I am convinced that the best and most effective economic policy is to have a proper research policy. Research is the pre-requisite for new services and innovative products.

In the new German *Länder* (federal states), we were horrified to see in 1993 that a large part of our industry had foundered because our products and technologies were not competitive. Exposure to international competition has made us aware of the need to develop new and innovative products if we wish to survive in international markets. New areas of technologies are emerging, and they obviously require considerable input. Europe's entire economic future therefore depends on research. Europe must also play an active role in Research and Technological Development (RTD) because of a number of developments inherent in this sector itself such as:

- high level research is increasingly complex and interdisciplinary;
- this is increasingly costly and requires a constantly increasing "critical mass".

There are very few individual research teams or laboratories or companies who can reasonably claim to be able to respond to these challenges. Even entire countries find it increasingly difficult to play a leading role in the many important areas of scientific and technological progress. As a result of the development of modern research in a global environment it has become necessary:

- to organize co-operation at different levels both within Europe and internationally,
- to co-ordinate national and European policies,
- to increase the mobility of individuals and ideas.

Without determined action at a European level, the present fragmentation of Europe's efforts cannot be overcome.

3. A POLICY FOR THE "EUROPEAN RESEARCH AREA"

Taking up this challenge the European Commission, Member States, the scientific community and industry are committed to working jointly towards the creation of a "European Research Area" (ERA). The Sixth Framework Programme for Research and Technological Development is the main financial and legal instrument for creation and implementation of the European Research Area. The Framework Programme must serve two main strategic objectives:

- strengthening the scientific and technological bases of industry;
- encouraging its international competitiveness whilst promoting research

activities in support of other EU policies.

The overall budget covering the four-year period 2003 to 2006 is 17.5 billion Euros. That is an increase of 17% from the Fifth Framework Programme and makes up 3.9% of the Union's total budget (2001), and 6% of the Union's public (civilian) research budget.

Seven thematic priority areas of research have been chosen within the Sixth Framework Programme. These areas are:

- genomics and biotechnology for health;
- information society technologies;
- nanotechnologies and nanosciences;
- aeronautics and space;
- food safety;
- sustainable development;
- and economic and social sciences.

Let me pick out two of these areas and explain why successful research is bonded to European cooperation.

3.1 Nanotechnology

Nanotechnology comprises both the research of lifeless matter, and the realm of the living. The ability to arrange atoms in such a way that they form nanosystems with exceptional physical, chemical, or biological characteristics, could open up applications that mark the beginning of an absolutely innovative technological era. Nanosciences could dramatically alter our entire technological environment.

For example, nano-electronics could offer a springboard for developing the molecular and quantum computers of tomorrow. Or the nano-synthesis of fundamental molecular modules of life could open up new perspectives for biomedicine and bio-pharmaceutics.

In the materials sciences, nanotechnologies offer infinite innovation potential for industrial use. In the engineering sciences the dynamic properties of certain atom arrangements could enhance the development of nano-motors, nano-pumps, and nano-engines with remarkable properties in terms of sustainability and energy conservation.

However, tremendous investments in fundamental and applied research, as well as multidisciplinary expert activity, would be required before the expectations placed in nanotechnologies could be met. The EU has to engage in a proactive European approach if we wish to use the opportunities that this third industrial revolution offers.

This revolution will take place during the next two to three decades, and will be characterized by the interpenetration of fundamental and applied research. The boundary between the two will become increasingly blurred, and will eventually disappear – such as was the case with developments in microelectronics.

These nanosystems require experts with an exceptional insight into the world of the atom, as well as engineers capable of designing test rigs and instruments with technical properties so far unheard. The wide range of applications, demands that an exceptional array of scientists (such as electronics experts, chemists, and biologists) engage in interdisciplinary cooperation.

We need a European Research Area for this massive mobilization of experts and resources from science and industry. In view of the enormity of the challenge there is no European country that could seriously consider doing this alone.

In the U.S.A., a broad, nationwide nanotech-research center network is already in place. In 2002, the US administration funded these academic and private sector activities with public loans worth 650 million Euros. In Europe the continental network is in its initial phase. A recent study reported that there are 86 cross-border co-operation initiatives involving about 2000 academic and private partners. The investment volume is estimated at 300 million Euros this year, of which two-thirds originate from national agencies. So the Europeans still need to catch up with the U.S. research activities.

3.2 Aeronautics and Space Technology

Let me now touch on an area which can obviously no longer be handled by a single national state: aeronautics and space technology. Space technology still holds tremendous development potential for the information society, and for environmental monitoring. Moreover, it is a good strategic tool for political security. Thanks to globalization it will be one of the most dynamic economic sectors for many decades to come. These opportunities obviously generate a certain research momentum.

In the world of aviation, the European Airbus is a huge success story. The message for Europe is clear: If we pool our resources we can catch up with the world's top player whose dominant market position once seemed unassailable. Here European cooperation is the key to success.

By 2020, air traffic will triple. This will correspond with a 5% per annum growth in passenger numbers, and a 6% growth in freight volume. On a global scale, this corresponds to an increase in demand for new aircraft of 15.500, worth roughly 1.3 trillion Euros.

Aviation and space technology are two outstanding sectors in which Europe should be able to assert its scientific and technological competence and economic efficiency. Airbus accounts for 50% of aircraft ordered worldwide; Ariane holds the same market share for commercial satellites. These success stories are the fruit of continuous research investment (both private and public), made possible by broad-scale coordination. In this area

Europe can create added value. As such, this task is among the priorities of the Sixth Framework Programme.

4. CHALLENGES AND IMPLICATIONS FOR EUROPE

So much for the scientific challenge, ladies and gentlemen. But what about the political reality in a Europe that is moving closer together?

In 1990, the countries of Western, Eastern, and Central Europe entered into a phase of joint development. Isolation and demarcation are a thing of the past; they have been replaced by interchange, integration, and peaceful co-existence. Since the first of May 2004, nine Eastern European countries have become real partners in the EU. Despite great enthusiasm for this, there are still a number of obstacles to overcome. The barriers impeding this development are not only of a linguistic and national type. There are problems relating to comprehension, differing horizons and different experiences between those in the East and in the West.

Financial constraints, lack of mutual understanding, and different national traditions can delay the transformation process. Old and new partners need to analyze these factors very critically if they wish to make progress. Conditions within the EU need to be carefully reviewed as well. We should therefore thoroughly analyze the recent German unification so as to avoid similar mistakes in the process of European integration.

In the European community there are many different research models within the national systems. We have now reached the stage where we must pool our development resources. This requires the establishment of mutually acceptable criteria. But can these criteria be limited to efficiency and technology transfer? What about flexibility, versatility, and open-mindedness? This is where our young Eastern European neighbors, who have come a long way in recent years, have set impressive examples. We need new incentives. Which system offers a maximum of creativity in terms of new ideas and concepts? How do we best organize and finance the transformation of ideas into products? There are diverging approaches in Europe, and it will be up to us to offer plausible answers that are compatible with our federal systems.

Although we may believe that these answers depend mainly on financial capacity, they will be just as much determined by structural elements. The new member states hope for economic growth through increased research and technological development. This is proper and acceptable, and as such, excessive bureaucracy must be avoided. I believe that there are many aspects that could expedite the exchange of information, and improve academic instruction, regardless of whether we are looking at Western or Eastern Europe.

We need to take an unbiased look at this when devising our framework programmes. I realize that during the somewhat rushed transformation process of the two German systems, many advantages in terms of organization and communication were not sufficiently taken into account. I know that it is extremely difficult to change organizations and structures, even if doing so would be conducive to greater efficiency. We should therefore seize the new opportunities offered by EU enlargement.

Our new members will enrich both the culture of communication, and the structures within the EU. Rather than erect new obstacles we should strive to dismantle existing ones. By this I mean that there was much better networking between research institutes and industry in many East European countries than in West European countries. The transfer between manufacturing companies and research institutes used to be a lot simpler, both on a personal and scientific level. Today the EU must look to Eastern Europe for new incentives.

In the East, science areas were much more simply organized. In most countries there were universities, polytechnics or specialist schools, and academic institutes offering various disciplines. The latter engaged both in fundamental and applied research. Despite the negative effects of their privileged status, their straightforward organization and their simple mode of finance offered undeniable advantages which perhaps should be re-assessed in the context of unification and globalization.

Equally exemplary were the structures of the school and university system. Diplomas and degrees were uniform and mutually recognized, as were entrance examinations. Although I appreciate the diversity within the European Community, I feel that we are under considerable time pressure. A certain amount of streamlining and de-regulation would certainly boost the rapprochement and mutual understanding of people living in the East and West European countries.

We will only master the road to a new united Europe once we have analyzed the divisions of the past, and understood their implications. Together we must draw up new criteria for the development of European research and education in the era of globalization. Globalization with its technological and industrial ramifications is economy-driven, and poses a tremendous challenge to the EU in its entirety. The countries and regions within the EU are not equally well-prepared for this process. There is now an urgent need for a discussion about the framework – and science must speak with one voice.

During these discussions, each country (and each government) will reassert the importance of their respective systems of education, innovation and research. This is not only our most valuable asset, but is also an asset of global strategic importance. The question for Europeans is therefore how our systems can exercise that strategic role to our best advantage. We will need to create a pan-European network of "centers of competence" that will share their technology and market know-how.

Networks thrive on links and nodes; if these are strong, the network will be viable. The essence of nodes and links in Eastern and Western Europe is still different. Because the link will be of little value if the nodes are weak, new member countries will have to review the capabilities of their institutes.

Perhaps in the future, funding could be directed towards strengthening infrastructure and mobility and co-operation.

Another important element will be the ranking of technological challenges. For example, one could ask about the future role of nuclear energy research in Europe. All of Eastern Europe, and large parts or Western Europe, will be reliant on nuclear energy for many years to come. Which of these research projects will need to be continued in order to prevent the existing nuclear power plants from becoming a threat to humanity? What will be the role of final storage and re-usability? It is up to scientists from East and West to conduct fruitful and objective dialogue, since ideological isolation is no longer an issue.

In the face of high unemployment in Europe, traditional structures need to be re-assessed. Which specifically East European systemic approaches to this problem could be meaningful? In the past there were different socio-political approaches, and divergent theories. Perhaps an open and unbiased comparison could offer new insights, and even alternative employment models.

We expect openness and transparency from our new EU partners when they analyze their specific problems and devise solutions. Such a pan-European network can only become a genuine centre of competence if its rules, parameters and strategies are mutually agreed upon. This requires communication and information – This requires communication and information – two components which were unequally weighted in the former East and West European countries.

This imparity will obviously not disappear from one day to the next. As a scientist I feel the need to point out that societal processes (like physical processes) have times of relaxation. A physicist would say that different systems of vibrations are bound to have different relaxation times.

Whether networking and research can be organized in a more objective manner will depend largely on the individual scientist, and his or her feeling of responsibility towards society.

However, every scientific community is also rooted in subjective perception. After decades of isolation, it will be difficult to shed these roots in favor of a more objective outlook.

As a member of UNESCO's World Ethics Commission, I believe that every scientist who produces results has a personal accountability to society. In a Europe that is moving closer together this is of crucial importance. The Europe we believe in derives its strength from high technological competence, which is not equivalent to mere technology transfer and economic efficiency. This Europe should, rather, be one of creativity and original ideas, one in which science will have a respected place of its own."

Chapter 4:

U.S. FEDERAL POLICIES FOR INNOVATIVE START-UPS: LESSONS IN SOCIAL CAPITAL FORMATION AND THE ROLE OF THE RESEARCH UNIVERSITY

James Turner
House Committee on Science, U.S. Congress

I. INTRODUCTION

Social capital formation, the universe of programs that make an economy work more efficiently, is an important aspect of U.S. innovation policy. While other topics such as science funding priorities, tax policy, and business assistance are also essential, the United States approach to social capital formation over the past quarter century, has helped create the environment that both permitted funds to be well-spent and United States productivity to reach record levels.

I have chosen to concentrate on four policy changes that have led to increased social capital: patent policy as it relates to university research, policies related to access to federal laboratories, antitrust policy as it relates to joint research and manufacturing, and immigration policy. Each of these topics is narrow enough to illustrate a major difference between the American approach and the European approach to innovation, that is, the United States reliance on social frameworks and the European reliance on programmatic frameworks. This is a story of three eras: the time before 1980 when the first of these policies became law, the period between 1980 and 2000, and the present era which began with the inauguration of President Bush in January 2001. I have also included a brief discussion of the emergence and some of the changes in the U.S. research university from World War II to date.

Positive changes in social capital tend to be win-win solutions pushed by the political center that increase overall efficiency of our economy by making it easier for companies or even segments of the economy to work together. The key time period for the social capital developments I discuss, 1980 through 1992, was, primarily a period of divided government where the fiscally conservative Republican Party controlled the White House and the Democratic Party controlled at least one House of the Congress. At the same time, there was an intense feeling in the United States that U.S. industry was slipping in international competition. The resulting political dynamic made major funding of public/private partnership programs unlikely and required moderate bipartisan agreement on any policy changes. Therefore, it is not surprising that social capital formation flourished at this time.

I began to work on these issues in the second half of the 1970s. Today what we were doing might be called enhancing social capital or permitting economic clusters to form, but these were terms that did not exist yet. We were pre-theory, but not without big thinkers. Congressman George Brown took a leadership role in these areas for years. Bruce Merrifield, who went on to be Professor of Entrepreneurship at the Wharton School at University of Pennsylvania created the environment in the Department of Commerce that led to Administration support. Pat Windham and Cassie Phillips of the Senate Commerce Committee staff and Jonathan Yarowsky of the House Judiciary Committee were among the many Congressional staff members who both provided vision and worried about details. We were able to work hand-in-glove partially and even occasionally make major changes in law without a dissenting vote because our solutions were new and had not developed a partisan hue. Perhaps it helped that we were not focusing on a framework when we made these changes; instead, we were looking for low-cost, no-cost ways to make our small areas of the economy work more smoothly. When such solutions are found, they tend to have broad appeal.

For 20 years, there has been a policy consensus in these areas, but times may be changing. The approach of the current Bush Administration is much different than what prior administrations' approaches have been. Its emphasis is heavily on macroeconomics and tax policy and there are few in the Administration who is actively involved with these issues. Furthermore, the populist forces that stepped aside in 1980 are regrouping. I personally feel it is still an open question whether some of the policies set in motion in 1980 and which have followed a fairly straight trajectory for 20 years are still sustainable in their current form or whether major changes are coming.

2. THE SITUATION BEFORE 1980

Before the Bayh-Dole Act became law in 1980, the federal government owned all patents that came from federal research. At the time of the Act's passage, the federal government held title to over 20.000 patents. It was rare for the patents arising from federally funded research to be licensed exclusively or for commercial products to be based on federal research. Federally funded patents looked very good on the inventors' walls, but did not look very good in terms if economic impact.

Pre-1984 antitrust policy pertaining to research was equally counterproductive. Two lower court cases that had been decided against corporations doing research together. These decisions were not definitive, but there was enough uncertainty and danger that corporate lawyers were advising their clients not to take a chance and do research together. The presumption that it was illegal for companies to work together was probably even stronger regarding joint manufacturing activities.

Before the mid-1980s, federal laboratories were islands of research. In 1983, I was working for a company that was competing to win the contract to run Oak Ridge National Laboratory (ORNL) and related production facilities. Oak Ridge, since World War II, had housed some of the federal government's premier research facilities. Its budget was hundreds of millions of dollars a year. By 1983, Oak Ridge had been in existence for forty years, but in all that time, only two companies had spun out from Oak Ridge research, and the total amount of royalties from licenses of 40 years of Oak Ridge patents was less than one percent of the current annual royalty stream for NIH patent licenses. The universities, the national laboratories, and industry in 1980 were effectively three separate worlds. The universities supplied talent to the other two sectors, but they did not supply commercial ideas.

3. FEDERAL PATENT POLICY: THE BAYH-DOLE LEGACY

The Bayh Dole Act of 1980 signaled a dramatic change in federal patent policy that in prior years had met strong resistance. Bayh-Dole's major reform was to allow inventors to own their inventions. This may seem like common sense now, but in 1980 some legislators considered inventions made with federal tax dollars to be a national treasure. To them, the taxpayers who paid for the research should own the fruits of that research. It did not matter that patents are a legal monopoly that exists to provide the incentive to develop technology and products based on the invention. Other members felt that a patent owned by the public was worthless because if everyone had an equal right to license a patent, the financial incentive to apply the invention in the commercial marketplace would be greatly diminished. An entrepreneur who spent significant resources commercializing an innovation based on a non-exclusive license to a federal patent would have no way to protect that investment from those who would jump into the market shortly after the entrepreneur had done the hard work.

In 1978, The Committee on Science, for which I worked then and now, had tried to include a provision in an energy bill that allowed inventors to hold patents arising from their research funded by the Department of Energy. I attended the conference meeting where Congressmen and Senators worked out the differences in their respective versions of the legislation. Members talked for two hours about this provision before they realized change was not possible; one powerful Senator had the power to keep the status quo.

In the next Congress (1979-80), the early versions of the Bayh-Dole Act gave patent rights to entities doing research for the government regardless of size. Any contractor or grantee could insist on owning the rights to his or her invention. Opponents of the bill in its original form did not want large businesses to be eligible for free patents, but were willing to allow the Bayh-Dole Act move forward if the law's benefits applied only to small businesses and non-profit organizations. A relatively small group of universities including Purdue, the University of Wisconsin, Stanford, and the University of California were the core of the outside group encouraging the Congress to pass the Bayh-Dole legislation. Since all research universities in the United States are nonprofits, the compromise Bayh-Dole Act allowed them to own patents arising from the federally funded work of their employees. Furthermore, the Senator who had blocked changes in 1978 had announced his retirement, and he no longer stood in the way. Bayh-Dole became law in November 1980, shortly before the Congressional term ended.

Congress' goal through Bayh-Dole was to make sure patent ownership got as close to the inventors as possible because the body of knowledge that is the basis for the patent resides in the individuals who are smart enough to come up with the idea and their involvement is generally necessary for successful commercialization. Wisconsin, Stanford, and the University of California were also leaders of the small group of universities who had already established patent licensing offices. While the Act permits inventors to hold title to their own inventions, other universities quickly followed the lead of these universities and started adding technology transfer offices and began requiring as a condition of employment for university employees to sign over rights in inventions made as university employees. Resultant royalties were usually split 50-50 between the university and the inventor.

University patenting under the Bayh-Dole Act started slowly but has increased dramatically over time. There were 464 patents granted to universities in 1982, 1184 granted in 1990, and 3151 granted in 1998. I expect the current number is somewhere between 3500 and 4000. Royalty income from university licensing took longer to develop, but it grew from $130 million in 1991 to $675 million in 1999; this increase is three times as fast as the rate of growth of university research budgets during that period. Evidence that this trend is likely to continue can be found in the increased attendance at the Association of University Technology Manager's annual conference. Before 1980, perhaps 50 people would attend their meetings; this year's conference topped 5000 in attendance.

The changes at universities have been equally dramatic. One effect, we sometimes call the Porsche effect, is when a professor whose invention has been licensed uses part of the proceeds to buy a Porsche, then other professors start thinking about the potential financial rewards to them of commercialization of their own work. Major universities now have many faculty members who have one foot in the academic world and the other in the business world.

Most Bayh-Dole Act university inventions are not commercialized initially by big companies. A more recent phenomenon is university involvement with start-up companies. In 1994, 175 U.S. start-up companies were formed with university generated patents; in 1999, the 275 companies were formed. Small businesses are different financially from more established companies. They do not have the cash flow to pay royalties; this has led to payment for Bayh-Dole Act inventions through university ownership of equity positions in small companies rather than cash royalty payments. Start-up businesses need nurturing environment; the Association of University Research Parks was founded only 15 years ago, but now it has 250 members including virtually every major research university in the country. There is a payoff for universities who have happy rich alumni. If you look at the campus at MIT, last year, 40 percent of the campus was new buildings under construction and funded by people who had made their fortunes during the technology boom. Similarly, the increased research and development capabilities of universities is leading to a series of accommodations for larger companies who with increasing frequency are locating personnel and resources on or near research university campuses. For instance, Carnegie Mellon has put up a building where 28 different companies working with the university are located.

4. FEDERAL LABORATORY POLICY

The first significant changes in laboratory policy also date back to 1980 when the Stevenson-Wydler Act became law the month before Bayh-Dole. This Act required each of the federal laboratories to establish technology transfer positions on their staffs. President Carter lost the election two weeks later and President Reagan did not provide funding for the other programs contained in the Act the most important of which would have established public-private partnerships. It took eight years for a variant of these programs to be revived. The 1986 amendments to the Stevenson-Wydler Act addressed made it possible for companies to do cooperative research with the federal laboratories by creating a new type of legal agreement, the Cooperative Research and Development Agreement (CRADA).

Before this Act, a company wanting to do joint research was subject to all of the requirements faced by federal contractors. The bureaucratic costs of cooperation generally outweighed potential benefits. After the Act was passed, most of the requirements were swept away. Some laboratories can finish a standard CRADA in a week or less. If a company provides its own funding and the laboratory provides its own funding and there is a meeting of the minds, a company can propose a project on Monday and later on that week the company and the laboratory can be working together.

The 1986 Stevenson-Wydler Amendments also provided incentives to federal laboratory employees to help with the commercialization of their inventions. Federal employees, who made an invention to, in addition to their paycheck, could keep part of the royalty stream from the licensing of their invention. We set the limit of the royalty payment to a federal inventor at what was then the salary level of the president. We thought we might face a backlash if laboratory inventors were by far the highest paid federal employees in the government. There is a handful on federal laboratory employees who are at the top level in a given year at this point and no one is complaining. This provision has turned out to be a major reason why federal laboratory inventions are now commercialized. These changes, along with changes in the patent law, have led to incubators and technology parks being located at federal laboratories and to the communities where the laboratories are located now looking at their laboratories as an engine of local economic development.

5. ANTITRUST

Congress through the National Cooperative Research Act (NCRA) changed the antitrust rules related to joint research, in 1984. This may be the most profound of the social capital changes we have made. The two lawsuits that had questioned whether companies could do research together had had such a chilling effect that every corporate counsel in the country was advising their companies not to do research with other companies. By 1984, the cost of doing research in the semiconductor industry was becoming burdensome for individual companies and the United States was rapidly losing market share. The Department of Defense felt the need for domestic sources of state-of-the-art chips and was willing to invest in the SEMATECH consortium but before joining, the chip making companies felt the need for antitrust protection. It took us almost a year to work out the provisions which finally became law. Those convicted of violation of antitrust laws before 1984 had to pay three times the amount of actual damages they had caused plus the attorney's fees for all parties to the case. NCRA said that if a company registered with the Justice Department and the Federal Trade Commission and publicly disclosed their areas of joint research and the company did not commit a per se violation of the antitrust laws such as price fixing, the company would not have to pay more than actual damages for an antitrust violation. There has not been a single, successful antitrust lawsuit dealing with research since NCRA became law. Yet without this change, corporate counsels would still feel the necessity to discourage joint research.

In 1993, NCRA was amended to permit joint manufacturing. Toyota and General Motors had proposed manufacturing cars on the same assembly line and one day they would be branded as a Geo Prism, the next day as a Toyota Corolla. However, neither company would go forward, despite the obvious benefits of this cooperation, without protection from treble damages under the U.S. antitrust laws. Now it is very, very common for companies to manufacture jointly.

This year, we are in the process of extending NCRA protections to the engineering societies and other standards development organizations (SDOs) that develop voluntary consensus standards. These standards are essential to the functioning of manufacturing and most other businesses, but the antitrust laws have been used to try to force the SDOs to reference technologies in standards that are unable to prevail through the consensus standards process.

It is difficult to understate how profound a change clarifying the antitrust laws has been. Before NCRA, major companies like IBM or DuPont had major research and development facilities that were their primary sources of innovative ideas. Before NCRA, each of these companies had only a handful of collaborations. Within a few years of NCRA passage, large companies had thousands of research collaborations and small high technology companies sprung up to help meet their research needs. Today, no company would dare depend solely on its own research; to stay competitive, companies have to seek out state-of-the-art knowledge wherever it can be found. We have had the same experience following NCRA's extension to joint manufacturing. Now that we have a green light to cooperate and the communications and software technologies to make it possible, cooperation in manufacturing is becoming standard operating procedure and we are moving rapidly towards virtual companies.

6. IMMIGRATION POLICY

The fourth policy contributing to U.S. social capital is immigration policy. At least until recently immigration law has favored scientists and science and engineering students who wish to come to the United States to work in a company, to start a company, or to study. In recent years, it has not been unusual for half of the graduate students in science and engineering at prominent U.S. graduate schools to come from outside the United States and HI-B visas have readily been available to international technical workers. This has meant that we have had ideas from all over the world. In Silicon Valley at its peak, there were over 2000 businesses that had been started by Chinese and Indian immigrants and probably more businesses were started by people who were born outside the United States. So that free market in people has been a truly amazing development in the strength of the universities and in the strength of business clusters.

Some areas like Pittsburgh that see high technology industries as their future have set up committees to decide how they make the city's culture more international as well, to make sure that they have mosques and temples, library collections, cultural exchanges and art exhibits that reflect the culture of the people who are coming in to make them feel comfortable. Technological immigration has made the United States more of an international community and cities like Pittsburgh that because of the steel industry had two generations of immigrants from Middle to Eastern Europe now is a city with nationalities from around the world.

7. RESEARCH UNIVERSITIES

Until the 1950s, American universities did very little research other than agricultural research at land-grant colleges. The National Science Foundation was not founded until 1950. Serious energy research began with the founding of the Atomic Energy Commission in 1954. Both NASA and the Defense Advanced Research Projects Agency were founded in 1958 in reaction to Sputnik. The National Institutes of Health, while founded in 1887, did not expand dramatically until the 1980s. Overall since 1953, the increase in the volume of research done at universities has been two orders of magnitude. From the beginning, the federal government has been the dominant funding source of university research. While industrial research done at universities increased by an order of magnitude between 1953 to 1980, and by another order of magnitude between 1980 and 2000, companies still fund only about 10 percent of U.S. university research. Therefore, federal spending on research, and the laws that favor commercialization of the fruits of that research, work together to produce a climate of innovation.

Except for a period of decline in the late sixties/early seventies, university research has been increasing year after year after year. However it's not been increasing evenly. I think there is a misconception in Europe regarding the areas on which our universities and our governments spend these research dollars. In 1970, the National Science Foundation, the Department of Defense, NASA, and the Department of Energy funded over 50% of federal university research and provided most of the money universities used for research in the physical sciences, mathematics, and traditional engineering disciplines. Health research, coming mainly from the NIH, was already over a third of total. In the year 2000, after much of the doubling on NIH's budget had occurred, a full three-fifths of the money spent by the government in universities is in the biological and the medical sciences and related engineering disciplines. If you look at the physical sciences, they now receive half of what health research does.

University programs follow the money; if the government wants more health care research, which is what will be provided. However, the changes go further. The NIH juggernaut really is affecting both our schools of science and our schools of engineering. For instance, at the University of Virginia's School of Engineering, a bioengineering major did not exist three or four years ago. The University of Virginia now has 230 bioengineering majors at the undergraduate level and is starting the graduate program. There has been a contraction with traditional engineering programs and nuclear engineering no longer is taught there. The aerospace engineering program shrunk and has become part of mechanical engineering. These changes are partially supply and demand for students and partially alignment of the school's priorities with available research dollars. The United States must address the mix of degree candidates and research funding areas if we are going to have an adequate supply of talent in the physical sciences and in traditional engineering disciplines when the current generation of engineers retires.

I have already mentioned the internationalization of universities. At our major research universities, there also is a de-emphasis on undergraduate education and more of an emphasis on graduate schools. Another very positive trend is the movement towards interdisciplinary research which is driven in part by National Science Foundation funding opportunities. Departments still control universities, but there are a lot more interdisciplinary efforts where departments collaborate. There is a magazine called *U.S. News & World Report* that produces a widely followed ranking of U.S. graduate schools. *US News* has started including research funding and funding from industry totals as components in their rankings so I think this will only accelerate the trend towards industry-driven interdisciplinary research.

The biggest limit on expanding the research budget at most U.S. universities is not the available research dollars but the availability of laboratory space. The federal government traditionally has not spent much on construction grants, so new buildings often come from three sources: wealthy donors, cooperative ventures with industry, and municipal bond funding. My guess is all three sources will push universities closer to industry which is positive because 90 percent government funding of university research is not sustainable over the long term.

8. CURRENT TRENDS AFFECTING INNOVATION

The aftermath of September 11 is having major impacts on innovation policies. Perhaps the most major effect to date is the change in immigration policies. It is currently much more difficult for a brilliant Pakistani, Indian, or Chinese student to enter the United States in a timely fashion and in the current academic year there was a noticeable drop-off in applications and matriculations from these countries. Visa problems make international collaboration more difficult and U.S. based international conferences are difficult to stage. Hopefully, these are temporary changes, but the

U.S.'s decreased popularity in Mid-Eastern and Asian could erode the increased social capital that our enlightened immigration policies have created.

I have alluded to a Bayh Dole backlash. Bayh-Dole patent policy is being tied to the cost of drugs. A consumer advocate is trying to use Bayh-Dole march-in rights to force pharmaceutical companies to lower prices for drugs that have benefited from federal research. If successful, this could have a chilling effect on the willingness of pharmaceutical companies to commercialize the results of federal research because there would be no guarantee of a reasonable rate of return on the development costs of such drugs.

More subtle challenges include state budget cuts and repeal of the estate tax. Our estate tax has been one of the big incentives for rich people to give buildings to universities. It is unclear whether people are still going to be willing to make large contributions if there are no longer major tax advantages for doing so.

In summary, progress is not linear. There is a large constituency for the changes that have occurred over the past 25 years and universities have become a major political force, in no small part because they are the largest employers in many Congressional districts.

The outcome of the Presidential race also will have an impact. The current Bush Administration also has less interest than previous Administrations in innovation policies and the next President, whether Bush or Kerry, must get our major deficits under control. If President Bush is re-elected, if he continues to push for tax reductions, and if he continues to pursue two wars, it is difficult to see how university research and most other discretionary programs can maintain historic levels of funding in Administration budgets. While some of the cuts will be restored by Congress, maintaining university research and innovation program will be much easier under a President who is committed to these programs. I am optometric that forward steps will be taken, but I am also well aware that some setbacks may occur. However, then nature of our system is to learn from both our successes and failures and I expect that you will be able to do the same.

Chapter 5:

ENTREPRENEURSHIP AND THE INNOVATION ECOSYSTEM POLICY LESSONS FROM THE UNITED STATES

Charles W. Wessner, PhD[1]
U. S. National Academies

1. INTRODUCTION

Germany and the United States face a common challenge in promoting innovation and entrepreneurship to maintain their leadership in global markets, with the economic growth and employment both societies seek. To this end, innovative policies at national and regional level are needed so that entrepreneurs—our local heroes—can be more successful in bringing the fruits of innovation to commercial reality. There is no prescribed formula to respond to this challenge. To foster the innovation process, public policies have to recognize and facilitate entrepreneurship within the multiple local contexts within which innovation takes place. For policies to be effective, they must focus less on aggregate input measures such as R&D percentages and more on the problems and incentives facing innovative entrepreneurs.

The United States is widely seen as one of the world's most innovative economies. Yet, the U.S. innovation system is not the well-oiled machine, smoothly generating innovation after innovation, as some European observers seem to believe. Indeed, many U.S. analysts doubt that the United States is maximizing its innovative potential. One reason for this perceived underperformance may be a lack of appropriate policy support, given that U.S. policymakers often do not understand the complex nature of the innovation process. They often regard new products simply as an outcome of the natural operation of the market, requiring little or no government role.

Even those familiar with the notion of a *National Innovation System* (NIS) often have a mechanistic (rather linear) view of the innovation process, understating the interactive processes actually taking place in the economy.[2] The NIS concept is often interpreted to imply that specific inputs into the innovation system can yield specific predicted results. This view is widespread in Europe as well, where there is a recognized need to generate more companies, more growth, and more employment.

The policy solution in Europe has often focused on pumping more money into basic research to fill the research deficit with the United States[3] and generate, by 2010, "the world's most competitive economy."[4] Funding basic research is of course essential for a modern industrial economy, but the added euros will not have their desired impact unless policymakers also address the incentives facing Europe's local heroes within their own cultures and political systems. Without focusing on the institutional framework and incentive for innovation, greater R&D inputs will not translate into the desired outputs of employment and growth (Wessner and Shivakumar 2002).

2. A NATIONAL INNOVATION ECOSYSTEM

A slightly different approach, but one that captures important nuance, is to understand the economy as a national innovation *ecosystem.* This approach can help us understand, first, that the system is not fixed but evolutionary, growing and evolving according to new needs and new circumstances and, second, that this system is susceptible to change as a result of new policy initiatives. The ecosystems approach highlights the complex *inter-linkages* among a variety of participants in an innovation economy (including individual entrepreneurs, as well as corporate actors such as large businesses and universities) and the importance of the *incentives* the various actors encounter as they push towards an "innovation friendly environment." Innovation, like regional competitiveness, will not be achieved by fiat but rather through a combination of public and private initiatives.

As we will see in the U.S. context below, an ecosystem approach to innovation policy draws special attention to the role of small businesses in economic growth and job creation. The analysis below should help dispel common myths about the nature of innovation and the positive role that government support can play. We also describe how innovative policies, like the U.S. Small Business Innovation Research (SBIR) program, have helped motivate new entrepreneurship and have helped entrepreneurs bridge the gap in early-stage technology funding, bringing as a result new, wealth creating ideas to commercial reality. The ecosystem concept is useful because it highlights both the changes that take place in an innovation system and the need for policy innovations to address the complex challenges that Germany and the United States face in promoting their local heroes in the global village.

3. SMALL BUSINESS AND INNOVATION

It is now widely recognized that small businesses are a key driver of the United States economy.[5] They have generated sixty to eighty percent of net new jobs annually over the past decade and employ nearly forty percent of the United States' science and engineering workforce (Small Business Administration 2004). These scientists and engineers, working in small businesses, produce fourteen times more patents than their counterparts in large patenting firms. These patents, moreover, are of high quality and are twice as likely to be cited.[6]

Another characteristic of small firms is that relatively small increments of investments can have a very high payoff in terms of long-term growth (Branscomb and Auerswald 2001). Such investments in early-stage technology development refresh the nation's economic foundations by transforming its science and engineering knowledge into valuable, sometimes "game-changing" innovations. In many cases, critical early investments in demonstration projects, new technology development, and R&D have been provided by the U.S. government. This important government role is not widely recognized in the United States. Yet as tab. 5.1 below illustrates, many major innovations were made possible through government funding for early-stage technology development.

Tab. 5.1: Precedents for public role in commercialization of science in the U.S.

- 1798 – Grant to Eli Whitney to produce muskets with interchangeable parts, founds first machine tool industry.
- 1842 – Samuel Morse receives award to demonstrate feasibility of telegraph.
- 1903 – Wright Brothers fly, fulfilling the terms of an Army contract.
- 1915 – National Advisory Committee for Aeronautics plays an instrumental role in the rapid advance in commercial and military aircraft technology.
- 1919 – Radio manufacturing (RCA) founded on the initiative (Equity and Board Membership) of the U.S. Navy with commercial and military rationales.
- 1940s, '50s, and '60s – Government investments in Jet Aircraft, Semiconductors, Computers, Satellites, Nuclear Energy lay the "Foundations of the Modern Economy" (Cohen and Noll 1992).
- 1969-1990s – Government investments create the forerunners of the Internet (Arpanet) and build the Global Positioning System.
- Today: Current investments are mainly found in genomic and biomedical research, and advanced computing and new materials, (e.g., nanotechnology initiatives).

Despite these and other achievements, many in the United States argue that it is "un-American" to intervene in the market by providing public support for private companies. This view suggests that in the United States, as elsewhere, the messy realities of the innovation process are often disconnected from how our political establishments and many influential people think about it. This disconnect has led to (what might be gently referred to as) curious ambiguities in public policy. For example, despite having noted the contributions of small firms to the economy, small firms are penalized, in effect, for their contributions through disproportionately large regulatory burdens. For instance, small firms (those with less than twenty employees) spend sixty percent more per employee than large firms to comply with federal regulations (Crain and Hopkins 2001).

Another example of this ambiguity concerns the frequent disputes over public support for early-stage technology development. New firms struggle for adequate funding, with over eighty percent of them relying on various forms of formal credit. Given the increase in public welfare that arises from successful innovation, early stage funding for innovation by the government would appear to be in the national interest—and, as tab. 5.1 shows, it has frequently been so. The Advanced Technology Program (ATP), a well-designed but modestly funded merit based federal initiative, fulfills just this role. Over the years, it has developed an impressive track record of support for new technology development and commercialization, ranging from fuel cells to proteomics to medical diagnostics. In fact, ATP has been given very high marks by the National Academies and has been cited internationally as a best practice model (National Research Council 2001).

Yet the House of Representatives has called for the elimination of the program every year since 1996. These calls are normally based on the argument that the government should not "pick winners and losers." In the American lexicon, this means that government should not "intervene" in the economy. Opponents of the program assume that markets work well and that good ideas will therefore also be funded by the market.[7] Such myths about the innovation system are widely held both in the U.S. and Europe. Understanding the underlying reality behind these myths is important for effective policymaking on both sides of the Atlantic.

4. MYTHS AND REALITIES ABOUT GOVERNMENT SUPPORT OF INDUSTRY R&D

Myths concerning government support for industry research and development often arise from a simple mechanistic understanding of, what is in reality, a complex innovation ecosystem. The linear model of innovation (See fig. 5.1) is as pervasive as it is erroneous. It creates the impression that increasing public and private investments in research will automatically result in greater commercialization, strengthening, in turn, national competitiveness in global markets. While its appeal lies in the elegance of its exposition, it is easy to forget that this simple model severely understates the complex interactions that actually take place within the innovation process.[8]

Fig 5.1: The myth of the linear model of innovation

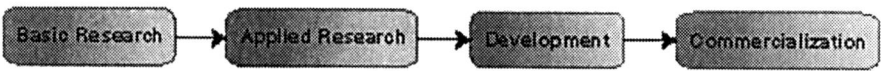

In the real world of research and innovation, distinctions between basic and applied research are rarely clear cut. (As Alan Bromley, the first President Bush's Science Advisor famously remarked, whether the work is considered basic or applied frequently depends on the researcher's intent at a given moment in time.) Many discoveries have a serendipitous element. Much learning occurs by trial and error. Many good ideas simply do not make it to the market place. The process from discovery to innovation to commercialization involves consecutive challenges and market signals that can often be indistinct or even absent.

A more sophisticated representation of the innovation process (though still, it must be emphasized, a model) includes feedback loops through which learning occurs. These loops—portrayed in fig. 5.2—suggest that technological breakthroughs may proceed, as well as stem from, basic research. This representation questions—though does not preclude—the implicit primacy of curiosity driven research, unrelated to markets or social needs. In the real world, many questions worthy of research are in fact derived from industry or social needs (Stokes 1997).[9]

Fig. 5.2: A non-linear model of innovation

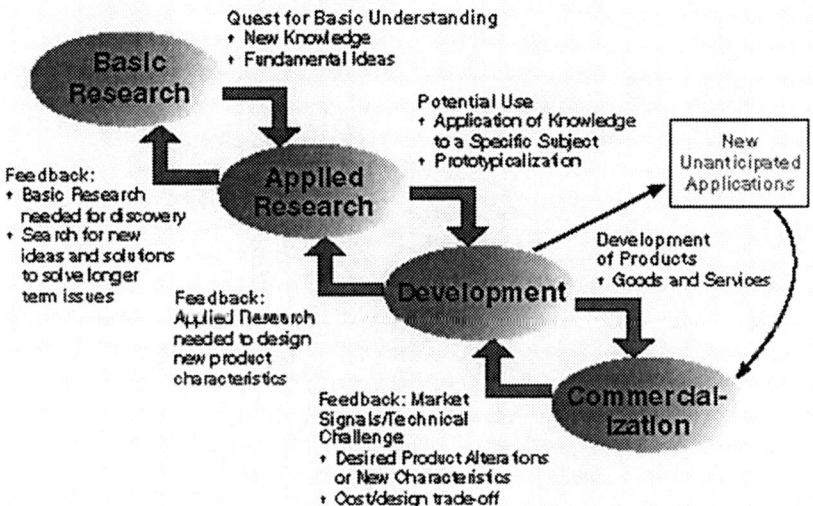

4.1 Is There a 3% Solution?

This complexity of innovation means that numerical targets for research expenditures must be accompanied by policies and actions that focus on the incentives and intermediating institutions designed to focus researchers' attention more on problems needing science-based solutions rather than on science for its own sake.

In the understandable desire to encourage innovation, and demonstrate a commitment to competitiveness, the European Council's Barcelona Declaration set an ambitious objective of increasing the Union's global research expenditure to approach three percent of Gross Domestic Product by 2010 with the specific goal of achieving greater firm growth and innovation.[10] Yet questions about the efficacy of this approach are widespread. One difficulty is that some European countries, like Sweden, already have high R&D expenditure as a percent of GDP with very limited *new* firm growth or innovation (outside large firms) to show for the high R&D expenditures. The case of Sweden strongly suggests that there is no correlation, must less causality, between levels of input expenditures on R&D and desired levels of innovation-led growth (Henrekson and Rosenberg 2001).

It is important to keep in mind that Europe is one of the world's foremost centers for research. The quality of European research is not in question. The problem facing many European countries relates more to how they may capitalize on the *existing* R&D investments. While the three percent target, described by some as a political goal, has the virtue of focusing public attention on the need for innovation, its actual import has been limited at best. The practical challenge is for policymakers to focus on creating better incentives for researchers in companies and universities to encourage them to convert their ideas into innovations and, eventually, into promising products for the global market.[11] Promoting a better understanding among policymakers of the realities of the innovation process is a major and necessary step in facilitating innovation while providing the opportunity to generate measurable returns on incremental R&D investments.

4.2 They Myth of Military Spin-Offs

In the same vein, understanding the sources of U.S. strength in innovation is important, especially if policy prescriptions for Europe are to draw from U.S. practice. One aspect of the U.S. innovation system that seems particularly susceptible to misinterpretation is the role of U.S. defense spending. There is, of course, a commonly held myth in Europe that U.S. defense research and procurement directly funds civilian technologies.

The myth appears to be rooted in selected examples in history that, to the extent they were accurate, no longer hold useful insights concerning the operation of the U.S. innovation system. Military support for aircraft, for example, is often cited as evidence for military-civilian spin-off. While it is true that defense procurement initiated research that helped Boeing develop the 707 (and to a lesser extent the 747) commercial aircraft, this happened over 50 years ago and in the context of an intense threat to European and U.S. security. These and other investments helped achieve a key U.S. policy goal (i.e. a credible capacity to transport troops and equipment rapidly), thereby making the need to do so less likely. These investments provided massive positive spillovers by deterring conflict and also fueling the boom in tourism that continues to enrich the lives of travelers and hosts around the world

It is important to understand that this spin-off model is less and less relevant to U.S. innovation. Indeed, many U.S. analysts argue that in today's world, U.S. defense related investments tend at best to yield only modest civilian benefits. For example, the hugely expensive development of Stealth technology for aircraft appears to have no foreseeable civilian market even though it provides significant military advantage. Extremely reputable U.S. analysts have argued that the requirements of military secrecy, military specifications, and long lead times associated with Pentagon procurement all act to slow the diffusion of new defense related technologies.[12]

The problem for the American defense establishment, moreover, is that the procurement-based innovation system no longer works well. Many argue that U.S. defense programs desperately need "spin in"—that is the ability to draw technologies rapidly from the commercial sector—a process that is impeded by a cumbersome procurement system that tends to protect a de facto oligopoly of established companies.[13]

The potential for military spin-off in the United States is also limited in part because the scale of the U.S. defense industrial sector has shrunk significantly following the end of the cold war, with the number of major U.S. defense contractors down from fifteen to five. To put this in perspective, consider that Intel Corporation is today valued at a hundred and fifty billion dollars—larger than the top three defense groups combined. This scaling-down means that the impact of defense R&D expenditures in the United States has a more modest impact on civilian innovation than commonly believed in Europe, and generally hoped for in the United States. Belief in this spin-off model can have negative consequences if it prompts additional budget support for defense R&D—support that is unlikely to yield the expected pay-offs in innovative civilian technologies and GDP growth.

4.3 The Myth of Perfect Markets

If some Europeans closely hold on to their belief that U.S. defense technology converts seamlessly to new commercial products, Americans themselves have deeply held myths about how their economy produces innovation. A common American myth is that "if it's a good idea, the market will fund it." In reality there is no such thing as "the market." Unlike the market model found in introductory economics texts, real world markets always operate within specific rules and conventions that lend unique characteristics to particular markets, and most markets suffer from seriously imperfect information.

Indeed, the problem of imperfect capital markets is particularly challenging for fledgling entrepreneurs. The knowledge that an entrepreneur has about his or her product may not be fully appreciated by potential customers—a phenomenon that economists call *asymmetric information*. This asymmetry can make it hard for small firms to obtain funding for new ideas because, as Michael Spence a recent winner of the Nobel Prize points out, new ideas are inherently hard to understand.[14] Few investors in the 1980's, for example, understood Bill Gates vision for Microsoft.

> **Box 1: Why US R&D spending on defense does not spill-over into civilian technologies**
>
> A recent study by PREST's Andrew James for the European Commission underscores the limitations of U.S. defense spending to the competitiveness of American commercial technologies. While the paper seems designed to support the view that the U.S. defense R&D spending contributes to U.S. competitiveness, to his credit, James nonetheless documents the concerns of U.S. analysts who argue that role of defense R&D is seriously overstated.
>
> - First, given that the bulk of the RDT&E[a] budget remains directed at development funding of traditional platforms (such as of combat aircraft) there are limited opportunities for civilian spin-offs—such as from heavy investments in stealth technologies noted earlier.
> - Second, U.S. analysts question whether current funding for R&D is the right R&D for economic growth. U.S. analysts note that federal R&D funding has skewed in recent years towards the life sciences. Overall U.S. spending for R&D appears high because of growth in funding for Defense development and for Homeland Security development, while the major federal sponsors of physical sciences and environmental sciences have seen budget stagnation, real cuts, or at best modest growth. The affected agencies would include the Department of Energy Office of Science, Department of Defense S&T programs, NASA, NSF, the National Oceanographic and Atmospheric Administration, the Department of Interior, and the National Institute of Standards and Technology.
> - Third, "the premise of spending money on defense R&D in the hope of gaining spin-off benefits is an ineffective policy at best. While there are some spin-offs, US analysts point out that this is hardly an efficient means of enhancing commercial competitiveness. The bulk of defense R&D spending remains focused on engineering development, testing, and evaluation where the prospects of spin-off benefits are relatively limited."
>
> Source: James 2004
> [a] Research, Development, Testing and Evaluation. Heavy expenditure takes place in the latter two phases.

Market entry is thus a challenge for new entrepreneurs with new ideas for a potentially disruptive product. These entrepreneurs tend to be unfamiliar with government regulations and procurement procedures, and more broadly may be unacquainted with commercial accounting and business practices. Many small firms are therefore at a disadvantage vis-à-vis incumbents in the defense procurement process, and face especially high challenges with regard to finance.[15]

Another hurdle for entrepreneurs is *the leakage of new knowledge* that escapes the boundaries of firms and intellectual property protection. The creator of new knowledge can seldom fully capture the economic value of that knowledge for his or her own firm. This spillover can inhibit investment in promising technologies for large and small firms—though it is especially important for small firms focused on a promising product or process (Mansfield 1986).

The challenge of incomplete and insufficient information for investors and the problem for entrepreneurs of moving quickly enough to capture a sufficient return on "leaky" investments pose substantial obstacles for new firms seeking capital. The difficulty of attracting investors to support an imperfectly understood, as yet-to-be-developed innovation is especially daunting. Indeed, the term, *Valley of Death* has come to describe the period of transition when a developing technology is deemed promising, but too new to validate its commercial potential and thereby attract the capital necessary for its development[16] (see fig. 5.3). This simple image of the "Valley of Death" captures an important point, namely that technological value does not lead inevitably to commercialization. Many good ideas perish on the way to the market.

Fig.5.3: The valley of death

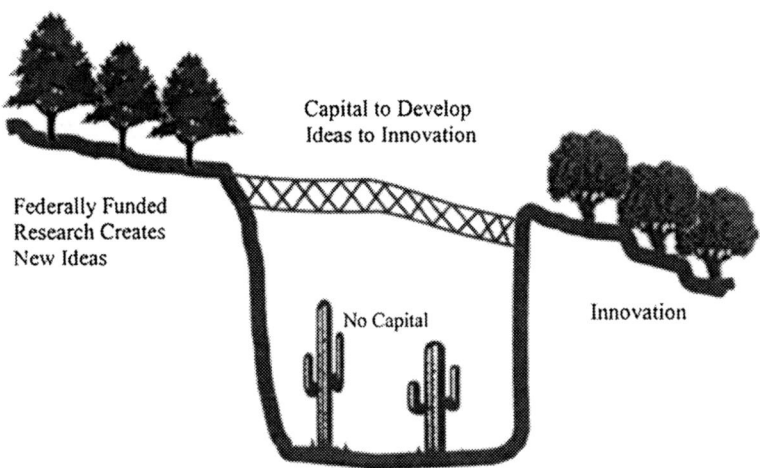

4.4 The Myth of U.S. Venture Capital Markets

A related myth is that the U.S. venture capital markets are so broad and deep that there's no need for government awards. In reality venture capitalists not only have limited information on new firms, as we have seen, but are also prone to herding tendencies, as witnessed in the recent dot.com boom and bust (Jacobs 2002 : 973).

Venture capitalists also, quite naturally, risk averse. Their goal, after all, is not to develop the nation's economy but to earn significant returns for their investors.[17] Accordingly, they tend to focus on later stages of technology development, because there is more information at this stage in the process about the commercial prospects of the innovation (and hence less risk to their investment.) And the amount of venture capital made available varies enormously, depending in no small part on the health of the stock market, which is the normal outlet for Initial Public Offerings where venture capitalists recoup their fund's investments. As fig. 5.4 below shows, venture capital fundraising and investment collapsed because the opportunities to harvest a private equity investment through Initial Public Offerings closed following the dramatic stock market declines of March 2000 (Megginson 2004).

Fig.5.4: Total equity investments into venture backed companies

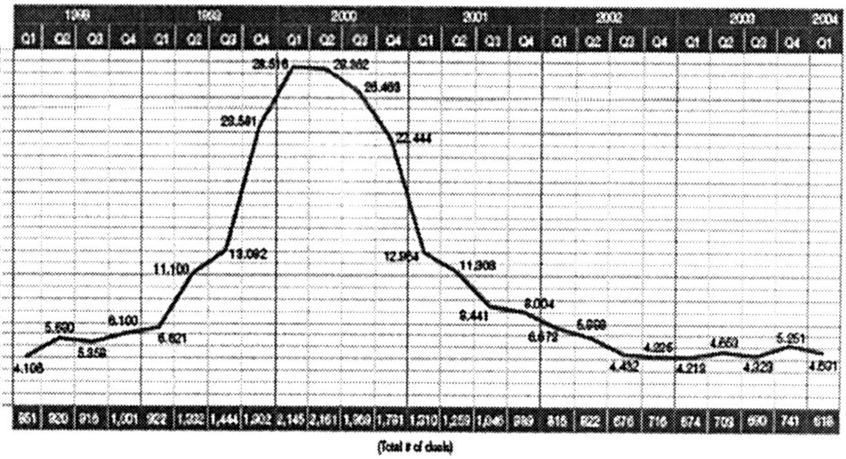

Source: PricewaterhouseCoopers et al 2004: 1

Another frequently overlooked limitation to the contribution of venture capital is that the average size of venture capital investments has gone up. Because of their reward structure, most venture firms find it uneconomical to fund and monitor small investments (Lerner 1999). The problem is that most small companies do not need and/or do not qualify for sums on the order of $6 million. Small companies more often require funds in the range of $500.000 to $1.5 million. For these reasons, there is frequently no venture capital solution to meet the needs of new technology firms. The realities behind the venture capital myth, as that of other myths, require public policies that support entrepreneurship and encourage or provide seed funding for new firms.

5. U.S. POLICIES FOR INNOVATION LED GROWTH

What is often left out of European discussion of the U.S. innovation system are its systemic aspects—i.e., the environment for innovation. In the United States, the environment for innovation is shaped by policies concerning areas such as taxation, capital markets, intellectual property, as well as a host of regulations—often critical for new firms—concerning market entry, labor standards, and of course bankruptcy. Such policies and regulations define the risk-reward ratio for aspiring entrepreneurs. Together, they condition the willingness of entrepreneurs to take on the risk of firm creation. They can also condition the willingness of investors to support entrepreneurs as they move an idea from the laboratory to the marketplace.

The generally supportive nature of these policies (buttressed by accommodating social and cultural attitudes) is one of the defining features of the U.S. innovation system.[18]

Tab. 5.2: Policy incentives for local heroes

- Innovation grants provide seed capital for entrepreneurs to start new firms—e.g. SBIR
- Competitively reviewed awards create information for markets, encouraging private capital investment in early-stage development—e.g., SBIR and ATP
- Intellectual property rights encourage invention by securing the fruits of invention
- Non-confiscatory tax policies preserve the rewards of entrepreneurship, and hence motivate entrepreneurship
- Labor flexibility provides firms the confidence to hire new workers—firms that can't fire won't hire.
- Gentle bankruptcy laws that enable entrepreneurs to assume the risk of a start-up without betting their homes and their futures.

5.1 Multiple Sources of Funding

Funding for innovation is another important component of U.S. innovation policy. The funding is substantial if limited in relation to the economy as a whole, and the sources of finance are quite diverse. Although business angels and venture capital firms, along with industry, state governments, and universities provide funding for some aspects of early stage technology development, the federal role seems to be larger than is generally thought. Recent research by Branscomb and Auerswald estimated that the federal government provides between 20 to 25 percent of all funds for early stage technology development—a substantial role by any measure and one surprising to Americans in its dimensions (see fig. 5.5).[19]

This contribution is rendered more significant in that competitive government awards address segments of the innovation cycle that private investors often find too risky. Because technology-based firms are a significant source of innovation and competitive advantage for the United States, it is important to improve our understanding of the role public-private partnerships policies—in this case, innovation awards—play in encouraging small-firm growth in the United States (National Research Council 2002).

The availability of early stage financing and its interaction with other elements of the U.S. innovation process are the focus of growing analytical efforts.[20] As we examine below, the Small Business Innovation Research Program (SBIR) is the largest example of the government's public-private partnership efforts to draw on the inventiveness of small, high-technology firms though competitive innovation awards. The potential of SBIR in this regard underscores the need to understand how it strengthens the nation's innovation ecosystem.

Fig. 5.5: Estimated distribution of funding sources for early-stage technology development

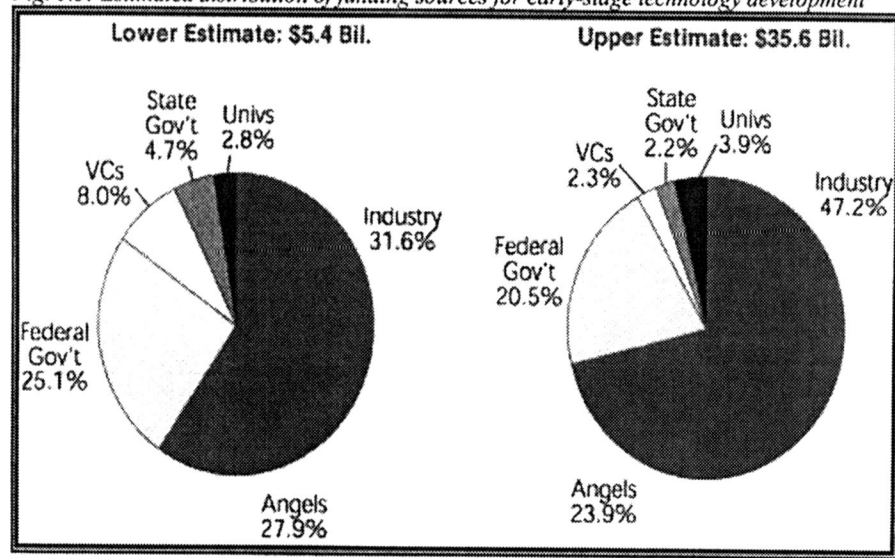

Source: Branscomb and Auerswald 2002: 23

6. THE SMALL BUSINESS INNOVATION RESEARCH PROGRAM (SBIR)

Created in 1982 and renewed in 1992 and 2001, SBIR requires agencies with an extramural research and development budget of more than $100 million to set aside 2.5 percent of this budget for innovation awards to small businesses. The program is structured in three phases:

- Phase I is essentially a feasibility study in which award winners undertake a limited amount of research aimed at establishing an idea's scientific and commercial promise. Today, the legislation anticipates Phase I grants as high as $100.000.[21] The program is highly competitive, with less than 15 percent of the applicants receiving awards.

- Phase II grants are larger—normally $750.000—and fund more extensive R&D to further develop the scientific and technical merit and the feasibility of research ideas; about half of the Phase I awardees receive Phase II funding.

- Phase III. This phase normally does not involve SBIR funds, but is the stage at which grant recipients should be obtaining additional funds either from a procurement program at the agency that made the award, from private investors, or from the capital markets. The objective of this phase is to move the technology to the prototype stage and into the commercial marketplace or government procurement, depending on the product.

Phase III of the program is often fraught with difficulty for new firms. In practice, agencies have developed different approaches to facilitating this transition to commercial viability; not least among them are additional SBIR awards.[22] Some firms with more experience with the program have become skilled in obtaining additional awards. Previous NRC research has shown that different firms have quite different objectives in applying to the program. Some seek to demonstrate the potential of promising research. Others seek to fulfill agency research requirements on a cost-effective basis. Still others seek a certification of quality (and the investments that can come from such recognition) as they push science-based products towards commercialization (Cramer 2000).

Features that make SBIR grants attractive from the firm's perspective include the fact that there is no dilution of ownership or repayment required. Importantly, grant recipients retain rights to intellectual property developed using the SBIR award, with no royalties owed to the government. The government retains royalty free use for a period, but this is very rarely exercised. Selection to receive SBIR grants also tend to confer a certification effect—a signal to private investors of the technical and commercial promise of the technology.[23]

6.1 Government Goals

From the perspective of the government, the SBIR program helps achieve agency missions as well as encourage knowledge-based economic growth (National Research Council 2004). By providing a bridge between small companies and the federal agencies, especially for procurement, SBIR serves as a catalyst for the development of new ideas and new technologies to meet federal missions in health, transport, the environment, and defense. It also provides a bridge between universities and the marketplace, thereby encouraging local and regional growth. Finally, by addressing gaps in early-stage funding for promising technologies, the program helps the nation capitalize on its substantial investments in research and development. While SBIR operations and accomplishments are sometimes discussed in general terms, the actual implementation of the program is carried out in agencies with quite distinct missions and interests. There is, therefore, significant variation in objectives and mechanisms.

Today, eleven agencies and departments grant SBIR awards totaling some $2 billion annually to support a wide variety of federal missions. While large, overall, SBIR is decentralized in terms of the agencies responsible for its implementation. This decentralization reflects the diversity of program goals and the variety of award recipients covered under SBIR. For example, SBIR awards by the National Institutes of Health (NIH) are often—although not exclusively— directed towards initiating long-term drug development. Those awarded by the Department of Defense (DoD) by comparison, are often directed towards shorter-term product acquisition and defense-only applications. It is important to note that there is important variation across and within agencies. For example, sub-units of large agencies such as NIH and DoD pursue their own distinctive organizational goals. Within DoD alone, these vary from outfitting Special Forces to supply management to the development of vaccines to protect troops to improving telecommunications. Reflecting this mission diversity, each agency typically also has its own manner of initiating solicitations, choosing awardees, and screening for applicants.

Tab.5.3: Contributions of SBIR concept

✓ Catalyzes the development of new ideas and new technologies
✓ Helps create new firms to capitalizes on substantial U.S. R&D investments
✓ Addresses gaps in early-stage funding for promising technologies
✓ Certification Effect—Government endorsement of technical quality acts as a positive signal, attracting private investment
✓ Provides a bridge between small companies and government agencies, especially for procurement
✓ Contributes new methods and new technologies to agency missions

Key among the contributions of the SBIR concept (summarized in tab. 5.3 above) is its certification effect. The fact the government is giving an entrepreneur an award based on a two-phase review of technical merits and commercial potential is a signal of quality that attracts private capitalists seeking to reduce the uncertainties associated with early-stage finance. This certification effect contradicts another common policy myth that innovation awards "crowd-out" private capital. Indeed, recent empirical research by Paul David, Bronwyn Hall, and Andrew Toole demonstrates that there is only, at best, equivocal empirical support for the contention that private capital is crowded out (David, Hall and Toole 1999).

Indeed, recent research commissioned by the National Academies has found that competitive innovation awards can "crowd-in" investment capital because of the halo effect of the government endorsement (Feldman and Kelley 2001). In sum, programs like SBIR can stimulate the commercial application of scientific research and help bridge the Valley of Death by providing seed capital and validation for private investors. As we see below, public-private partnerships like SBIR can also act as a catalyst for cooperation, linking university researchers, companies, and research institutions to bring new ideas to market.

7 THE ENABLING ROLE OF UNIVERSITIES

Research universities are a key component of the U.S. innovation ecosystem. Their role as focal points in the innovation system has evolved tremendously over the last twenty years. More than ever before, industry depends on university research for new ideas for improved products and processes, while university researchers frequently draw ideas from commercial trends to explore new veins of scientific inquiry.

The university role in the regional economy has also undergone significant change. Universities are increasingly recognized not only as centers of learning but also as poles of regional growth and employment. It is important to note that the distribution of university contributions to local economies is by no means even. There is significant variation across states and regions in the United States, with some universities such as MIT and Stanford now recognized as global centers of innovation, while others are much less active and less effective in commercializing new technologies. The contribution of U.S. universities to innovation and growth is, nevertheless, widespread. In Pittsburgh, Pennsylvania, for example, the University of Pittsburgh and Carnegie-Mellon University have become the largest employers in the region and are spurring the creation of innovative new firms, helping to replace the reliance of the regional economy on the steel industry.[24]

Box 2: Universities as engines of economic growth

"To suggest that, somehow, universities are not and should not be engines of economic growth is missing the central point of how our economy grows and how we create jobs."

Robert Birgeneau, Chancellor, UC Berkeley
Quoted on NPR Morning Edition, Date: 08-09-04

The growth of the U.S. biotech industry to its position of world leadership is associated by some with the close links between American universities and industry. This type of cooperation is increasingly found in Germany as well. The University of Munich, for example, spun off a series of private companies during the dotcom boom, suggesting that with the right leadership and incentives, German universities can contribute to the creation of innovative new companies as well (Washburn 2000: 9).

Universities, in turn, also benefit from their connection to their communities. Encouraged by the Bayh-Dole University and Small Business Patent Act—a 1980 federal law that permits government grantees and contractors to retain title to federally funded inventions and encourages universities to license inventions to industry—universities are now encouraged to license technologies for commercial exploitation.[25] This, however, has, sometimes led to protracted disputes about patent valuations between inventors and investors. In order to better align the interests of universities with those of their licensees, universities are now taking equity positions with increasing frequency (Feldman, Feller, Bercovitz and Burton 2002). When the SBIR program was created in the early 1980s, universities strongly objected to the program, seeing it as a source of competition for federal R&D funds.

In the course of the decade of the 1990s, this perception of the program significantly evolved. In the commercialization-sensitive environment created by Bayh-Dole, SBIR awards were increasingly seen as a source of early-stage financial support for promising ideas.

Fig 5.6: How ideas are commercialized: transferring university technology to firms

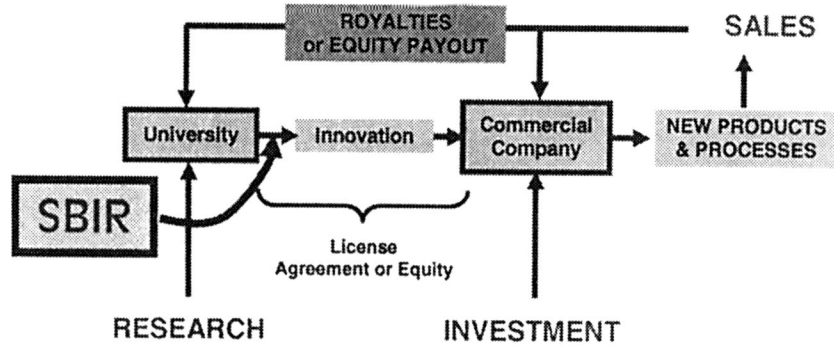

Source: Adapted from C. Gabriel, Carnegie Mellon University

The role of SBIR in encouraging professors to found companies based on their research appears to be growing in importance.[26] Importantly, the availability of the awards and the fact that a professor can apply for an SBIR award without actually having a firm, encourages applications from academics who would not otherwise be likely to commercialize directly their own technologies. Initial National Academy of Sciences research has shown that SBIR awards directly cause the creation of new firms, with positive benefits in employment and growth for the local economy.[27]

Contrary to what one might expect, the awards generally do not seem to detract from the teaching role of the university professor. On the contrary, the real life application of research with the attendant recognition in academic, technical, and financial terms can serve as a source of inspiration for students to pursue the real-world applications of their studies. Similarly, well-constructed agreements can provide access to otherwise cost-prohibitive technological resources thus enhancing the relevance of the students' educational experience.[28] University innovation along with early-stage funding by the government have spurred the growth of many successful technology companies, promoting a positive symbiotic relationship between the university and the regional economy.[29]

8. COMMON CHALLENGES IN INNOVATION POLICY: THE NEED FOR CIVIC ENTREPRENEURS

Policymakers around the world are focused on the challenges of making their economies more innovative. Many face genuine obstacles in encouraging university-industry cooperation and other types of public-private partnerships for the development of new technologies. Policymakers in both Germany and the U.S. face a common challenge in capitalizing on the substantial investments in R&D made by their nations. This is especially true with regard to the commercialization of publicly-funded research and development.[30]

Can the lessons gained from the U.S. experience be adapted for Germany? There are certainly cultural differences between Germany and the United States, yet the claims by some of American exceptionalism seem unwarranted. Our view is that there is a great deal of quality research and that there are many potential entrepreneurs on both sides of the Atlantic. The issue is how to provide the necessary incentives on one hand and reduce bureaucratic and regulatory obstacles on the other.

The concept of the innovation ecosystem draws attention to the need for civic entrepreneurs willing to take the steps necessary to clear the path and generate opportunities for private entrepreneurs. Effective policies to promote innovation-led growth and employment will require the political flexibility to change institutions so that incentives facing individuals are more closely aligned with broader social goals of economic dynamism and the political choices it offers nations and communities.

9. LESSONS FROM THE SBIR PROGRAM

The SBIR program, an example of civic entrepreneurship, has evolved over its twenty year history to provide major incentives to potential and existing entrepreneurs in the Untied States, while enabling the government to achieve important social missions in the environment, transportation, defense, health, and space exploration more efficiently.[31] As one of the most effective U.S public-private partnerships, the SBIR program provides some important lessons for comparable initiatives in civic entrepreneurship in Germany and elsewhere:

- *Focus innovation programs on the individual entrepreneur.* After all, countries don't innovate; firms do. Industry initiation and management of projects is essential. Providing broad solicitations to attract a variety of approaches towards achieving a given government mission is one of the SBIR program's strengths.
- *Limiting the government's participation.* Ensuring that government funds are granted on a competitive basis, with real and transparent competitions, is essential. Requiring industry cost share, and limiting public commitments in funds and time are important to maintain the

entrepreneur's commitment to a successful commercial outcome and to identifying technical failure early in the development cycle.
- *Improving markets by encouraging private initiative.* Government innovation awards such as SBIR do not replace the market. They can improve imperfect investment markets by creating new information about the quality of an innovation (through government and private review) and the commercial potential (by government interest and/or implicit endorsement) of the product. Another one of SBIR's major advantages is its bottom-up approach, relying on self-initiation by entrepreneurs with ideas for technologies applicable to government needs or commercial markets.
- *Match policies to market realities.* SBIR focuses on market processes—the environment where real entrepreneurs make real decisions—rather than on policy inputs—the realm of economists and their models of innovation. Without attention to market processes, more inputs into the innovation process (such as the European Commission's 3 percent solution for innovation-led growth) will not necessarily deliver better results.
- *Take advantage of Constructive Confusion.* While a harmonized policy looks well ordered from the policymaker's point of view, it often fails to make sense from the entrepreneur's perspective and can easily understate the diverse public needs and institutional processes. Policies that provide points of coordination for multiple and localized industry initiated efforts, by contrast, can exploit the richness of diversity in a nation's innovation ecosystem. A strength of the SBIR program is that it is administered flexibly, allowing the program to adapt to the various agency missions, scientific opportunities, and commercial imperatives. A centrally managed system with the attendant bureaucratic procedures and controls could well stifle the program.
- *Foster a culture for innovation.* Fostering a culture of innovation requires a change in the incentives facing entrepreneurs and others in the innovation ecosystem. Encouraging more professors to start new companies to commercialize their research ideas, for example, will come about only when the university supports and rewards such behavior in one form or another. This need for a change in university culture is often easier to recognize than to effect. One way to address this is to encourage parallel research institutions that encourage and reward cooperation on research relevant to industry needs.

These lessons, while important, provide no one-size-fits-all solution; there is no American panacea for the innovation challenge facing European economies. Germany, however, recognizes the nature of its challenge, and Chancellor Schroeder's attention to the role innovation merits broad national support. As we have seen, SBIR can promote local heroes as part of a national strategy for realize greater returns on national investments in research while strengthening the research and regional growth so necessary for Germany's future.

NOTES

[1] The author would like to recognize the many important contributions of his colleague Dr. Sujai Shivakumar of the National Academies Board on Science, Technology, and Economic Policy to the preparation of this paper.

[2] The National Innovation System (NIS) approach concerns how knowledge is created, diffused, and used in an economy. In particular, the NIS research agenda focuses on complex mechanisms promoting knowledge distribution, national and regional policies, economic and knowledge infrastructures, and international linkages and comparisons. Richard Nelson has played a leading role in developing and disseminating the concept of a national innovation system (Nelson 1993).

[3] For example, see COM 2003, European Commission, DG Research. (Luxembourg). *Third European Report on Science and Technology Indicators* (www.cordis.lu/indicators).

[4] The 2010 goal is stated in the European Union's Lisbon Strategy. See http://europa.eu.int/comm/lisbon_strategy/index_en.html.

[5] Birch's work exercised major influence on the perception of the role of small firms. David Audretsch and Zoltan Acs have also pioneered research on the role of small firms in the economy (Acs and Audretsch 1990).

[6] Ibd.

[7] Although program proponents have so far saved the program, the yearly uncertainty over funding is not desirable, by any definition, for an R&D program requiring companies to prepare complex submissions to justify funding. The fact that applications have risen in recent years attests both to the value and perceived quality of ATP and to the dearth of alternate sources of early-stage funding.

[8] While, as the limiting case, the innovation process can be relatively simple, such examples are rarely found in the real-world.

[9] The complementarities between applied and basic research was persuasively argued in Stokes 1997.

[10] See European Council, Presidency Conclusions—Barcelona, 15 and 16 March 2002, SN100/1/02 REV 1, Page 20.

[11] Wessner and Shivakumar op cit. For the challenge of transforming ideas into innovations, see Branscomb and Auerswald, op. cit.

[12] Alic documented this phenomenon in 1992 (Alic 1992).

[13] This problem is succinctly described in a White Paper by Senator Lieberman's office. See "White Paper: Nation Security Aspects of the Global Migration of the U.S. Semiconductor Industry." Office of Senator Lieberman, June 2003, p. 1-2, http://lieberman.senate.gov/newsroom/whitepapers/semiconductor.pdf.

[14] The Nobel Committee cited Spence's contribution in highlighting the importance of market signals in the presence of information asymmetries. For his seminal paper on this topic, see Spence 1974.

[15] Innovators in large firms also face a similar problem, where multiple options, established hurdle rates, and technological and market uncertainties militate against even promising technologies. As noted by Dr. Bruce Griffing, the laboratory manager responsible for developing mammography diagnostic technology for General Electric noted, *"There is a valley of death for new technologies, even in the largest companies."* (Griffing 2001). With regard to the challenges small firms face in obtaining funding, see Branscomb and Auerswald,

Taking Technical Risks, op. cit. See also Josh Lerner, "Public Venture Capital," in National Research Council, *The Small Business Innovation Program: Challenges and Opportunities*, C. Wessner, ed. Washington, D.C.: National Academy Press, 1999.

[16] See Vernon J. Ehlers, *Unlocking Our Future: Toward a New National Science Policy, A Report to Congress by the House Committee on Science* (Washington, D.C.: GPO, 1998). Accessed at http://www.access.gpo.gov/congress/house/science/cp105-b/science105b.pdf.

[17] "The goal of venture capitalists is to make money for our fund investors – not to develop the economy." Personal communication with David Morgenthaler, founder Morgenthaler Ventures and past President of the National Venture Capital Association.

[18] See, for example, Nelson 1997.

[19] It is important to remember that these are estimates. The authors stress the "limitations inherent in the data and the magnitude of the extrapolations..." and urge that the findings be interpreted with caution. They note further that while the funding range presented for each category is large, these approximate estimates, nonetheless, provide "valuable insight into the overall scale and composition of early-stage technology development funding patterns and allow at least a preliminary comparison of the relative level of federal, state, and private investments." For further discussion of the approach and its limitations, see Branscomb and Auerswald 2002 : 20-24.

[20] The growth and subsequent contribution of venture capital have begun to attract the serious study needed to illuminate the dynamics of high-technology firm evolution. See for example, the work of Jeffrey Sohl and colleagues and the University of New Hampshire's Center for Venture Research, described at http://www.unh.edu/cvr.

[21] With the accord of the Small Business Administration, which plays an oversight role for the program, this amount can be higher in certain circumstances; e.g., drug development at NIH, and is often lower with smaller SBIR programs, e.g., EPA or the Department of Agriculture.

[22] NSF, for example, has what is called a Phase II-B program that allocates additional funding to help potentially promising technology develop further and attract private matching funds. As with venture-funded firms, Phase III is likely to include some mix of economically viable and non-viable products, ultimately to be determined by the relevant agency mission requirements or private markets.

[23] This certification effect was initially identified by Lerner 1999., "Public Venture Capital," in National Research Council, The Small Business Innovation Program: Challenges and Opportunities, C. Wessner, ed. Washington, D.C.: National Academy Press, 1999.

[24] See remarks by Christina Gabriel in National Research Council, *The Small Business Innovation Research Program, Program Diversity and Assessment Challenges*, op cit.

[25] David Mowery and Bhaven Sampath note that success in applying the Bayh-Dole concept more widely depends on the attention given to the structural differences in the educational systems of other nations. See Mowery and Sampath 2004. , "The Bayh-Dole Act of 1980 and University-Industry Technology Transfer: A Model for other OECD Governments?" in *Ivory Tower and Industrial Innovation: University-Industry Technology Transfer Before and After the Bayh Dole Act*, Palo Alto: Stanford University Press, 2004.

[26] This remains to be empirically determined, although there is substantial anecdotal evidence supporting this trend. For an illustrative case, see Audretsch et al. 2000.

[27] See National Research Council, *The Small Business Innovation Research Program, An assessment of the Department of Defense Fast Track Initiative*, op cit.

[28] Cooperation with private companies is not without risk and requires careful management; yet even controversial agreements like the 1998 Berkeley agreement with Novartis seemed to have provided significant benefits to the university with no loss to academic freedom. See Rausser, G.C.: Letter to the Editor of *Atlantic Monthly*, May 19, 2000. Accessed at www.cnr.berkeley.edu/pdf/dean_rausser/Atl_ltr_edt_5_2000.pdf.

[29] See Henderson and Smith 2002. It is important to reemphasize that not all universities have a commercialization culture, and among those that do, not all have a successful

commercialization process. For a discussion of some of the reasons for this variation, see Siegel, Waldman and Link 2004.

[30] See the Opening Statement by House of Representatives Armed Services Committee Chairman Duncan Hunter concerning the lack of return on US R&D investments at the Committee Hearing on the Impact of Defense Offsets, held on 8 June 2004.

[31] The concept of early-stage financial support for high-risk technologies with commercial promise was first advanced by Roland Tibbetts at the National Science Foundation (NSF). As early as 1976, Mr. Tibbetts advocated that the NSF should increase the share of its funds going to small business. This civic entrepreneurship led ultimately to the establishment of the SBIR program. For an overview of the origins and history of the SBIR program, see Turner and Brown 1999.

REFERENCES

Acs, Z.J and Audretsch, D.B. (1990). *Innovation and Small Firms.* Cambridge, MA: MIT Press.

Alic, J. (1992). *Beyond Spinoff: Military and Civilian Technologies in a Changing World.* Boston: Harvard University Press.

Audretsch, D.B. et al. (2000). "Does the Small Business Innovation Research Program Foster Entrepreneurial Behavior? Evidence from Indiana." In National Research Council. *The Small Business Innovation Research Program, An Assessment of the Department of Defense Fast Track Initiative*, C. Wessner (ed.), Washington DC: National Academy Press.

Birch, D.L. (1981). "Who Creates Jobs?" *The Public Interest* 65: 3-14.

Branscomb, L.M. and Auerswald, P.E. (2001). *Taking Technical Risks: How Innovators, Managers, and Investors Manage Risk in High-Tech Innovations.* Cambridge MA: MIT Press.

Branscomb, L.M. and Auerswald, P.E. (2002). *Between Invention and Innovation, An Analysis of Funding for Early-Stage Technology Development.* Gaithersburg, MD: NIST GCR 02-841, November 2002.

Cohen, L.R. and Noll, R.G. (1991). *Technology Pork Barrel.* Washington DC: Brookings Institution Press, June 1991.

Crain, W.M. and Hopkins, T.D. (2001). "The Impact of Regulatory Costs on Small Firms." In U.S. Small Business Administration, Office of Advocacy, Research Summary 207, October 2001.

Cramer, R. (2000). "Patterns of Firm Participation in the Small Business Innovation Research Program in Southwestern and Mountain States." In National Research Council. *The Small Business Innovation Research Program, An Assessment of the Department of Defense Fast Track Initiative*, C. Wessner (ed.), Washington, D.C.: National Academy Press.

David, P.A., Hall, B.H. and Toole, A.A. (1999): *Is Public R&D a Complement or Substitute for Private R&D? A Review of the Econometric Evidence.* In NBER Working Papers, No 7373.

Feldman, M. and Kelley, M.R. (2001): "Leveraging Research and Development: The impact of the Advanced Technology Program." In National Research Council. *The Advanced Technology Program, Assessing Outcomes*, C. Wessner (ed.), Washington, D.C.: National Academy Press.

Feldman, M., Feller, I., Bercovitz, J. and Burton, R. (2002). "Equity and the Technology Transfer Strategies of American Research Universities." *Management Science*, 48 (1).

Griffing, B. (2001). *Between Invention and Innovation, Mapping the Funding for Early Stage Technologies.* Carnegie Conference Center, Washington, DC., 25 January 2001.

Henderson, J.A. and Smith, J.J. (2002). *Academia, Industry, and the Bayh-Dole Act: An Implied Duty to Commercialize.* In White Paper, Center for the Integration of Medicine and Innovative Technology, Harvard University, October 2002.

Henrekson, M. and Rosenberg, N. (2001). "Designing Efficient Institutions for Science-Based Entrepreneurship: Lessons from the U.S. and Sweden." *Journal of Technology Transfer*, 26 (3).

Jacobs, T. (2002). "Biotech Follows dot.com Boom and Bust." *Nature*, 20 (10).

James, A. (2004). *US Defence and R&D Spending: An Analysis of the Impacts*. Rapporteur's Report for the EURAB Working Group ERA Scope and Vision, PREST, University of Manchester, January 2004.

Lerner, J. (1999). "Public Venture Capital." In National Research Council. *The Small Business Innovation Program: Challenges and Opportunities*. C. Wessner (ed.), Washington, D.C.: National Academy Press.

Mansfield, E. (1986): "How Fast Does New Industrial Technology Leak Out?" *Journal of Industrial Economics* 34 (2): 217-224.

Megginson, W.L. (2004). "Towards a Global Model of Venture Capital?" *Journal of Applied and Corporate Finance* 16 (1) Winter 2004.

Mowery, D. and Sampath, B. (2004). "The Bayh-Dole Act of 1980 and University-Industry Technology Transfer: A Model for other OECD Governments?" In D. Mowery et al. *Ivory Tower and Industrial Innovation: University-Industry Technology Transfer Before and After the Bayh Dole Act*. Palo Alto: Stanford University Press.

National Research Council (2001). *The Advanced Technology Program, Assessing Outcomes*. C. Wessner (ed.), Washington DC: National Academy Press.

National Research Council (2002). *Government-Industry Partnerships for the Development of New Technologies, Summary Report*. C. Wessner (ed.), Washington, D.C.: National Academy Press.

National Research Council (2004). *The Small Business Innovation Research Program, Program Diversity and Assessment Challenges*. Washington DC: National Academies Press.

Nelson, R. (ed.) (1993). *National Innovation Systems*. New York: Oxford University Press.

PricewaterhouseCoopers, Thomson Venture Economics and National Venture Capital Association (2004). *Money Tree Survey-Q1 2004 Results U.S. Report*. February 2004: http://www.pwcmoneytree.com

Richard Nelson (ed.) (1997). *National Systems of Innovation*. New York: Oxford University Press.

Siegel, D., Waldman D. and Link, A. (2004). "Toward a Model of the Effective Transfer of Scientific Knowledge from Academicians to Practitioners: Qualitative Evidence from the Commercialization of University Technologies." *Journal of Engineering and Technology Management* 21 (1-2): 115-142.

Small Business Administration, Office of Advocacy (2004). *Small Business by the Numbers*. June 2004.

Spence, M. (1974). *Market Signaling: Informational Transfer in Hiring and Related Processes*. Cambridge: Harvard University Press.

Stokes, D. (1997). *Pasteur's Quadrant, Basic Science and Technological Innovation*. Washington DC: Brookings Institution.

Turner, J. and Brown, G. (1999). "The Federal Role in Small Business Research." *Issues in Science and Technology* Summer 1999: 51-58.

Washburn, J. (2000). "The Kept University." *The Atlantic Monthly* 1 March 2000.

Wessner, C.W. and Shivakumar, S.J. (2002). *The Role of Macro Targets and Micro Incentives in Europe's R&D Policy*. IPTS Report 69 (11).

PART THREE

ASSESSMENT OF ENTREPRENEURSHIP POLICIES

Chapter 6:

ENTREPRENEURIAL BEHAVIOR IN DIFFERING ENVIRONMENTS

Friederike Welter
Rheinisch-Westfälisches Institut für Wirtschaftsforschung (RWI), Essen, and Jönköping International Business School (JIBS), Sweden

1. INTRODUCTION

External influences on entrepreneurship and entrepreneurial behavior gain importance in unfamiliar and fragile environments such as new sectors, or the transformation countries in Eastern Europe where institutional reforms have not yet been thoroughly implemented. We can distinguish between factors of influence on the macro level (e.g. the political, juridical and economic framework, cultural norms and religious traditions), on the meso level (e.g. business associations, industry-specific practices and codes of conduct, standardization and trade unions) and on the micro level such as personal beliefs and values, contracts and organizational cultures. They are reflected in individual economic actions such as strategy formulation, regulation of inter- and intra-firm relationships, recruitment practices or networking as well as in the general patterns of consumer, saving and investment behavior in different cultures and societies. In this context, institutional forces influence the nature and pace of entrepreneurship, as Knight (1997: 696) pointed out, saying that "we cannot assess the rationality of individual action without taking account of the institutional and cultural context in which everyday decisions are made." This takes on special importance, when comparing entrepreneurial behavior in different contexts.

In order to analyze the impact of the environment on entrepreneurship and entrepreneurial behavior, the evolutionary branch of New Institutional Economics, especially the concept of formal and informal institutions introduced by Douglass North (1990), combined with institutional theory approaches emphasizing strategic responses to institutional pressures (Oliver 1991, Scott 2001) appears to be particularly suited. Institutional theory allows us to identify the constraints and enabling factors influencing entrepreneurship in different environments, in order to explore entrepreneur's reactions to these institutional pressures.

This chapter is structured into four main sections. Part 2 introduces the main elements of institutional theory, analyzing the institutional embeddedness of entrepreneurship, enforcement mechanisms and entrepreneurial behavior. In part 3 these elements are employed to explore both institutional pressures and strategic responses of new and small firms in differing environments, drawing on selected empirical evidence from collaborative projects in both transition countries and mature market economies, mainly Germany (for an overview on methods and samples cf. Welter 2003). Part 4 summarizes the selected empirical evidence, emphasizing patterns, processes and changes of entrepreneurial behavior, whilst part 5 summarizes the results, indicating conclusions and open questions.

2. INSTITUTIONAL THEORY AND ENTREPRENEURSHIP
2.1 The Institutional Embeddedness of Entrepreneurship

Institutional theory allows to analyze the influence of different levels of the environment on patterns of entrepreneurship and entrepreneurial behavior (Hoskisson et al. 2000), thus drawing attention to the institutional embeddedness of entrepreneurship. North (1990, 1995) understands institutions as the incentive structure of a society, because they assist in reducing uncertainty and risk for individual behavior as well as the transaction costs connected with entrepreneurship. They "define what actors can do, what is expected from them, or they must do, and what is advantageous for them. In this way, they give stability and predictability to economic interaction." (Dallago 2000: 305). Applying North's concept to entrepreneurship, institutions are the 'formal' and 'informal' constraints and enabling forces on entrepreneurship. In this regard, Scott (2001: 52) identifies 'three pillars of institutions', which are enforced by different mechanisms. He distinguishes between regulative institutions, enforced by coercion, normative institutions, enforced by normative pressures, and cultural-cognitive institutions, which are enforced by mimetic mechanisms.

With regard to entrepreneurship, both formal or regulative institutions such as policy- and economy-related rules and organizations and informal institutions such as norms and values of a society influence the extent of entrepreneurship as well as the nature of actions taken by entrepreneurs. Examples of formal institutions influencing entrepreneurship include the political and economic constitution, the legal framework and the financial system. Informal institutions refer to codes of conduct, values and norms, i.e., those uncodified attitudes which are embedded in a society, regulating individual behavior. Codes of conduct and values reflect the collective, tacit interpretation of individual mental perceptions (Denzau and North 1994). As North (1990) put it: "They [the informal institutions] come from socially transmitted information and are part of the heritage that we call culture."

Whilst informal institutions are the culturally accepted basis legitimating entrepreneurship, the formal institutions contribute the regulatory frame (Wade-Benzoni et al. 2002). In other words, formal institutions provide the regulatory frame for entrepreneurship, thus creating opportunity fields for entrepreneurship, and informal institutions, which legitimate entrepreneurship in a society, determine the collective and individual perceptions of entrepreneurial opportunities (Welter and Smallbone 2003).

However, a clear-cut distinction between formal and informal institutions is difficult to achieve. Both informal and formal institutions are mutually dependent, whilst mental perceptions of individuals and informal institutions co-evolve. Partly, informal institutions result from formal institutions, which they in turn (could) modify. In this regard, they evolve as a culture-specific interpretation of formal rules. For example, whilst each legal framework normally contains explicit regulations for implementing laws7, over time these regulations are complemented by an implicit understanding of their content. This refers to unwritten rules, i.e., informal institutions fill in legal gaps which become apparent only through applying laws and regulations to daily life. In addition, informal institutions also contribute to the enforcement of the formal framework. Although legal sanctions such as penalties for unlawful behavior play an important role in implementing new rules of the game, these means are far from being sufficient. In this context, North (1990) himself states that "we need to know much more about culturally derived norms of behavior and how they interact with formal rules to get better answers...".

Fundamental *formal or regulative institutions* such as private property rights are a major influence on the existence of entrepreneurship whilst the legal frame determines its nature and extent. This refers to laws relating to bankruptcy, contracts, commercial activities, taxes, but it also involves organizations with the capacity to implement them. Laws might create new opportunity fields for entrepreneurship. For example, in Germany the introduction of rules for environmental protection fostered venture creation in recycling industries. Other key institutions include the financial system or sectors in the sense of sector specific technological standards. Here, technological progress allows for customized mass production, thus creating new market opportunities in sectors, which were previously dominated by economies of scales and scope and consequently larger enterprise sizes.

Normative and cultural-cognitive elements of institutions reflect what North labels *informal institutions*. Normative elements are apparent on different levels: on the level of society, where norms and values determine the appropriateness of entrepreneurship, on the level of sectors, where normative institutions are reflected in codes of conduct as set down by business associations and professions, and on the level of communities such as religious, kinship or ethnic groups. Normative elements contain the collective sense making, whilst cultural-cognitive elements refer to the individual understanding.

With regard to informal institutions on society level, Busenitz et al. (2000) refer to a 'normative dimension', which measures the degree to which a society admires entrepreneurial activities. Empirical studies such as the Global Entrepreneurship Monitor demonstrate that this image of entrepreneurship differs across countries, thus explaining differences in the extent of entreprencurship: "Among the many factors that contribute to entrepreneurship, perhaps the most critical is a set of social and cultural values along with the appropriate social, economic and political institutions that legitimize and encourage the pursuit of entrepreneurial opportunity" (Reynolds, Hay and Camp 1999: 43). In this context, cultural norms, which tolerate and foster entrepreneurial activities, affect the number of people with previous entrepreneurial experiences, thus creating role models (Shane 2003). Cultural institutions also influence whether a society has a practice of saving for the future or a focus on "living and spending to enjoy the moment" (Morrison 1998: 9), which in turn determines the amount of personal savings available for a business start-up. Moreover, cultural norms decide whether a society tolerates profit making behavior as one prerequisite for entrepreneurship. For example, South Asian 'producer' economies stress values such as economical behavior or long-term orientation whilst European societies could be classified as 'consumer' economies (Weber 1997).

2.2 Enforcement Mechanisms and Entrepreneurial Behavior

Drawing on institutional theory, the behavior of entrepreneurs in different environments is explained by analyzing their reactions to institutional pressures. This refers to the enforcement mechanisms, i.e., coercive, normative and mimetic pressures, of the institutions outlined above, which might generate different strategic responses of the entrepreneurs (Oliver 1991, Scott 2001).

The *regulative element of institutions* is enforced by *coercive mechanisms*. Entrepreneurs may experience coercive pressures as forces they have to deal with, or as a more informal code of conduct such as unwritten codes of behavior, for example with regard to planning a new venture, thus explaining the overall occurrence of business plans (Honig and Karlsson 2004). With regard to entrepreneurial behavior, regulative institutions and coercive pressures mainly are reflected in the formal rules as set out by governments, such as regulations for registering enterprises, tax payments and social security and sanctions for not adhering to these rules.

Normative and cultural-cognitive institutions are enforced by normative and mimetic mechanism regulating individual behaviour. *Normative mechanisms* explicitly or implicitly force entrepreneurs to adhere to the codes of conduct as set out by a specific community, for example, industries, business associations, families or ethnic groups. They assist in creating legitimacy, which is of particular importance for nascent entrepreneurs and entrepreneurs in unfamiliar environments, who face a high degree of liability of newness. Mechanisms to ensure normative behaviour include formal regulations such as certification or accreditation (Scott 2001), but normative institutions are also enforced by informal mechanisms such as trust.

Trust also assists in enforcing regulative institutions, which will only operate successfully if individuals are able to establish a basic level of trust in the reliability of any exchanges, but also in sanctions and penalties. Thus, the maintenance of trust supplements formal institutions, acting as an enforcement mechanism. Trust assists in lowering the transaction costs of commercial actions, which do not have to be (fully) based on formal regulations (such as contracts) in those cases where the participants know each other either personally, or by name. Trust and the institutional environment are mutually dependent, where "transactions that are viable in an institutional environment that provides strong safeguards may be nonviable in institutional environments that are weak (...)." (Williamson 1993: 476).

Mimetic mechanisms assist entrepreneurs in coping with uncertainty and unfamiliar situations, as they allow or even force them to draw on generally accepted models, such as organizational models, growth strategies or existing business ideas. Whilst previous research has stressed industry as the major source of mimetic behaviour (Honig and Karlsson 2004), this needs to be extended when looking at entrepreneurship. Here, additional sources of mimetic behaviour as reflected in the business idea are professional background of the entrepreneur, and her general experiences. Moreover, the role of mimetic behaviour might vary in different environments. For example, new ventures need to create legitimacy, which could be done through mimicking business ideas or business models of successfully established firms. This differs with regard to innovative new entrepreneurs, who bring new forms or activities into a market (Aldrich 2000: 218), or for nascent entrepreneurs in new and unfamiliar environments respectively. Aldrich points out that innovative entrepreneurs are likely to find themselves in a bootstrapping situation, where they have to develop an identity as a trustworthy person without being able to draw on established models. In such environments, mimetic behaviour would be both more important, but also less feasible.

Whilst these mechanisms reflect the general means identified by institutional theory to enforce institutions, Oliver (1991), in her study on *strategic responses to institutional pressures*, emphasizes individual responses. She distinguishes between five general strategies, including conformity (or acquiescence), compromise, avoidance, defiance and manipulation. Conforming responses include habitual and mimetic actions and agreement, whilst compromising refers to balancing, placating and negotiation. Avoidance is characterized by tactics such as concealment, buffer attempts, which often result in decoupling parts of a structure, and evasion (Scott 2001). Defiance refers to openly formulated resistance, challenging and attacking regulations, norms and values, whilst manipulation contains responses such as co-optation, where institutional interest groups are simultaneously integrated and weakened, influencing and controlling.

At a first glance, one would expect similar strategic responses of entrepreneurs in similar business fields across country environments, as the cognitive principles of decision-making and strategizing are the same regardless of environment. However, ways of understanding are specific to particular cultures and periods of time, depending on the "particular social and economic arrangements prevailing in that culture at that time" (Burr 1995: 4). They also reflect the individual interpretation of one's environment as well as individual personal and professional backgrounds. This in turn may result in differences in entrepreneurial behavior despite of a similar 'micro' environment in terms of sector.

In this regard, the concept of path dependency helps to explain behavior which "...may bear little resemblance to the legitimate courses of action stipulated by the formal rules" (Nee 1998: 86). Especially normative and cultural-cognitive institutions are persistent and changing slowly (Williamson 2000). Therefore, the persistency of informal institutions influences entrepreneurial behavior in those situations where a new regulatory frame and previous codes of conduct do not fit any longer (Mummert 1995, 1999). In this context, conflicting formal and informal institutions encourage individuals to recur to a familiar course of action, which as a rule reflect their previous experiences and tacit knowledge. This tends to reinforce trusted and known codes of conduct, resulting at the individual level in an escalating commitment of entrepreneurs to viable, but not necessarily the best courses of actions (Whyte 1986). From a macroeconomic point of view, these lock-in effects may foster a sub-optimal resource allocation (Arthur 1994). Thus, in a situation where individual behavior no longer fits the prevailing business codes of conduct, this might lead entrepreneurs to over-conform, in order to re-establish legitimacy in a new order, but it might also result in avoidance and defiance patterns.

3. STRATEGIC RESPONSES IN DIFFERING ENVIRONMENTS: SELECTED EMPIRICAL EVIDENCE

How do entrepreneurs in new and small firms behave in differing environments? In which ways do they react to institutional pressures? Does this differ across environments? This section sets out to explore entrepreneurial behavior in new and small firms both in emerging market economies (so-called transition or transformation economies) and in Germany as an example for a mature market economy, looking at their strategic responses to institutional settings.

3.1 Strategic Responses in Transition Countries

Entrepreneurial behavior is guided by the same cognitive principles, although empirical results demonstrate that strategic responses of new and young firms appear to differ across environments and countries. This is mainly due to different institutional settings. Informal institutions, i.e., normative and cultural-cognitive factors, have a far greater impact on individual behavior in transformation countries compared to mature market economies (Peng 2000, Smallbone and Welter 2001). This is re-enforced by deficits in the regulative environment. Here, inadequate institutions foster entrepreneurial behavior, which is unproductive from a macro economic point of view, but which ensures enterprise survival, thus being rational from the entrepreneur's point of view.

One such example refers to strategic responses to regulative institutions and enforcement mechanisms. Especially in early stages of transition, laws are either lacking, they are not implemented properly or they change frequently. In order to cope with an environment, which exerts great and unforeseen regulative pressures, entrepreneurs mainly employ avoidance strategies, which also contain some elements of defiance and manipulation. 'Typical' avoidance behavior refers to tactics such as evasion and concealment. This includes, e.g., tax avoidance through setting up a second business and transferring payments between businesses, or to splitting payments to employees into a minimum wage part, which is paid officially, and bonus payments 'under the table' (Welter and Smallbone 2003). All this is done in order to preserve the financial resource base of the enterprise in an environment where new and small firms experience major difficulties in accessing external finance. Although tax avoidance is not unknown in mature market economies, in transition countries, especially those at an early stage, it is a 'common' and widely tolerated behavior, which assists new and small firms in surviving an inadequate and often hostile environment. For example, according to a survey of Russian SMEs, in October 1998 50% of the surveyed SMEs did not pay any taxes at all, those who did, declared a mere 30% of their turnover and 10% of their wages (Tschepurenko 1999: 151).

Whilst most strategic responses used by small firms in fragile environments such as portfolio and serial entrepreneurship in order to finance more capital intensive businesses (Welter and Smallbone 2003) contain a certain element of manipulation in the sense that they influence values and attitudes of government and society, a direct manipulation response refers to a mixture of tactics such as control, influence and co-optation (Oliver 1991). This is rarely to be observed in small and new firms, which lack the power and standing in dealing with governments and other interest groups. Here, bribes and presents, which often are required to start a business in fragile and hostile environments such as transition economies in early stages, appear to reflect a compromise strategy on behalf of the entrepreneur. This is illustrated by an example from Uzbekistan, where a woman entrepreneur set up a detergent company in 1995:

> In order to start production the entrepreneur needed to register with the Standards Office (involving recording the technical specifics of materials). The license application required permits from local government, the local environmental health office, the fire office. Moreover, she needed a laboratory test of her products. This part of the process is required for the Standards Office to provide a certificate (which needs to be annually renewed) and took approximately 3-4 months. Finally, she obtained her license from the Ministry of Health, valid for five years. In order to speed up the process, the entrepreneur paid bribes in form of presents, e.g., flowers and candy for woman, brandy for man. She accepts these 'shadow expenditures' as part of doing business. Being an Uzbek woman, it was not openly suggested how much she should pay but she chose to offer presents to 'oil the wheels' of the process. She thinks male officials are more open about the amount of bribes required from male entrepreneurs.

In this context, research on transition economies (e.g., Gustafson 1999, Smallbone and Welter 2001) indicates that inadequate legal and financial systems during transition often re-enforced socialist norms of behavior such as the Soviet "legacy of non-compliance" (Feige 1997: 28), thereby explaining rent-seeking forms of entrepreneurship or informal entrepreneurship, which often are a result of avoidance and manipulation strategies, but also of compromise tactics. The social context inherited from the former socialist period appears to affect both the attitudes and behavior of entrepreneurs and the attitudes of society at large towards entrepreneurship.

Here, strategic responses include elements of defiance in situations where entrepreneurs (openly) ignore new norms and values (Oliver 1991). One example refers to the wide spread use of networking strategies in nowadays business, which goes back to the concept of mutual favors (blat), employed during Soviet times to cope with daily shortages (Ledeneva 1998). Nowadays networking is used to enter markets, to find customers and to develop markets, to get access to scarce resources or to recruit employees, as the following case illustrates (Welter and Havnes 2000):

> In the late eighties Michal, a candidate of computer science and reader at the state university in N, set up the business in which he and colleagues develop and sell computer-aided design programs as well as work on customer specific computer problems. The business idea was jointly developed by Michal and some of his colleagues from different university faculties in an attempt to earn (extra) money and because of the then uncertain perspectives at the university. Michal employs eight employees on part-time basis; he as director and a female colleague are the only ones working full-time at the business. All employees know each other from the university, and so far Michal never recruited an external person. The job in the computer business is a second employment for all of them with the first job described by Michal as the "*secure jobs*". The business rents five rooms in the university buildings. Rent

is paid in kind with extra labor of Michal at the university. Customers were initially sought through mouth-to-mouth information and eventually also through advertisements in the so-called 'red pages'. Michal also claims to have a dealer network reaching across major Russian cities without specifying these relationships. Nevertheless, customers mainly appear to be found randomly. As Michal put it: *"Our customers know how to find us."* Old contacts also assist in securing new projects. For example one of his colleagues at the university knew a shipbuilder who got interested in their design systems and commissioned a contract.

Several studies confirm that in transition countries networking contacts play an important role for new and small firms (e.g., Tschepurenko 1994, 1999, IPSSA 1998, Peng 2000, Smallbone and Welter 2001, Welter and Smallbone 2003, Yan and Manolova 1998). In countries with a hostile or fragile environment these reciprocal contacts assist in solving diverse business problems. Here, personal trust substitutes for insufficient formal and informal institutions such as weakly specified legal regulations and inadequate law enforcement. However, it also forces entrepreneurs to employ strategies, which in the long run might restrict business development and growth, as entrepreneurs limit themselves to doing business within a known circle.

3.2 Strategic Responses in Mature Market Economies

In comparison, entrepreneurship in mature market economies mainly takes place in an environment, where society has accepted entrepreneurship as an integral part of the economic well-being. Institutions are known and well established, and entrepreneurs know how to deal with them. This also implies that strategic responses are generally tested, and entrepreneurs can easily draw on sets of strategic options. Moreover, sanctioning mechanism for rule-deviant behavior are implemented and known to all players.

Therefore, in familiar environments with strong coercive pressures (e.g., a functioning law system) one would expect new and small firms to mainly employ conforming and compromising strategic responses to institutional pressures, mainly influenced by regulative, less so (at least less explicitly) by normative and cultural-cognitive institutions. Moreover, mimetic behavior is much more common in these environments compared to transition countries, where business models had to be built up from scratch, whilst in a mature market economy tested sets of business models and strategic options exist. This is apparent in that nascent and young entrepreneurs interviewed in Germany often used 'standardized' advice such as handbooks and popular business books in creating their initial business strategy (Welter 2003).

However, also in mature and stable environments normative and cultural-cognitive institutions can play an important role. This refers to milieu-typical institutions as reflected in family business, particularly so in craft-based firms, which implicitly are based on a century old institutional system, which is coupled with and re-enforced through family traditions. The following two examples of family-owned businesses demonstrate two typical strategic responses, where the institutional pressure on entrepreneurial behavior originating from the family background either forces them to openly defy the norms as set by the family or to look for ways to conform and compromise. Entrepreneurs in family businesses show either a rigid business orientation or a strong family orientation (cf. Reid et al. 1999 for the distinction of Ward). This is reflected in entrepreneurs with a business orientation being more risk-orientated and showing strategic awareness, whilst family-oriented entrepreneurs prefer maintaining the 'status-quo', although this might be detrimental for their firm.

The first case outlined below falls into the first category. The evidence presented here illustrates a defiance response, where the entrepreneur actively re-orientates the business, despite normative and cultural-cognitive pressures from his family. The entrepreneur demonstrates a clear business orientation, which assists him in defying family expectations and traditions, instead concentrating on satisfying his aims and developing his firm.

This craft firm is a family business in the 3rd generation, having been founded in the 19th century. The business is a craft business in carpentry. They design and produce interiors (such as kitchen, bathrooms and bedrooms) on an ecological basis, for example without using noxious varnishes. Currently, Eugenie and her husband David work in the business. David took over in 1981 after himself having been trained as a carpenter in Bavaria (i.e. far away from his home town which is located near the border to Luxembourg). Taking over the family business had always been David's aim, and he asked his wife Eugenie to join him as co-entrepreneur. A major problem during the take-over was the open antagonism David faced from his father and their employees of many years, as soon as he announced and then proceeded to introduce the product reorientation. The company formerly worked mainly as construction carpentry, producing stairs, doors and the like. David always wanted to specialise in ecological made products, and he finished a specialised further training. However, it took him years to persuade his father, employees and colleagues of the benefits for the craft business.

The second case presents a situation, where the entrepreneur had difficulties in overcoming the institutional pressures allegedly set by her family. Her entrepreneurial behavior can best be described as being a reactive and short-term response to institutional pressures. She shows a clear family-orientation in her strategies, trying to conform to her family's expectations, whilst at the same time attempting to find a compromise between family traditions, her aims and the need to remodel her firm. The entrepreneur was forced to take over the family business after the sudden death of her father. During the interview, she showed herself as not having taken this decision voluntarily, which is reflected in remarks such as *"I did not only take over the store, but also his debts and credits"*.

This young woman entrepreneur took over her father's retail business on his death in 1998, after working for the company for eight years. The business sells porcelain products and serves both local and regional markets. The company is a family business in the 2nd generation. The company was set up by Katja's father who could not take over his father's business, as the father was reluctant to leave the firm. Therefore, Katja's father moved to another town, where he bought an already renowned company in the same trade line. According to Katja, her father did never claim officially that he expected his children to follow him into business or take over his company. In her training and studies, she nevertheless specialised in the company's business field and in management studies, whilst her brother will now take over their grandparents' shop in M. She herself was trained as a retail trader, specialising in porcelain. She then studied business administration, after which she started working in the family's business.

Katja seems to be torn between the perceived wish of her family to continue a family tradition and her desire to lead her own life as a mother and sales person. Family tradition, which she herself acknowledges when stating *"We are a family with a background in porcelain"*, forces her to get more and more involved in managing the company, although she would prefer selling her products. Without so many words, she prides herself on being an excellent sales person. On the other hand, she appreciates the 'freedom' that being her own boss gives her, especially with respect to her child's needs. She feels that she would have difficulties in finding a comparable part-time job, also due to her limited working experience which she described as *"working as father's daughter in a family business"*. She does not picture herself as a career woman, which results in her wanting to keep a low profile in business, although she concedes a need for more active marketing: *"Currently, our firm exists because of the name and reputation of my father."*

Both cases illustrate the normative and cultural-cognitive pressures as frequently experienced by entrepreneurs in businesses with a family dimension. In this context, informal institutions appear to exert a dominating influence on entrepreneurial behavior. The strategic (non-)responses of both entrepreneurs draw attention to the "social dimension of entrepreneurial decision-making" (Taylor and Thorpe 2004: 210), thus emphasizing the role of informal institutions in understanding entrepreneurial behavior across different environments. It is in this context, that Aldrich and Cliff (2004) suggest a "family-embeddedness perspective" on new venture creation, which should be extended to research entrepreneurial behavior in general.

4. PATTERNS, PROCESSES AND CHANGES OF ENTREPRENEURIAL BEHAVIOUR

Which strategic processes are underlying entrepreneurial behavior in new and young firms? Are strategic responses to institutional pressures planned or emergent? Are there typical strategy processes and patterns across different environments? What triggers changes in entrepreneurial behavior? These questions are explored in the next section, in order to summaries and condense the empirical evidence presented in the previous chapter.

4.1 Patterns and Processes of Entrepreneurial Behavior

Research has shown that entrepreneurs in new and small firms often improvise and *'muddle-through'* (e.g., Baker et al. 2001, Covin and Slevin 1989, Welter 2003, Yan and Manolova 1998), with 'strategy' typically being emergent and 'strategic vision' more commonly demonstrated than strategic planning. (Gibb and Scott 1985) Regardless of environments, entrepreneurs react from day-to-day, neglecting the longer term development of their business. Over time, decision-making processes tend to become increasingly routinized, as entrepreneurs fall back on behavior they once have applied successfully, as long as they are facing familiar situations, for which 'closed loop' learning can provide the basis for making an adequate response. Entrepreneurs muddle through by using a decision-making method of successive, restricted comparisons, where decision-making and acting occur simultaneously (Lindblom 1959).

This pattern is often to be found in new enterprises, non-growth oriented ones (Baker et al. 2001), micro firms, and enterprises, which operate in new business fields or adverse economic environments. In newer and younger enterprises, which often are headed by younger entrepreneurs, this is due to a lack of business and entrepreneurial experience. Small firms rely on informal decision-making and an informal organisation, both of which might impede a more structured strategy style. With regard to environments, it is adverse, unfamiliar and fragile environments, where entrepreneurs keep a low profile, mainly avoiding to adhere to official regulations whenever possible, or conforming as far as possible, which is made difficult in environments with rapid institutional changes. Thus, environments with institutional gaps generally favour a muddling-through process (Barrett 1998). This refers to both regulative institutions, as reflected in political environments, as well as to normative institutions such as to be observed in business fields and sectors. New and unfamiliar environments lack the basic strategic options, which have to be learned in a trial and error process, going from simple to more complex patterns over time. In fragile and turbulent environments, entrepreneurs have to decide and (re-)act rapidly, whilst the deficient institutional settings re-enforce institutional mistrust.

Here, cognitive biases inherent in decision making processes could re-enforce muddling-through and unstructured behavior of entrepreneurs. The conflict theory of decision making explains this in terms of 'avoidance' (Lyles and Thomas 1988). Once an entrepreneur has settled on a particular course of action, she will only change her behavior in cases where current actions lead to negative results, which are higher than the risk coupled with taking an unknown course of action. If new actions and options are considered as too risky and costly, entrepreneurs will not change their behavior, hoping that "the problem will eventually go away." (Lyles and Thomas 1988: 136).

The opposite pattern would be a *design* approach, where entrepreneurs actively search possibilities to improve and develop their business actions and strategies. External conditions or situations may trigger this entrepreneurial behavior, albeit they do not exercise a decisive influence. The entrepreneur actively uses feedback and reactions on previous actions in order to evaluate her strategies. This is often done intuitively, reflecting less a formal, visible planning and decision-making process than more the 'strategic awareness' of entrepreneurs in small firms (Gibb and Scott 1985). A more deliberate entrepreneurial behavior is used more frequently in growth-oriented small enterprises, in established firms and/or by older entrepreneurs who can draw on years of entrepreneurial experiences and tested sets of strategic options, and in larger enterprises, where a formalized organization structure favors this strategy style. Moreover, a design approach assists in coping with complex environments such as mature markets or established sectors as well as in later stages of the transformation process.

Empirical studies demonstrate that the majority of new and small firms do not employ 'pure' patterns, but instead they mix phases of muddling-through behavior with phases of a more active behavior (cf. Welter 2003 both for an overview of relevant studies and empirical evidence). Nevertheless, most new and small firms show a foremost reactive behavior. Even in mature environments small ventures prefer to react instead of proactively exploit opportunities. Whilst such a behavior is not surprising in an unstable and fragile transition environment, where institutions do not (yet) function properly, in more stable environments this pattern apparently also reflects overly complex institutional settings, which have developed over time.

Interestingly, environmental factors have a different impact on strategy patterns, depending on the respective country settings (Welter 2003). In transition countries, entrepreneurial behavior is predominantly influenced by the regulative and political environment, especially during the early stages of transition, and by prevailing informal institutions such as 'old' codes of conduct. In mature market economies, macro economic and structural conditions play a much more important role in determining entrepreneurial behavior.

4.2 Changing Entrepreneurial Behavior

Behavioral change could be a result of institutional change, which has a positive influence on entrepreneurship, where it removes or lowers barriers to market entry and market exit, thus creating opportunity fields for entrepreneurs, and vice versa. Examples for positive changes include the introduction of private property rights at the beginning of the transformation process in former socialist countries, or the efforts to deregulate industries in mature market economies. Seen from an individual, cognitive-based perspective, behavioral change is based on learning, which is reflected in changing 'theories-in-use' (Schön 1975), or the process of 'effectuation', as suggested by Sarasvathy (2001).

However, learning itself is affected by the environment and/or access to resources. It is here, where internal or external events act as triggers for a change in entrepreneurial behavior, provided they exceed a 'threshold', above which the entrepreneur gets irritated and recognizes an urgent need for behavioral changes (Koch et al. 2000). This threshold obviously depends on the entrepreneur's background and experiences and his/her business objectives.

Triggers resulting in a more active entrepreneurial behavior are to be found in situations, where entrepreneurs can no longer rely on their proven strategic responses. Not surprisingly, entrepreneurs like to stick to successful actions and strategies, although this behavior might restrict enterprise development and growth, especially where entrepreneurs rely on informal sources of assistance and capital, or where they partly or wholly operate in the shadow economy. *Internal triggers* of strategic change include the general business orientation, business objectives, new business opportunities, tight liquidity positions and the like. *External triggers* are for example drops in demand, fundamental economic and political system changes such as the transition to a market economy included, etc.

When entrepreneurs *change* strategies and their behavior, this either happens incrementally, reflecting entrepreneurial learning, or *abruptly*, reflecting an internal or external crisis. The latter situation is reflected in a case, which was interviewed in autumn 2000 (Smallbone and Welter 2003):

Nadja, a Russian entrepreneur who owns a small travel agency specializing in business study tours, had difficulties in expressing her current motives for continuing in business. She described herself as being not ready to answer that question just now because her company experienced hard times until spring 2000. Only at the time of the interview, was she able to start thinking about her plans, which she described as pursuing limited growth, but also looking for possibilities to diversify. Her aspirations had been higher after her initial business success, but after the Russian crisis she stopped thinking about any future plans, as demand for her product depends on the economic situation of her customers. The Russian crisis of summer 1998 caused a majority of her customers to cancel their signed contracts for the coming autumn. Business was worse for approximately half a year, although the firm had enough money to cover current expenses. Moreover, Nadja used this to seriously beginning market research: *"Before that I always talked about broadening our field and considering a policy for my firm, but I had no time until the crisis came"*.

The case below illustrates a more *incremental mode of strategic change*, based on the actions taken by a young entrepreneur during his business formation process. As Welter and Havnes (2000) state, the case "illustrates the variety of approaches used by the entrepreneur to control environment elements during the start-up of his high-tech business. Importantly, the influence of random factors results in seemingly unplanned activities which in turn are clearly supportive to the development of the business." This entrepreneur's decision to set up his own business was triggered by several events, including the visit to one of the leading fairs, a successful application to a support program and an evolving partnership with another small company because of his interesting product plus finally a co-operation with a leading US company in his particular business field.

Gerd founded a limited liability company in February 1998, with initially two partners and him as managing director. He started his business part-time as a free-lancer at the beginning of 1996 while he was still writing his dissertation. Gerd is a specialist on memory metals and shape memory alloys. His former professor always told him to start an own business, but Gerd never took him seriously, although he apparently carefully deliberated the idea. The Hanover fair was a key event where G met a Swiss professor who taught him a number of 'marketing tricks' to sell his scientific results. The excellent feed back at the fair stunned Gerd, and he gave his own business a serious thought after that. He successfully applied for the NRW-program PFAU at the end of 1996 when he had finished his degree. This funded his part-time job as research assistant until May 1999, during which time he managed to get his firm off the ground. Early in the establishing process he approached a company which produced ovens to ask them to construct his oven. The owner of the company (a well-established manufacturing firm with around 40 employees) found Gerd's ideas interesting and suggested a financial partnership. This offer enabled Gerd to establish his business in 1998. Gerd rented an office within the partner company with room for a secretary, which is in the neighborhood of his own construction halls.

Gerd offers a whole range of activities related to the product 'memory metals': research and development, production of small quantities (maximum batch size 300-500), trade in specific metals, advice and consultancy. Gerd took up the trade line after having signed a co-operation agreement with an American company at the end of 1998. This was done in order to alleviate problems with material supplies, as his customers asked for a constant quality and reliable supply of materials, which he could not provide using the university's suppliers (the quantities used in laboratories are much smaller and are not necessarily of a constant quality).

Although all of these events at first glance might appear random and not deliberate, they also illustrate a more or less implicit shift towards a more structured behavior in order to master environmental complexities. Thus, the entrepreneur obviously moves from simple reactions to the challenges and pressures from the environment to a more complex behavioral pattern (Welter 2003). Such entrepreneurial behavior, that evolves from simple to complex patterns, indicates an emergent process of individual learning, which depends on the mixture of institutional factors such as personal experiences and background (cultural-cognitive institutions), the socio-cultural and sectoral milieu (normative institutions), and regulative settings. Strategic responses in new and small firms thus are part of an ongoing learning process, during which entrepreneurs constantly and simultaneously reflect and interpret their behavior (Taylor and Thorpe 2004).

5. CONCLUSION

To summaries: an imperfect or overly complex environment favors an entrepreneurial behavior, which appears rationally from the entrepreneur's point of view, but which consists of short-term oriented entrepreneurial responses, aimed at dealing with external institutional pressures. Personal trust dominates business relations. Entrepreneurs muddle through, paying more attention to solving daily business problems instead of planning their business development in the longer term. All this results in forms of unproductive entrepreneurship (Baumol 1990), constraining enterprise growth prospects and the contribution of entrepreneurship to economic development.

The formation of entrepreneurial patterns in new and small ventures is a complex and interactive process, where entrepreneurs and their environment co-evolve. Here, institutional change can be favorable, as it opens up new fields which entrepreneurs can pursue. However, institutional change also may be detrimental for economic development at the macro level in situations, where it triggers and/or reinforces norm-deviant behavior on the individual level. Conflicts within the institutional settings encourage entrepreneurs to recur to familiar and known courses of actions, which are based on the requirements of the previous institutional environment and which in turn influence the environment.

In this context, vicious circles might develop. One such example concerns the avoidance strategies as outlined above, resulting out of an adverse economic and tax environment. However, their widespread use also reinforces the negative attitude of governments towards small and private firms, which in turn might impede the development of a more consistent institutional frame. Thus, although this entrepreneurial behavior might support firm performance and/or survival in the short run, it might be detrimental in the long run, restricting the ability of the firm to grow and develop. In this context, entrepreneurs operating in environments where they know the rules of the game, have far greater possibilities to manipulate their environment and avoid following (all) rules.

Generally, entrepreneurial behaviour of new and small firms reflects both a deliberate and structured approach as well as seemingly spontaneous and emergent processes. The latter plays a more important role in explaining entrepreneurial behaviour than approaches that mainly focus on 'rational' behaviour and 'homo economicus'. Moreover, entrepreneurial learning becomes apparent in strategy processes and behavioural patterns in new and small enterprises. Learning itself is shaped, but not strictly determined by cultural-cognitive and normative institutions, reflecting both the socialisation and background of entrepreneurs as well as their subjective interpretation of reality. In this regard, entrepreneurial behaviour evolves through a continuous 'dialogue' of entrepreneurs and their environments, throughout which entrepreneurs play a more or less active role, filtering impulses from their environments and making sense of institutional pressures. Here, path-dependency plays a role, as the entrepreneur's 'life issues' (Kisfalvi 2002) such as her background and experiences are reflected both in the strategic awareness as well as patterns of entrepreneurial behaviour.

Political and economic factors dominate behavioral patterns in new and small firms in the short run, whilst cultural-cognitive and normative institutions are a longer term influence. The latter are also difficult to change. This plays a role in those cases where previously 'learned' habits and routines negatively influence entrepreneurial behavior. In this context, governments need to pay specific attention to developing a consistent institutional frame, which incorporates country-specific cultural codes of conduct as well as the implementation of institutional changes. In this context, a consistent institutional environment allows entrepreneurs to shift from a muddling-through approach to more pro-active entrepreneurial behavior, as they no longer need to focus their scarce resources on solving day-to-day problems.

Whilst there is a relationship between the institutional frame, institutional legacies and entrepreneurship, it is nevertheless difficult to isolate dominant factors of influence because of its complex and recursive nature. Entrepreneurship and entrepreneurial behavior result from a dynamic inter-relationship between internal (i.e. both organizational and personal characteristics) and external conditions which also include other factors besides the institutional environment. In this context, future research is needed in order to learn more about distinctive factor combinations influencing entrepreneurship development in different environments. This in turn will have important practical implications for those involved in supporting entrepreneurship.

REFERENCES

Aldrich, H. (2000). "Entrepreneurial Strategies in New Organizational Populations." In R. Swedberg (ed.). *Entrepreneurship: The Social Science View*. Oxford: University Press, 211-228 (reprinted from Bull, I., H. Thomas and G. Willard (eds.) (1995). Entrepreneurship: Perspectives on Theory Building: Pergamon).

Aldrich, H.E. and Cliff, J.E. (2004). "The pervasive effects of family on entrepreneurship: toward a family embeddedness perspective." *Journal of Business Venturing* 18: 573-596.

Arthur, W. Brian (1994). *Increasing returns and path dependence in the economy*. Michigan: University Press.

Baker, T., Miner, A.S., and Eesley, D.T. (2001). *Fake it until you make it: improvisation and new ventures*." Paper presented at the Babson-Kauffman Entrepreneurship Research Conference, 13.-16. June 2001, Jönköping.

Barrett, F.J. (1998). "Creativity and Improvisation in Jazz and Organizations: Implications for Organizational Learning." *Organization Science* 9 (5): 605-622.

Baumol, W. (1990). "Entrepreneurship: Productive, Unproductive and Destructive." *Journal of Political Economy* 98 (5): 893-921.

Burr, V. (1995). *An introduction to social constructionism*. London: Routledge.

Busenitz, L.W., Gómez, C. and Spencer, J.W. (2000). "Country Institutional Profiles: Unlocking Entrepreneurial Phenomena." *Academy of Management Journal* 43 (5): 994-1003.

Covin, J.G. and Slevin, D. P. (1989). "Strategic Management of Small Firms in Hostile and Benign Environments." *Strategic Management Journal* 10: 75-87.

Dallago, B. (2000). "The Organisational and Productive Impact of the Economic System. The Case of SMEs." *Small Business Economics* 15: 303-319.

Denzau A.T. and North, D.C. (1994). "Shared Mental Models: Ideologies and Institutions." *Kyklos* 47 (1): 3-31.

Feige, E. (1997). "Underground Activity and Institutional Change: Productive, Protective, and Predatory Behavior in Transition Economies." In Nelson, J.M., Tilly, C. and Walker, L. (eds.) *Transforming Post-Communist Political Economies*, Washington, D.C., 21-34.

Gibb, A. and Scott, M. (1985). "Strategic Awareness, Personal Commitment and the Process of Planning in the Small Business." *Journal of Management Studies* 22 (6): 597-629.

Gustafson, T. (1999). *Capitalism Russian-style*. Cambridge.

Honig, B. and Karlsson, T. (2004). Institutional forces and the written business plan. *Journal of Management* 30 (1): 29-48.

Hoskisson, R.E., Eden, L., Lau, C.M. and Wright, M. (2000). "Strategy in Emerging Economies." *Academy of Management Journal* 43 (3): 249-267.

IPSSA (1998). *Small Business in Russia*, Moscow.

Kisfalvi, V. (2002). "The entrepreneur's character, life issues, and strategy making: A field study." *Journal of Business Venturing* 17: 489-518.

Knight, J. (1997). "Social Institutions and Human Cognition: Thinking about old Questions in new Ways." *Journal of Institutional and Theoretical Economics* 153: 693-699.

Koch, T., Thomas, M. and Woderich, R. (2000). *Angekommen? Privatwirtschaftliche Selbständige in Brandenburg im zehnten Jahr. Kontextbedingungen, Prozessverläufe, Lernanlässe.* Berlin.

Ledeneva, A.V. (1998). *Russia's economy of favours: Blat, networking and informal exchange.* Cambridge: Cambridge University Press

Lindblom, C.E. (1959). "The Science of „Muddling Through"." *Public Administration Review* 19: 79-88.

Lyles, M.A. and Thomas, H. (1988). "Strategic Problem Formulation: Biases and Assumptions embedded in Alternative Decision-Making Models," *Journal of Management Studies* 25 (2): 131-145.

Morrison, A. (1998). *Entrepreneurship and Culture Specificity*, Paper presented at IntEnt98, Oestrich–Winkel, 26–28 July.

Mummert, U. (1995). *Informelle Institutionen in ökonomischen Transformationsprozessen.* Contributiones Jenenses, 2, Baden-Baden: Nomos.

Mummert, U. (1999). *Informal Institutions and Institutional Policy – Shedding Light on the Myth of Institutional Conflict.* Diskussionsbeitrag, 02-99, Max-Planck Institute for Research into Economic Systems, Jena.

Nee, V. (1998). "Norms and Networks in Economic and Organizational Performance." *American Economic Review* 88 (2): 85-89.

North D.C. (1990). *Institutions, Institutional Change and Economic Performance*, Cambridge.

North, D.C. (1995). "Structural Changes of Institutions and the Process of Transformation." *Prague Economic Papers* 4 (3): 229-234.

Oliver, C. (1991). "Strategic responses to institutional processes." *Academy of Management Review* 16 (1): 145-179.

Peng, M. (2000). *Business strategies in transition economies*, Thousand Oaks, London, New Delhi.

Reid, R., Dunn, B., Cromie, S. and Adams, J. (1999). „Familienorientierung oder Geschäftsorientierung in Familienbetrieben." *Internationales Gewerbearchiv* 47: 149-165.

Reynolds, P.D., Hay, M. and Camp, S.M. (1999). *Global Entrepreneurship Monitor: 1999 Executive Report,* Kansas City: Kauffman Center.

Sarasvathy, S.D. (2001). "Causation and effectuation: Toward a theoretical shift from economic inevitability to entrepreneurial contingency." *Academy of Management Review* 26 (2): 243-263.

Schön, D. (1975). "Deutero-learning in organizations: Learning for increased effectiveness." *Organizational Dynamics* 3: 2-16.

Scott, R.W. (2001). *Institutions and Organizations.* Thousand Oaks et al.: Sage.

Shane, S. (2003). *A General Theory of Entrepreneurship: The Individual-Opportunity Nexus.* Aldershot, UK: Edward Elgar.

Smallbone, D. and Welter, F. (2001). "The distinctiveness of entrepreneurship in transition economies." *Small Business Economics* 16 (4): 249-262.

Smallbone, D. and Welter, F. (2003). *Entrepreneurship in transition economies: necessity or opportunity driven?* Paper presented to the Babson College-Kauffman Foundation Entrepreneurship Research Conference, Babson, USA, 5.-7. Juni 2003.

Taylor, D.W. and Thorpe, R. (2004). "Entrepreneurial learning: a process of co-participation." *Journal of Small Business and Enterprise Development* 11 (2). 203-211.

Tschepurenko, A. (1994) „Das neue Russland: Die Kleinunternehmen und die große Politik." *Internationales Gewerbearchiv* 42: 260-265.

Tschepurenko, A. (1999). „Die neuen russischen Unternehmer: Wer sie sind, wie sie sind." In H.-H. Höhmann (ed.). *Eine unterschätzte Dimension? Zur Rolle wirtschaftskultureller Faktoren in der osteuropäischen Transformation*, Analysen zur Kultur und Gesellschaft im östlichen Europa, 9, Bremen: edition temmen, 139-152.

Wade-Benzoni, K. A. et al. (2002). "Barriers to Resolution in Ideologically based Negotations: The role of Values and Institutions." *Academy of Management Review* 27 (1): 41-57.

Weber, H. (1997). „Zwischen asiatischem und anglo-amerikanischem Kapitalismus - das deutsche industrielle System in der Klemme." In U. Bullmann and R.G. Heinze (eds.). *Regionale Modernisierungspolitik*. Opladen: Westdeutscher Verlag, 53-75.

Welter, F. (2003). *Strategien, KMU und Umfeld*. Schriftenreihe des RWI, 69. Berlin: Duncker & Humblot.

Welter, F. and Havnes, P.-A. (2000). "SMEs and environmental turbulence." In H.-J. Pleitner and W. Weber (eds.). *Die KMU im 21. Jahrhundert – Impulse, Ansichten, Konzepte*, St. Gallen, 41-50.

Welter, F. and Smallbone, D. (2003). "Entrepreneurship and Enterprise Strategies in Transition Economies: An Institutional Perspective." In D. Kirby and Watson, A. (eds.). *Small Firms and Economic Development in Developed and Transition Economies: A Reader*, Ashgate, 95-114.

Whyte, G. (1986). "Escalating Commitment to a Course of Action: A Reinterpretation." *Academy of Management Review* 11 (2): 311-321.

Williamson, O.E. (1993). "Calculativeness, Trust and Economic Organization." *Journal of Law and Economics* XXXVI (April): 453-486.

Yan, A. and Manolova, T.S. (1998). "New and Small Players on Shaky Ground: a multicase study of emerging entrepreneurial firms in a transforming economy." *Journal of Applied Management Studies* 7 (1): 139-143.

Chapter 7:

ENTREPRENEURSHIP IN GERMAN REGIONS AND THE POLICY DIMENSION - EMPIRICAL EVIDENCE FROM THE REGIONAL ENTREPRENEURSHIP MONITOR (REM)

Rolf Sternberg
University of Cologne

1. INTRODUCTION

Supporting entrepreneurs and start-ups has been part of the broader measures and goals of economic promotional policy in Germany and its regions for around 20 years. In the 1980s, technology centers and business incubators were the first instrument in the then West Germany which regional and local governments employed in order to achieve this goal. While these centers still exist in great abundance in Germany, many measures and instruments have since been added to the portfolio, intended specifically to support start-ups in particular technological fields (e.g. biotechnology), in selected regions, or launched by university graduates, or by female entrepreneurs. In addition to the local municipalities and individual federal states, the federal government is now also very heavily involved in supporting start-ups and entrepreneurs. As has been demonstrated by the annual country reports of the Global Entrepreneurship Monitor (GEM) since 1999, policy programmers are some of Germany's comparative strengths in terms of entrepreneurial framework conditions (cf. the latest country report for Germany, Sternberg, Bergmann and Lückgen 2004).

To date, empirically based results focusing on the impact of such political efforts on the number of start-ups, for example, or their survival rate are scarce (see Engel and Licht (2004) on the role of public programs to support venture capital activities dedicated to start-ups). It is very much apparent that the lack of data on start-ups is one of the factors which create considerable methodical problems for empirical measurement of the correlation between the availability and/or utilization of a start-up program on the one hand and the decision of an individual to launch a start-up and / or the development of a start-up (growth or just survival, early shut-down?)

on the other. There is a similar problem when, instead of investigating the impact of a promotional program on individual entrepreneurs or start-ups, the focus is to be on the impact on all entrepreneurs or start-ups in a region or country. This problem is further aggravated by the fact that there will very likely be time lags between the launch of a promotional program and any effects it may have, and that very little is known about the length of these time lags (which may also differ between individual states and regions). There are many questions still facing policy evaluation research in this field.

In this paper the policy dimension of entrepreneurship will be interpreted from a regional perspective. The decision of an individual to proceed with or refrain from launching a start-up is not only influenced by factors relating to the individual in question; it is also a regional event (Feldman 2001). The entrepreneur is part of – predominantly – regional, personal networks; he or she acts under the influence of the regional entrepreneurial climate and feels most directly the effects of measures regional policies to promote start-ups, while measures introduced by the federal government or even the government of the European Community are perceived to a considerably lesser extent. At the same time, the majority of the effects of successful start-ups are initially felt at regional level (e.g. effects on the level of employment). It is therefore logical that regional public policies in favor of start-ups should primarily be evaluated from a regional point of view and thus a correlation with innovative regional development established. While the general ceteris paribus effect of the region on an individual's decision to start or not to start a business has been analyzed empirically for German regions (e.g., Wagner/Sternberg 2004, Bergmann 2004), there is still a research gap in terms of the policy impacts.

If one has to assess regional public policy strategies dedicated to new firms, there is no choice but to interpret policy instruments as one of several regional factors that have an impact on new firm formation. The main question is why and how do regional environmental factors influence entrepreneurial activities and the entrepreneurial attitudes of the local population? In order to be able to answer this question, it is, again, necessary to come to an understanding of entrepreneurship as a regional event, dependent on and involving more than personal factors. Consequently and given the empirically well-proven spatial immobility of start-ups, a regional oriented entrepreneurship policy can be interpreted as an endogenous regional development policy. If policies to promote entrepreneurial activities within a region are to be justified in times when public coffers are low, it has to be shown what can be achieved with regional start-up promotion policies. Start-ups (i.e. young and – initially – small firms) are particularly well suited as catalysts and drivers of endogenous regional development, i.e. primarily influenced from within the region. As discussed by Sternberg (2003, 2004), entrepreneurial activities are primarily an element of *endogenous* development potential and entrepreneurial activities promote regional development in the area of economic growth (cf. Davidsson, Lindmark and Olofsson 1995 Carré and Thurik 2003, Carré et al. 2002, Wennekers and Thurik 1999, van Stel and Storey 2002, Ashcroft and Love 1996).

This paper addresses a small section of this field of research and focuses clearly on the regional, sub-national level. The aim is to analyze the influence of regional entrepreneurial framework conditions, taking into consideration the policy dimension in particular. All empirical statements relate to data gathered in the course of the Regional Entrepreneurship Monitor (REM). Although policy implications are not the focus of this research project, they can be derived directly or indirectly from results to date. This paper concentrates on ten German planning regions (*"Raumordnungsregionen"*). The data are from 2003, which differentiates this paper from a more recent publication by the same author (cf. Sternberg forthcoming), which was based on the first phase of the REM (data from 2001).

This paper starts with a short overview of functions, tasks and methods of action of public administrations and public institutions in promoting start-ups in Germany, although this presentation cannot remain restricted to the REM regions. This chapter will be followed by an introduction to the Regional Entrepreneurship Monitor. Then the core results of the second phase of REM (REM II, 2002-2004) will be presented where the focus is on the interregional comparison of entrepreneurial activities, entrepreneurial attitudes and entrepreneurial framework conditions. The focus will then shift to those results which relate specifically to the analysis and evaluation of existing public policy instruments for start-up entrepreneurs. Followed by an empirical based discussion of two of the eight entrepreneurial framework conditions (policy regulations, policy programs), the implications of regionally differing, politically related entrepreneurial framework conditions which can be derived from the REM will be analyzed.

2. WHAT IS REM?

The Regional Entrepreneurship Monitor Germany (REM) is a joint research project of the Institute of Economic and Social Geography, University of Cologne, and the Institute of Economics, University of Lüneburg and is led by Rolf Sternberg and Joachim Wagner. It is funded by the German Research Foundation (*"Deutsche Forschungsgemeinschaft"*, DFG) during the first phase (REM I, 2000-2002) and during the second phase (REM II, 2002-2004) within the scope of its program "Interdisciplinary Entrepreneurship Research". Additional funding came in either or both phases from Ernst & Young, the Munich and Upper Bavaria Chamber of Industry and Commerce (*"IHK München und Oberbayern"*), *"Kreissparkasse Köln"*, *"Kreissparkasse Recklinghausen"*, *"Sparkasse Gelsenkirchen"*, *"Castrop-Rauxel"* and *"Bottrop, Stadtsparkasse Gladbeck"*, the "*Norddeutsche Landesbank*" and the "*Landeszentralbank Niedersachsen*". For further methodological information about REM see Japsen (2002), Bergmann (2004, 2002) and Lückgen and Oberschachtsiek (2004).

The aim of REM is to present empirically based evidence for two questions:
- How much does the level of entrepreneurial activity vary between ten German regions?
- What makes a region 'entrepreneurial'? What regional characteristics are related to differences in entrepreneurial activity?

Most of the empirical results concerning entrepreneurial activities, entrepreneurial attitudes and assessments of entrepreneurial framework conditions in this paper are based on surveys carried out in the course of REM II, in 2003. Spatially, REM II examined ten out of 97 German planning regions, for which the results may be taken as representative. Similar surveys were carried out in 2001 in the course of the first phase of the research project ("REM I"), started in, 2000. It must be emphasized explicitly that the data collated in the course of REM should not be expected to generate representative results for the whole of Germany and all its regions. Rather, the declared objective is to select representative examples for various region types and to compare them with one another.

2.1 REM and GEM: Parallels and Differences

The Regional Entrepreneurship Monitor (REM) is based on the approach of the international "Global Entrepreneurship Monitor (GEM)" research project. Within the long-term GEM project (established in 1997), an international team of researchers documents and analyses the scope and causes of entrepreneurial activities and the complex relationship between entrepreneurship and economic growth in various countries and publishes the results each year. GEM started with ten participant countries; 31 countries were involved in the 2003 study (see www.gemconsortium.org. for details and all country reports and global reports)

Germany is one of the ten countries which have been involved in the GEM project from the very beginning. The German country team is led by the author, who also coordinates the REM team together with Professor Joachim Wagner (Lüneburg). The results of recent years have shown that entrepreneurial activities within a country are in statistical relationship with overall economic development and that interregional differences in entrepreneurial activities and attitudes are obvious (for further information see http://www.wiso.uni-koeln.de/wigeo/).

Although there are many parallels between GEM (see Reynolds et al. 2004 for details) and REM in terms of research questions, methodological approach and aims, REM compares (ten) sub-national regions instead of countries and provides more reliable information on (the ten selected) German regions than GEM due to the larger sample groups used.

Similar to GEM, four types of data have been assembled for the REM assessment in 2003 (see Lückgen and Oberschachtsiek 2004):
- Representative surveys of 1,000 persons between 18 and 64 years in age in each REM region,
- Detailed personal interviews with 54 regional experts on entrepreneurial framework conditions in the respective REM regions,
- Standardized questionnaires completed by 468 experts in the REM regions and
- Standardized data from secondary sources assembled on each REM region.

2.2 Methodological Approach, Data and Definitions

Within REM – and similar to GEM – we distinguish between three measures of entrepreneurial activity for each region, calculated on the basis of the 18-64-year old inhabitants: the proportion of nascent entrepreneurs, the proportion of young entrepreneurs (or new businesses) and the Total Entrepreneurial Activity rate (TEA).

An individual may be considered a "nascent entrepreneur" based on three conditions: first, if he or she has done something – taken some action – to create a new business in the past year, if he or she expects to share ownership of the new firm; and, third, if the firm has not yet paid salaries and wages for more than three months. In cases where the firm already exists and the interviewee is the owner and he or she has paid salaries and wages for more than three but less than 42 months, it is classified as a "new business" and the individual is classified as a "young entrepreneur". The TEA rate is the sum of the two previous measures; those persons who qualify as both a "nascent entrepreneur" and a "new business" are counted only once, however.

This paper takes into consideration both the population survey and the expert surveys. In the ten REM regions described below a random sample of 1.000 inhabitants was interviewed in the summer of 2003, leading to a data set with 10.000 cases. This questionnaire asked, beside other aspects, about a number of items related to entrepreneurial activities (e.g., whether the interviewee is the owner of a firm that is currently actively run by her or him, whether she/he is currently engaged in starting an own business) and entrepreneurial attitudes and motivations. Second, detailed personal interviews were conducted with regional experts in each of the REM regions followed by standardized questionnaires distributed to these and other regional experts. A deliberate procedure was used for the selection of the entrepreneurship experts. For the purposes of this study, those qualifying as entrepreneurship experts are or were for some time active in the fields of entrepreneurship promotion, advisory services or research in the regions to be examined. They should be in a position to give as soundly based an evaluation of the entrepreneurial framework conditions in their respective regions as possible.

The entrepreneurship experts were selected from the following institutions, organizations and companies by means of a distribution key:
- Business services (tax, corporate and insurance consultants, lawyers, universities and other institutions of higher education, etc.)
- District and municipal institutions for the promotion of economic growth
- Credit institutes (banks, building societies/ savings banks)
- Entrepreneurship initiatives, networks, other promotional institutions for entrepreneurs
- Confederations ("*Wirtschaftsjunioren*" (Associations of Young Business People)), entrepreneur federations, etc.)
- Chambers (Chamber of Industry and Commerce, Chamber of Handicraft)
- Technology parks, innovation centers, business incubators
- Technology transfer institutions, associated institutes at universities
- Scientists (entrepreneurship researchers) at universities and research institutions
- Capital venture companies, business angels
- Initiatives for the promotion of women in business (women's commissioners, networks for women)
- Labor exchanges.

A total of 54 interviews were carried out in the months of August to September 2003. The main purpose of the expert interviews was to identify regional characteristics of the start-up sector which it would not have been possible to ascertain by means of a standardized written survey. The experts were asked for their personal evaluation of the framework conditions for start-ups in their respective regions. They were encouraged to discuss, positive aspects and specific problems, as well as particular characteristics of the start-up sector in their region.

The purpose of the written survey using a standardized questionnaire was also to evaluate regional framework conditions for start-ups. The same questionnaire was used in all ten regions under examination, which enabled a regional comparison of the entrepreneurial framework conditions. All interview partners took part in the written survey, along with additional experts from each of the ten regions. As the number of experts from the twelve fields listed above taking part in the written survey varied from one region to another, measures were taken to ensure equal weighting was given to the statements of the various experts from each region. The weighting factors for the statements of the experts are the result of the quotient of the average number of experts per field in the ten regions and the actual number of experts from an individual region. This procedure ensures that the results from one region are not distorted by an above-average number of experts from a particular field compared with other regions.

Indices were calculated based on the evaluations of the experts, combining the individual statements for each entrepreneurial framework condition (e.g. the REM Index of Policy Programs). Following a reliability test (Cronbach's alpha) some of the statement variables were excluded from the further analysis so that each of the eight indices is based on between two and five individual questions or statements with a five-point scale to indicate the level of agreement (from 1 = disagree totally to 5 = agree totally), the responses to which were then collated to create (usually) a single index per framework condition. Each of the statements is included in the index with the same weighting.

2.3 The REM Regions

Even if we can not claim that the data are representative for Germany as a whole, the regions were selected in such a way that they mirror the spatial structure with regard to old and new federal states (i.e., western and eastern Germany), highly industrialized versus more rural regions, centre and periphery, etc. (see fig. 7.1 for the location of the ten regions). The REM regions were selected according to three criteria:
- Spatial distribution of population (western, eastern, southern, northern part of the country)
- Region types (larger urban agglomerations, urbanized areas, rural areas)
- Start-up rates 1996-1998 according to firm data of the Institute for Employment Research, Nuremberg (high, medium, low).

As a rough guide, information relating to the average in the selected regions can be considered to be a valid instrument for information on Germany as a whole. As the REM regions overall were intended to represent the region types in Germany as far as possible, it was clear from the start that economically strong regions (e.g. Munich, Stuttgart) would be set against economically weaker regions (e.g. Middle Mecklenburg/Rostock). It can be no surprise either that entrepreneurial activities are considerably stronger in Cologne and Munich, for example, than in Emscher-Lippe or Western Saxony. This result was predetermined by the selection of the regions. The core focus of REM is to quantify the extent of these differences and to find the reasons behind them.

Fig. 7.1: The REM case study areas

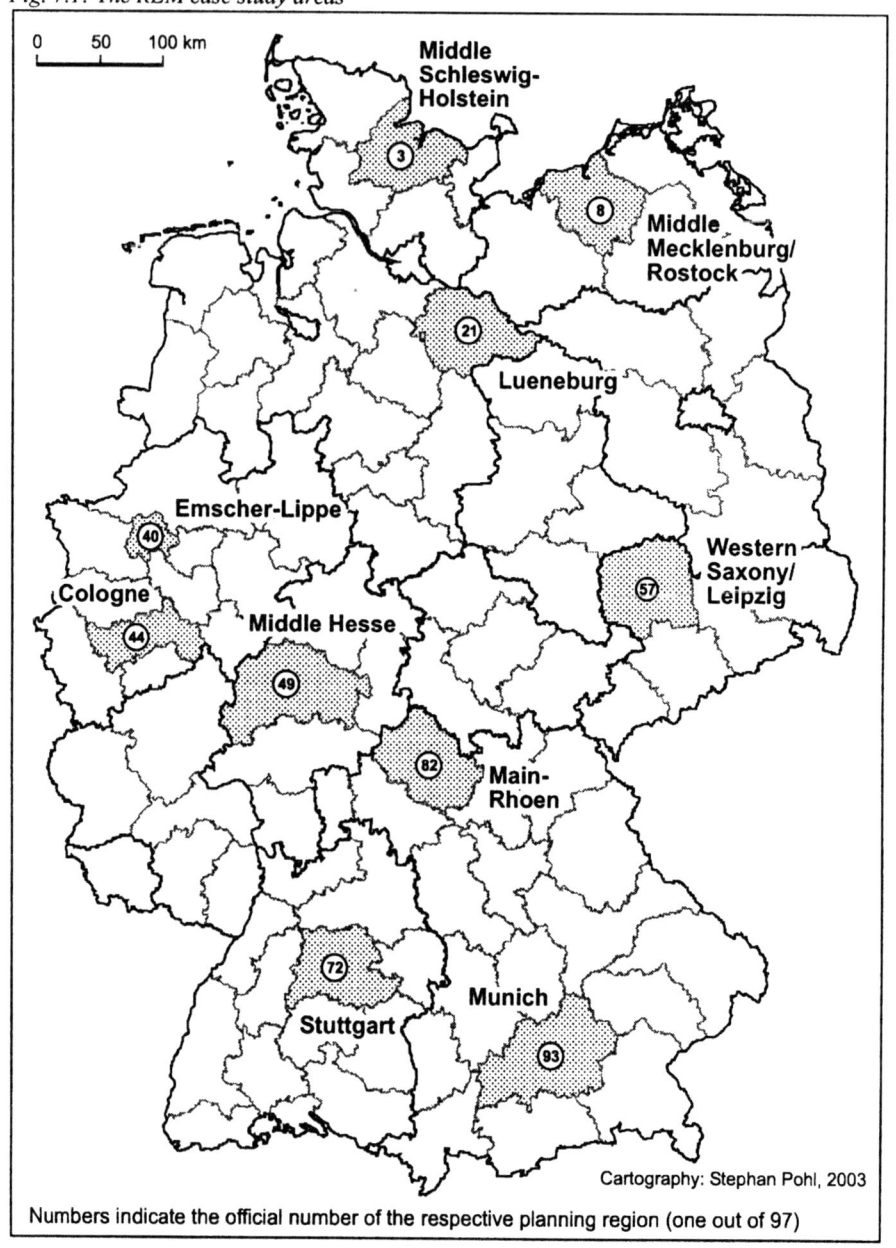

Numbers indicate the official number of the respective planning region (one out of 97)

3. ENTREPRENEURIAL ATTITUDES OF THE REGIONAL POPULATION AS DETERMINANTS OF ENTREPRENEURIAL ACTIVITIES

3.1 Entrepreneurial Activities

In REM entrepreneurial activities are measured using three entrepreneurial ratios: the proportion of nascent entrepreneurs, the proportion of young entrepreneurs and the Total Entrepreneurial Activity rate (see section 2.2 for definitions).

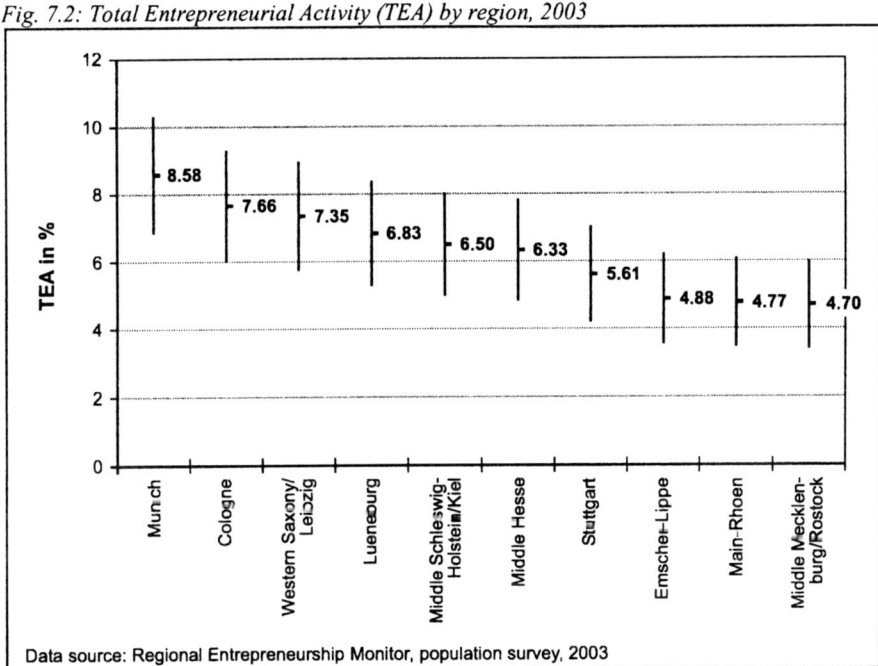

Fig. 7.2: Total Entrepreneurial Activity (TEA) by region, 2003

Data source: Regional Entrepreneurship Monitor, population survey, 2003

The level of entrepreneurial activities differs in the 10 regions – and these differences are at least partially statistically significant. Entrepreneurs obviously enjoy particularly good entrepreneurial framework conditions in Munich and Cologne, for the Total Entrepreneurial Activity rate is especially high in these regions. The mean average TEA rate is 6.32% (proportion of nascent or young entrepreneurs among all 18-64-year old inhabitants in the regions). The spread ranges from Munich (8.58%) and Cologne (7.66%) through to Main-Rhoen and Middle Mecklenburg with slightly higher than 4.70%. The vertical lines in fig. 7.2 represent the upper and lower limits of the 95% confidence interval, i.e. the limits within which the actual average of all inhabitants is, stated with 95% certainty. Provided the confidence intervals do not overlap, there can be said to be statistically significant differences between the regions. Correspondingly, there are statistically significant differences between the TEA rates of the two leading regions of

Munich and Cologne on the one hand and the worst-placed region of Middle Mecklenburg on the other. Compared with 2001, when the REM was launched, the eastern German region Western/Saxony/Leipzig in particular has succeeded in increasing its TEA rate considerably (from 4.96% to 7.35%), which results in a marked improvement in this region's ranking. The differences between the ten regions are narrower in 2003 than in 2001.

3.2 Attitudes of the Local Population

Important determinants for an individual's decision to start or not to start a business are the start-up opportunities in the near future and in the region where the individual lives. The decisive factor here is the individual perception of such opportunities, which may well differ from the actual opportunities as seen objectively, as people may consider opportunities to be more or less favorable than they actually are. The personal perception of start-up opportunities plays a very important role. Whereas, on average, only 17,5% of all people across all the REM regions believe the opportunities for starting a company will be or become favorable in the next six months in the regions where they live, an above-average proportion of people in the regions of Munich, Stuttgart, Cologne and Western Saxony hold this belief. In Munich, one third sees favorable entrepreneurial opportunities in the next six months. At the other end of the scale is Rostock, where only 8.6% of people see favorable opportunities for starting a company in the short term. The differences between the REM regions are very large for this variable, similar to 2001. The gap between the two high-rated regions and the two rated regions is enormous and the proportion of those seeing good opportunities for starting a company in Middle Mecklenburg/Rostock is only slightly higher than one fourth of that in Munich! The values for this variable have fallen – in some cases drastically – in all REM regions compared with 2001, a result which can also be derived for Germany as a whole from the results of the GEM in 2003 (see Sternberg, Bergmann and Lückgen 2004; Lückgen and Oberschachtsiek 2004). Similar to the results in 2001, the differences between the regions are, in most cases, statistically significant, which means that the perception of the start-up opportunities differs more from one region to another than actual entrepreneurial activities.

An individual who see good entrepreneurial opportunities in the near future will still not start a company if he or she harbors a considerable fear of failure in the venture. This fear of failure was more widespread in Germany than in any other GEM country in 2003 with the exception of Greece: 49.3% of all respondents confirmed that the fear of failure would prevent them from starting a business (see Sternberg, Bergmann and Lückgen 2004). This figure for Germany as a whole is slightly higher than the mean average for the 10 REM regions, which means that the fear of failure is somewhat more acutely felt in areas outside the REM regions.

Fig. 7.3: Perception of start-up opportunities by REM region, 2003

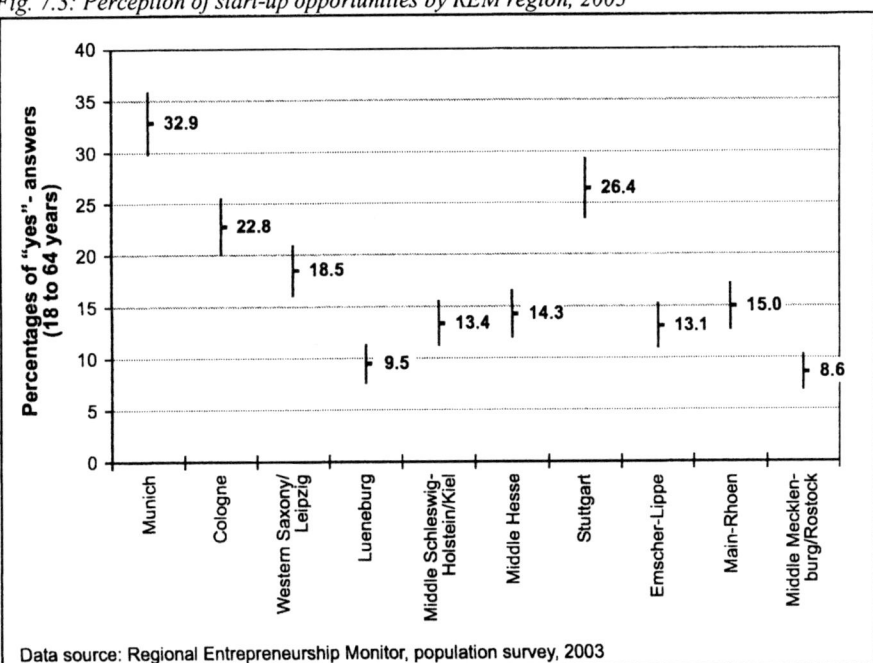

The differences between the REM regions are not quite so large concerning the fear of failure as they were regarding entrepreneurial opportunities, but considerably greater than in the responses to the question on individual entrepreneurial skills. As had to be expected, the fear of failure is particularly high in regions where the TEA rate is low. The particularly high fear of failure variable evidenced in Leipzig does, however, stand out, as this region has the third highest TEA value for 2003. The example of Middle Hesse demonstrates that the inhabitants of a region can have evidently more positive entrepreneurial attitudes than would normally be expected on the basis of expert evaluations of entrepreneurial framework conditions in those regions.

Of course, other attitude variable may have an impact on an individual's decision as well, namely the image of self-employed persons or the entrepreneurial skills of the interviewee. While REM regions differ for such variables as well, their statistical impact on TEA rate is lower than for both variables discussed before. Overall, the values of the variables on entrepreneurial attitudes demonstrate the existence of a causal and statistical link with entrepreneurial activities. Regions where the inhabitants see more favorable start-up opportunities and where the fear of failure is low also have higher levels of entrepreneurial activity. Most of the regions fit this picture.

Fig. 7. 4: Fear of failure by REM Region, 2003

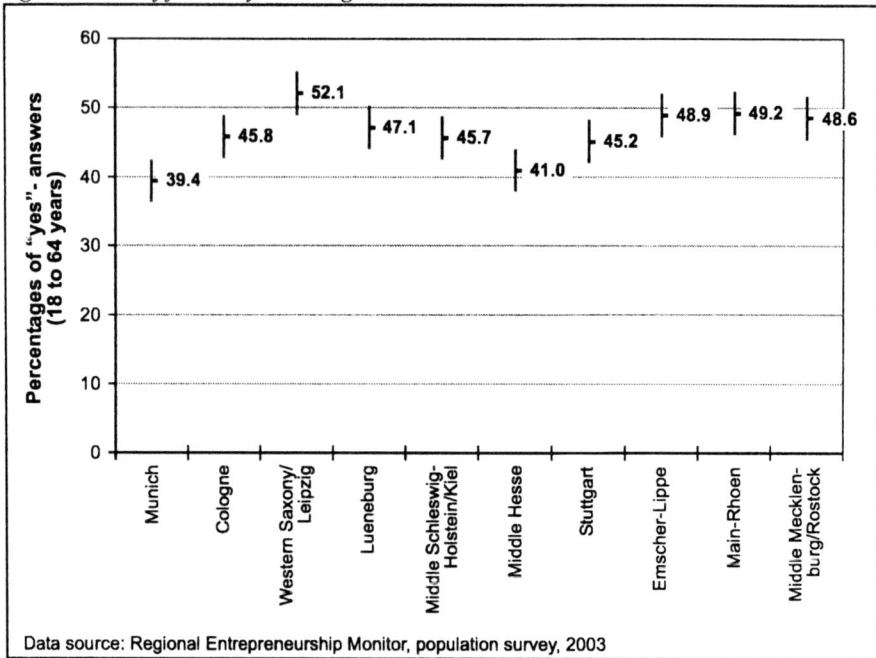

4. ASSESSMENT OF ENTREPRENEURIAL, POLITICALLY RELEVANT FRAMEWORK CONDITIONS IN THE REM REGIONS IN 2003

Decisions by the inhabitants of regions to launch a start-up are not solely determined directly by the attitudes of the individuals themselves, but – so the hypothesis – also semi-indirectly by entrepreneurial framework conditions. Some of these entrepreneurial framework conditions are uniform throughout Germany (e.g. some taxes); some of them, on the other hand, differ from one region to another – and these regional attributes matter for the decision to start a new business ceteris paribus, i.e. after controlling for sex, age, education etc. (cf. Sternberg and Wagner 2004). The following text deals exclusively with the latter regional framework conditions. It is a widespread view that the regions with the best framework conditions and the most favorable attitudes among the population generally also stand out with above-average levels of entrepreneurial activities or a particularly high proportion of self-employed people. This hypothesis has hardly been tested empirically to date, however.

The regional experts involved in the study mostly evaluated the local entrepreneurial framework conditions positively (five point scale from 1 (negative) to 5 (positive). Correspondingly, entrepreneurs in all ten REM regions overall enjoy rather good government programs aimed at supporting start-ups (the mean average index evaluation was 3.67) and regional networks in favor of start-ups (3.58). The weaknesses identified were the framework conditions in the fields of finance (mean average 3.03) and cultural values and social norms (3.17). Compared with the results from 2001, the differences between the mean average values for the individual entrepreneurial framework conditions vary less strongly in 2003.

Fig. 7.5: Assessment of eight entrepreneurial framework conditions by REM Region, 2003

	\multicolumn{8}{c}{Framework conditions[a]:}							
	Finance	Government policy	Government programmes	R&D transfer	Education	Labour	Norms, values	Networks
Munich	☺	☺	☺	☻	☺	☻	☺	☺
Cologne	☻	☹	☺	☺	☹	☻	☺	☻
Western Saxony/Leipzig	☺	☻	☻	☺	☻	☻	☻	☻
Lueneburg	☹	☹	☹	☹	☹	☹	☹	☺
Middle Schleswig-Holstein/Kiel	☹	☺	☺	☺	☺	☺	☺	☹
Middle Hesse	☻	☺	☹	☻	☺	☺	☺	☹
Stuttgart	☻	☻	☻	☻	☻	☺	☻	☻
Main-Rhoen	☺	☻	☺	☹	☺	☺	☻	☺
Emscher-Lippe	☺	☺	☻	☹	☻	☹	☹	☺
Middle Mecklenburg/Rostock	☹	☹	☹	☺	☹	☹	☹	☹
Mean value of column	3.03	3.42	3.67	3.30	3.45	3.38	3.17	3.58
Standard deviation	0.74	0.64	0.70	0.78	0.73	0.84	0.66	0.82

☻ Top 3 ranks   ☺ Mid 4 ranks   ☹ Lower 3 ranks

[a]: 5 point scale from '1' (unfavourable conditions) to '5' (favourable conditions)
Data source: Regional Entrepreneurship Monitor, expert survey, 2003

Differences, in some cases significant, were found in the regional comparison of evaluations of the framework conditions. Overall, the regions of Stuttgart and (to a lesser degree) Western Saxony achieves the best results, while Lüneburg and Middle Mecklenburg are at the bottom of the list. In contrast to 2001, metropolitan regions tend to enjoy better results, and rural and smaller urban areas generate poorer results on the whole. The differences between western and eastern German regions are less marked than two years previously. While Stuttgart has succeeded in reinforcing its claim to the top spot, Munich has lost some ground, without actually receiving a really poor evaluation for any one of the eight entrepreneurial framework conditions.

As the standard deviation values for fig. 7.5 show, the differences between the regions regarding the eight entrepreneurial framework conditions vary considerably, even though these differences are less marked than in 2001. They differ to a relatively large extent in labor as well as in R&D transfer, while the differences between the regions concerning the government programs are relatively small.

5. EVALUATION OF EXISTING PUBLIC POLICY INSTRUMENTS TO PROMOTE START-UPS

As shown earlier regional government programs and regional government policies in favour of start-ups should aim to influence the entrepreneurial attitudes of the population, as there is an evident link between these attitudes and entrepreneurial activities. Greater efforts should be made to promote the development of an entrepreneurially friendly culture. Action needs to be taken at regional level in the fields of financing, the structure of the promotional infrastructure and R&D transfer, as well as entrepreneurially focused education and training. The need for action in these individual fields varies considerably from one region to another. It is therefore not only the start-up itself that should be seen (also) as a regional event, but that, in the promotion of start-ups, the maxim is: space matters!

This chapter will demonstrate the general public policy measures being undertaken in Germany to initiate and promote start-ups and, subsequently, how these measures are evaluated in the REM regions themselves. It should be noted that the GEM country reports for Germany have for many years been consistent in their findings that Germany as a whole (i.e. independently of individual regions) has very good policies for the promotion of start-ups, when compared with other GEM countries (see Sternberg, Bergmann and Lückgen 2004).

For something over ten years now, there has been a large, and still increasing, number of promotional programs in Germany aimed explicitly or implicitly at supporting entrepreneurial activities. These programs, which take effect in Germany and its regions, have been established by the European Union, individual federal ministries (... for Economics and Labor, ... for Education and Research), ministries of the individual federal states and individual municipalities. The REM regions are divided up on the basis of the 97 planning regions, which do not represent any official delineation of regions. Consequently, there are no entrepreneurship promotion programs which apply exclusively to individual REM regions. It is therefore not possible to evaluate existing public policy instruments directly using REM data. The intention of this chapter is therefore to give a brief overview of the number and type of entrepreneurship promotion programs developed by the various governments and which <u>also</u> (even if not exclusively) apply in the regions.

Following Sternberg (forthcoming) it is helpful to consider data supplied by the promotion database of the Federal Ministry of Economics and Labor (from August 2003). Only programs relating to the promotional area of "establishing and maintaining start-ups" are analyzed. The areas covered by the programs are, in the case of the EU programs, all current Member States and, in the case of programs established by federal ministries, the entire Federal Republic of Germany, provided these are not regionally differentiated programs such as Exist or GRW. The same applies for the areas covered by the promotional programs of the individual federal states.

The programs of the European Union are clearly weighted towards innovative start-ups, as the programs "Innovation Relay Centres" (IRC) and the "European Business Incubator Network" (EBN) show. The total of 20 programs run by federal ministries offers a very broad spectrum which is administered by promotional organizations and is oriented towards broadly differing target groups. This allows unemployed people to be supported on their path to professional independence with bridging moneys. The federal government in Berlin also has several programs which are aimed at promoting particularly knowledge- and technology-intensive entrepreneurs, who have considerable potential for growth (e.g. BTU start-up program, INSTI-KMU patent campaign, FUTOUR 2000).

Some of the programs are regionally selective, i.e. only entrepreneurs in certain promotion regions are entitled to apply for support. This is particularly true of the "Exist – University-based start-ups" program, which was designed as a competition and in the first phase only support start-ups from universities in the five winning regions of Wuppertal, Karlsruhe, Stuttgart, South Thuringia and Dresden. The joint project between central and state government "*Verbesserung der regionalen Wirtschaftsstruktur*" (improvement of the regional economic structure) is similar, in that it only supports start-ups from the promotion areas covered by the joint project. Some programs are deliberately oriented exclusively towards eastern Germany, but apply for the whole region. Most programs cover the whole country, however.

One major strength of the decentralized promotional policy in Germany is that the support programs are distributed over several spatial areas. In particular, the individual federal states have established promotional programs of their own which are broadly similar, but which also include some state-specific characteristics. Eastern German states are particularly active, measured by the number of promotional programs in operation. An observer may interpret this as an indicator of the need for such promotional measures in a part of Germany which has, to date, been characterized by a relatively low level of entrepreneurial activities when compared with western Germany (apart from the most recent years since reunification of eastern and western Germany). Of course, the mere number of these promotional does not allow any conclusions as to their effectiveness.

The public policy instruments mentioned are aimed, implicitly or explicitly, at promoting start-ups from various types of incubator units. Incubator units are institutions where an entrepreneur was active before launching the start-up (and may still be, during – and even after – the launch of the start-up, in the case of part-time self-employment). This orientation towards the incubator unit can be very important as it has a not inconsiderable influence on the entrepreneurial propensity and capabilities of the individual. A former student, for example, may still benefit for a long time as a nascent entrepreneur or young entrepreneur from his or her former professor and the research team, through access to innovative personal networks, for example. Equally, the idea for the start-up may even have originated as a result of these contacts.

Literature on entrepreneurial research differentiates in particular between (other) companies, universities and other institutions of higher education, and extra-university research institutions (in Germany, for example, the institutes of the Max-Planck Society or the Fraunhofer institutes) as incubator units. In a purely qualitative sense, other companies are by far the more important (see Sternberg et al. 1997 on business incubators or innovation centers). Start-ups from universities and other institutions of higher education, as well as extra-university institutions are also of particular interest, however, due to the high level of transfer potential, and are promoted by various national and state-level programs (e.g. "*PFAU*" in North-Rhine/Westphalia, "*Flügge*" in Bavaria, "*Junge Innovatoren*" (young innovators) in Baden-Württemberg; see also the scientific evaluations of parts of these programs by the author, see Klose and Sternberg 2002, Müller and Sternberg 2004 or www.wiso.uni-koeln.de/wigeo).

Of course, there are also entrepreneurs who have launched a start-up without the explicit influence of an incubator organization – be that because they did not have access to one (e.g. entrepreneurs who were previously unemployed) or because, although the entrepreneur was in employment, the employer and the institution had no influence on the entrepreneurial idea.

6. EVALUATION OF PUBLIC POLICIES AIMED AT SUPPORTING START-UPS IN THE REM REGIONS

Following these general discussions of entrepreneurial activities as regional events, not related explicitly to REM regions, the focus will now once again be on the REM regions themselves. This cannot represent a direct evaluation of individual public policy programs (this is not the aim of REM), but the statements made by the average of 50 entrepreneurial experts from each region do allow an implicit evaluation of promotional programs in operation in the individual regions. As detailed in the methodological section, there are two regional entrepreneurial framework conditions which explicitly reflect the political framework conditions: regional government programs (5 statements) on the one hand and the quantity and quality of government regulations and bureaucratic rules (4 statements) on the other. On the following pages the statistical relationship for selected statements to the proportion of nascent entrepreneurs in the individual regions are examined. The hypothesis is that the favorable nature of the policy variables leads/has led to higher levels of entrepreneurial activity. Time lags between the implementation of political measures and their impact, although very obvious, are not taken into consideration, because its lengths are difficult to estimate.

A coordinate system was selected as the form of graphic representation, with the average of the indices of the political variables on the abscissa and the nascent rate on the ordinate. The point of intersection of the two axes symbolizes the average of the two variables across all regions. According to the stated hypothesis, most regions should be in the lower left and upper right quadrants. The upper right quadrant represents regions with above-average proportions of nascent entrepreneurs and an above average evaluation of the political variables, whereas both these values are below the regional average in the lower left quadrant. The two remaining quadrants represent high rates of nascent entrepreneurs with poor evaluations of the policy variables and vice versa. Five of the total of nine individual statements on political framework conditions was investigated for the following analysis. The results of these five statements can be taken as representative of the nine statements as a whole.

The correlation between public policies and entrepreneurial activity is surprisingly weak if the focus of the statement is on the priority attached to this issue by the state government. This priority is indeed perceived as very high in all REM regions (with 3.87, the second highest mean average of all the statements belonging to the two political framework conditions shown here). This said, only three of the ten REM regions are to be found in the expected quadrants. In Munich and Western Saxony in particular, the respective state governments are acknowledged as attaching a high priority to the promotion of start-ups and, at the same time, these regions enjoy high proportions of nascent entrepreneurs. The same applies in reverse to Middle Hesse. It is possible that the measures implemented by state public policies, which exist in sufficient quantity in every federal state (see previous chapter), are not known to an appropriate extent in all areas of the states. The gap between the best and the poorest value for this policy variable is particularly large.

Fig. 7.6: High priority for start-ups among state government and share of nascent entrepreneurs, 2003

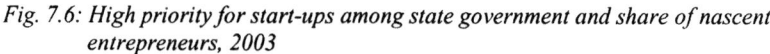

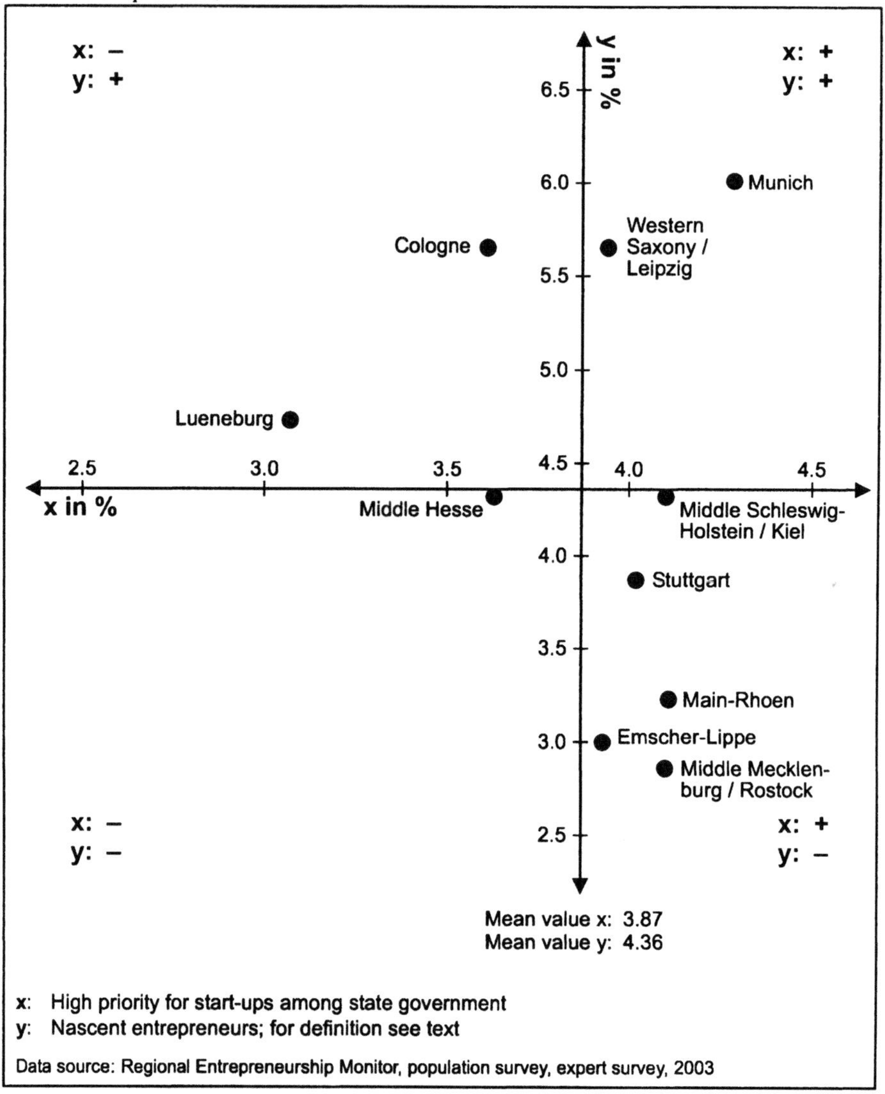

Statement analyzed in fig. 7.7 is much the same as in fig. 7.6, except that here the focus is on local analysis (city or county), rather than regional analysis (federal state). This figure shows a very similar pattern to the previous figure. Here, as in the previous figure, only three regions are to be found in the expected quadrants. Two of these three regions, Munich and Western Saxony, are the same as those in fig. 7.6. In contrast to the previous figure, however, the standard deviation of the values for this policy statement is considerably smaller. One possible interpretation of this result is that, at the local level, start-up experts apparently scarcely differentiate between measures implemented by regional and local governments in terms of the significance of start-ups. It would be interesting to find out whether entrepreneurs and potential entrepreneurs in the regions concerned share a similar perception. This is one of the aspects to be included as an addition for the third round of data gathering (REM III).

Common hypotheses of entrepreneurial research and policy in Germany have maintained for many years that bureaucratic obstacles and state regulation make it more difficult to actually launch start-ups. There has so far seldom been concrete, empirical evidence to back up claims of this kind, however, which are voiced in particular by representatives of the political parties and associations with scarcely concealed ulterior motives.

Initially, there is evidence of considerable deficits in this respect in the regions. None of the nine policy statements mentioned here receives a poorer average evaluation (mean average 2.88 on a five point scale, very small gaps between the regions). This particularly negative evaluation of this statement does not correspond, however, to the expected low start-up rates in the regions concerned. There is no statistical correlation with the proportion of nascent entrepreneurs: Half of the ten regions are to be found in the expected quadrants, and half not. The Cologne region (poor evaluation of the statement, but high proportion of nascent entrepreneurs) and Main-Rhoen (third lowest proportion of nascent entrepreneurs, but best evaluation of the statement) represent the most conspicuous deviations from the expected distributed. This result allows several conclusions to be drawn: The most plausible is that this kind of bureaucratic obstacle obviously has no effect on the number of nascent entrepreneurs. Obstacles may exist and obstruct entrepreneurs in many individual cases in some places. Seen overall, however, they cannot be taken as an explanation for the greater frequency of start-ups in certain regions than in others. Other empirical research work by the author, for example on start-ups originating from Cologne universities (cf. Backes-Gellner, Demirer and Sternberg 2002), demonstrates that the fear potential entrepreneurs have of supposed bureaucratic obstacles hindering the actual launch of their start-up is indeed very common, but is totally unjustified in many cases, as the legal regulations they are afraid of do not, de facto, exist.

The general evaluation of programs and services for start-ups is very positive: This statement receives this highest mean average value (4.03) of all nine policy statements while, at the same time, the standard deviation between the ten regions is low. The start-up experts therefore feel enough is being done. Here, too, however, there is practically no statistical correlation to be found with the start-up rates (only five regions are in the expected quadrants). It is especially surprising that although Cologne has the second highest level of nascent entrepreneurs, the proportion of respondents who feel that public policy offers a broad range of programs and services for start-ups is very low. The most positive response to this statement is in

Emscher-Lippe, the region with the second lowest proportion of nascent entrepreneurs.

Fig. 7.7: High priority for start-ups among local government and share of nascent entrepreneurs, 2003

x: High priority for start-ups among local government
y: Nascent entrepreneurs; for definition see text

Data source: Regional Entrepreneurship Monitor, population survey, expert survey, 2003

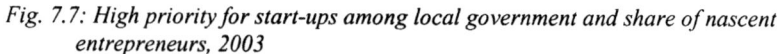

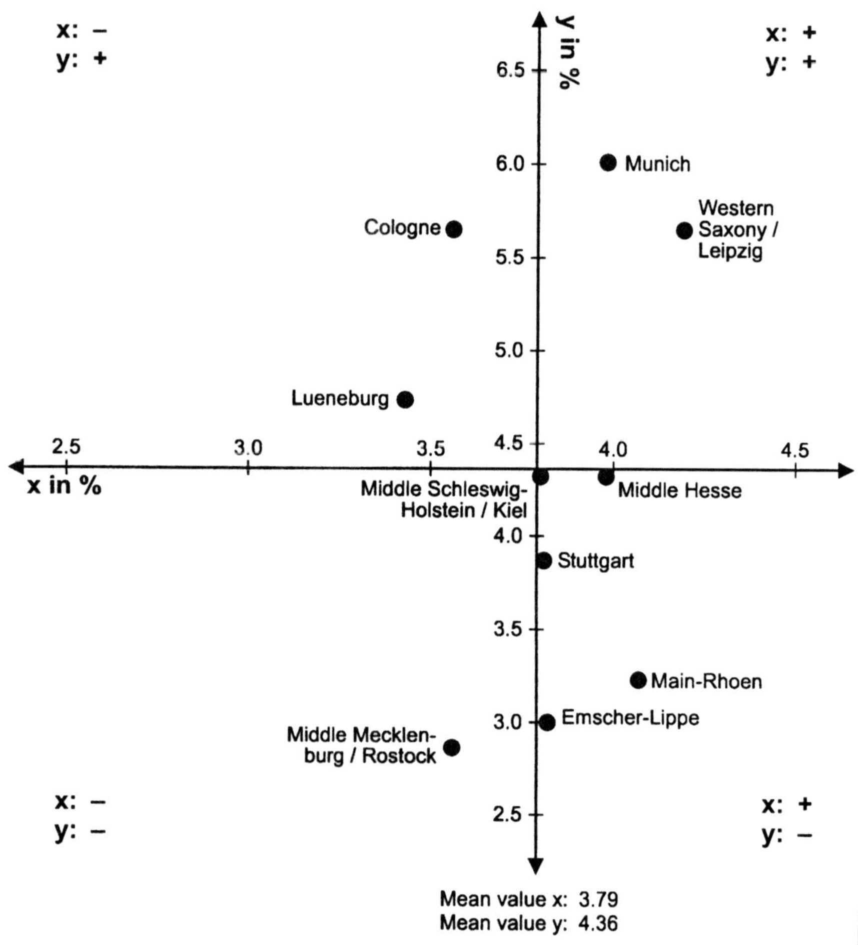

Entrepreneurship in German Regions 133

Fig. 7.8: Regulations/bureaucratic rules and share of nascent entrepreneurs, 2003

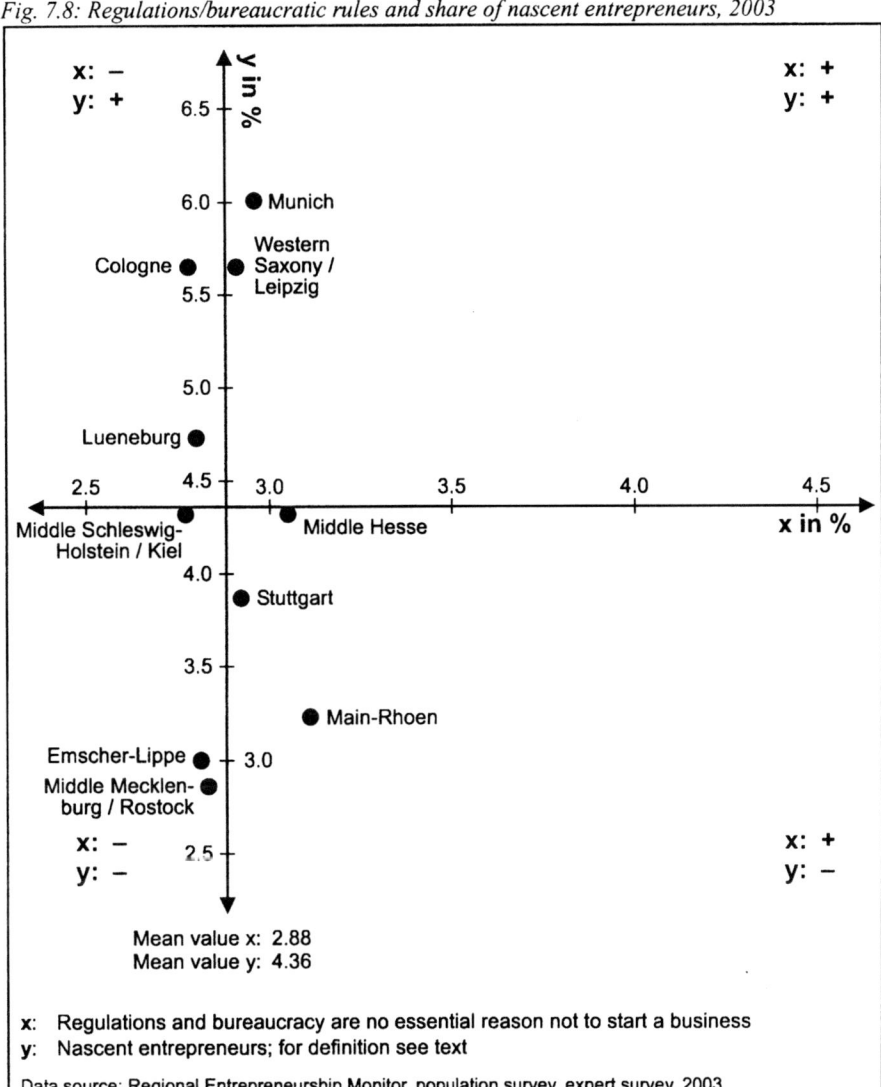

Fig. 7.9: Range of public policy programs and share of nascent entrepreneurs, 2003

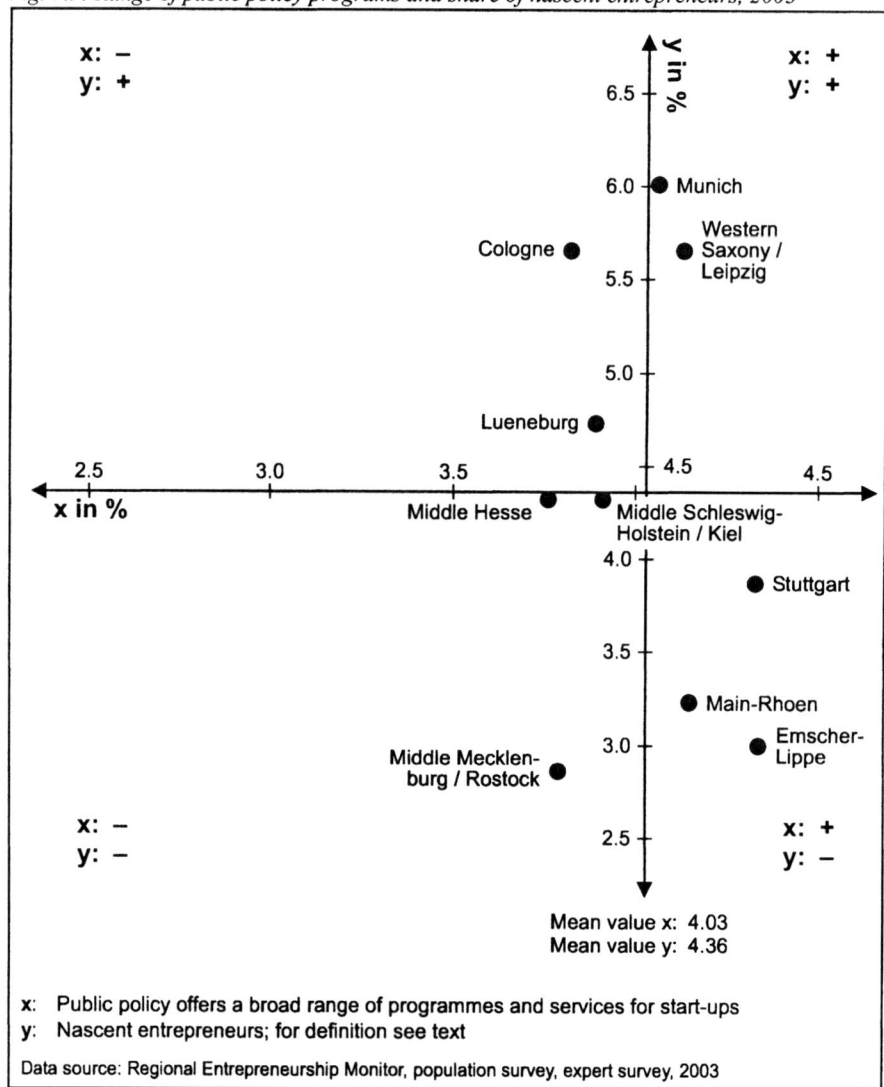

The most striking result is produced by the last graphic of this kind, which deals with the statement "In my region, entrepreneurs quickly find the right contact person within consulting services". Here the correlation is more negative in nature: With the exception of two regions (the two regions in Eastern Germany), all REM regions are to be found in the two quadrants thought less probable (upper left and lower right). In almost all regions with above-average proportions of nascent entrepreneurs, the entrepreneurs need a disproportionately long time to find the right contact person within consulting services. Correspondingly, almost all regions in which contact persons are found quickly have below-average proportions of nascent entrepreneurs. Despite the low standard deviation for this policy statement, it does allow us to draw the conclusion that rapid access to contact persons obviously does not have a positive impact on the level of nascent entrepreneurs.

In conclusion it may be said that the nature of government programs within the regions may have an influence on entrepreneurial activities, though this need not necessarily be the case. Time lags between the implementation of a measure to support entrepreneurial activities and the effect on entrepreneurial attitudes and entrepreneurial activities at regional level may be responsible for the fact that statistical correlations can scarcely be found, provided the same reference year is taken for dependent and independent variables.

Finally, the values of the correlation analysis (bivariate Pearson correlation) have been added to the graphic representations of figures 7.6-7.10. First, correlation coefficients are calculated for each of the nine given statements on the two policy variables, as well as the two dependent variables of the start-up rates (TEA and nascent entrepreneurs, respectively). As tab. 7.1 shows, a statistically significant correlation between the policy statements and the two start-up rates cannot be demonstrated in any single case. Obviously, a region which implements specific measures to support start-ups, measures which are evaluated by start-up experts as good and comprehensive, cannot assume that these measures will result in higher levels of nascent entrepreneurs than in regions which do not implement such measures. This conclusion is true at least when, as in this case, the same reference year (2003) is taken as a basis. If different reference years were taken, the result may turn out different as a result of the time-lag problem. The picture is very different, however, if the correlations between the policy statements are analyzed. Four statements demonstrate in some cases highly significant correlations with four of the other eight statements. This applies to the statements „In my region the support for start-ups is a high priority for policy at the local government level", „In my region government policies aimed at supporting start-ups are effective", „In my region, entrepreneurs can find the right contact person quickly within consulting services" and "In my region, promotional institutions work together in a coordinated fashion".

Tellingly, the statement "In my region the amount of trade tax and real property tax is NOT a burden for start-ups" is the only one which does not demonstrate a statistically significant correlation with any of the other statements. As the correlations between the policy statements as previously mentioned are all, as expected and without exception, positive, it would not be implausible to suspect that no individual statement has a direct influence on start-up rates, but that a combination of several policy statement may do so.

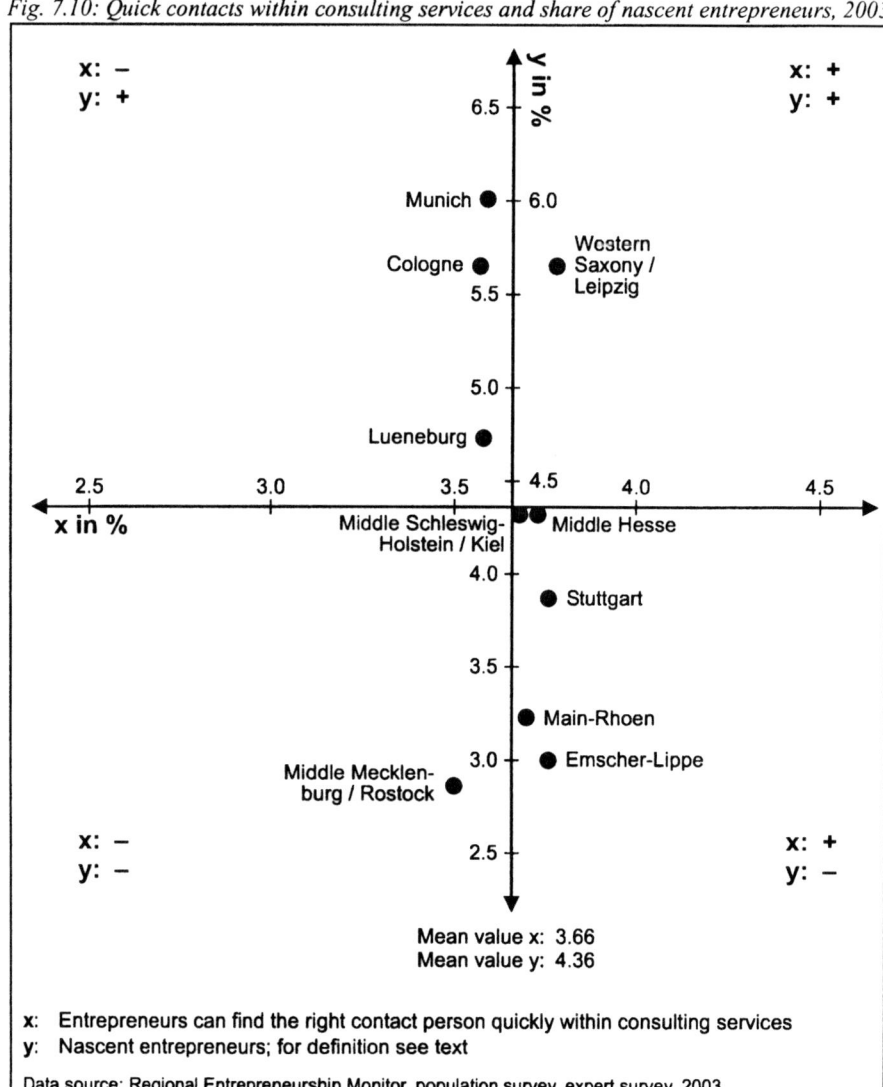

Fig. 7.10: Quick contacts within consulting services and share of nascent entrepreneurs, 2003

Entrepreneurship in German Regions

Tab. 7.1: *Correlations between the single statements of political framework conditions and entrepreneurial activity, 2003*

	TEA 2003 in %	Nascent 2003 in %	Priority state	Priority local	Taxes	Regulations	Support infrastruct.	Effectiveness	Quick contacts	Business incubators	Coordinated policies
TEA 2003	1.000										
Nascent 2003	0.982***	1.000									
Priority state	-0.111	-0.096	1.000								
Priority local	0.101	0.186	0.642**	1.000							
Taxes	-0.204	-0.187	-0.069	0.341	1.000						
Regulations	-0.132	-0.031	0.587*	0.898***	0.337	1.000					
Support Infrastructure	-0.307	-0.273	0.457	0.515	0.099	0.495	1.000				
Effectiveness	0.017	0.074	0.456	0.633**	0.169	0.509	0.861***	1.000			
Quick Contacts	-0.310	-0.231	0.377	0.655**	0.335	0.539	0.867***	0.836***	1.000		
Business Incubators	0.009	0.063	0.612*	0.239	0.014	0.125	0.090	0.234	0.209	1.000	
Coordinated	0.078	0.141	0.153	0.495	0.252	0.227	0.570*	0.584*	0.803***	0.274	1.000

Priority state (local) = In my region the support for start-ups is a high priority for policy at the regional (local) government level
Taxes = In my region the amount of trade tax and real property tax is NOT a burden for start-ups
Regulations = In my region, regulation and bureaucratic rules do not represent a major obstacle to entrepreneurship.
Support infrastruct. = In my region, the public promotional structure offers a broad range of promotional programs and consulting services for start-ups.
Effectiveness = In my region government policies aimed at supporting start-ups are effective
Quick contacts = In my region, entrepreneurs can find the right contact person quickly within consulting services.
Business incubators= In my region science parks and business incubators provide effective support for start-ups
Coordinated = In my region, promotional institutions work together in a coordinated fashion

Pearson correlation coefficients; *: $p < 0.1$; **: $p < 0.05$; ***: $p < 0.01$; N=97 planning regions; Data source: REM, population and expert survey 2003

Finally, in summary, the correlation between all nine entrepreneurial framework conditions and both indicators of entrepreneurial activity at the level of the REM regions is investigated (tab. 7.2). While the nine individual statements on the two policy variables were found not to demonstrate any statistical correlation with the two dependent variables in any single case, a statistical correlation does exist for the „labor" index, more precisely for both variables for entrepreneurial activity. Based on this finding, the positive conditions on the local labor market obviously coincide positively with start-up rates. The labor market index is calculated based on the two statements: "In my region, start-ups have access to a broad supply of qualified workers" and "In my region, start-ups can recruit highly qualified workers without significant difficulties". The index values of all other entrepreneurial framework conditions do not have any statistical correlation with the start-up rates. This also applies explicitly to the two policy framework conditions. There is, however, a statistically significant correlation between certain indices of the entrepreneurial framework conditions, as shown by tab. 7.2. In each of these cases, the correlations are positive, as expected. The two policy variables enjoy positively results in this respect. „Policy programs" demonstrates such a positive statistical correlation with five of the remaining seven entrepreneurial framework conditions, the correlation being particularly strong in the area of education. The latter also applies to the area of „regulations and bureaucratic obstacles", for which there also exist strong correlations with „cultural values and social norms" and with the second policy variable. This result may suggest that the policy variables – similar to almost all other framework conditions – may not have any single, direct statistical correlation with the regional start-up rates, but that they may work in combination with some of the other framework conditions, by which they are influenced and which, in turn, they also appear to influence. More empirical research is needed to close this gap.

7. CONCLUSIONS

The REM shows that politics in general and policies to promote start-ups in particular should aim to influence the public's attitudes towards start-ups; these attitudes are in clear correlation with entrepreneurial activities. More effort should be made to contribute to the development of a culture which is friendly towards entrepreneurship (see Lückgen and Oberschachtsiek 2004). Action needs to be taken at regional level in the area of financing, the structure of the promotional infrastructure and the transfer of research and development, as well as in the area of education and training relating to entrepreneurship. The need for action varies considerably from field to field in the individual regions. Furthermore, even if political efforts are increased, it cannot be assumed that there will be a positive influence in the short term on entrepreneurial activities for each and every facet of the political framework conditions and the public promotional infrastructure.

Tab. 7.2: Correlations between eight entrepreneurial framework conditions (indices) and entrepreneurial activity, 2003

	Nascent 2003 in %	TEA 2003 in %	Finance	Regulations, bureaucracy	Start-up programs	R&D transfer	Education	Labor	Cultural values, social norms	Network integration
Nascent 2003 in %	1.000									
TEA 2003 in %	0.982***	1.000								
Finance	0.263	0.189	1.000							
Regulations, Bureaucracy	-0.126	-0.188	0.111	1.000						
Start-up Programs	0.009	-0.070	0.574*	0.599*	1.000					
R&D transfer	0.370	0.367	0.300	0.354	0.403	1.000				
Education	-0.220	-0.253	0.095	0.765**	0.804***	0.372	1.000			
Labor	0.741**	0.723**	0.452	0.336	0.325	0.595*	0.071	1.000		
Cultur.values social norms	0.407	0.310	0.515	0.707**	0.697**	0.680**	0.484	0.749**	1.000	
Network Integration	0.489	0.395	0.554*	0.150	0.735**	0.456	0.418	0.385	0.614*	1.000

Pearson correlation coefficients; *: $p < 0.1$; **: $p < 0.05$; ***: $p < 0.01$; N=97 planning regions
Data source: Regional Entrepreneurship Monitor, population survey 2003, expert survey 2003

This rather sobering conclusion is backed up by the fact that, for the entrepreneurial framework conditions in general (with the exception of the labor market) and for the individual policy statements, no evidence can be found whatsoever of statistically significant correlations with the start-up rates at the level of the 10 REM regions. Such correlations can be demonstrated, however, for the attitude variables „fear of failure as a reason not to start a business" and „start-up opportunities". This result can be interpreted in many ways. First, it is possible that political measures do have an effect, but that it takes many years (an unknown number of years!) before these effects are felt. Second, it is conceivable that political measures alone do not lead to an increase in start-up rates, but only in combination with favorable characteristics among the other entrepreneurial framework conditions (which can only be directly controlled by policies to a limited extent). Third, it cannot be ruled out that political measures to promote entrepreneurial activities have neither direct nor indirect, neither immediate nor medium- to long-term effects on entrepreneurial activities. The question of the time lags, at least, may be answered by the REM research project at a later stage, when a longer history of data is available.

In this chapter it is only possible to generate rather general conclusions for Germany as a whole, but not conclusions that could be directly applicable to any of 10 REM regions individually. Previous chapters have shown that an individual's entrepreneurial propensity and activity depend on a range of factors. Some of these determinants depend on their social environment, such as the entrepreneurial propensity and attitudes towards start-ups among friends and acquaintances. Ultimately, entrepreneurial framework conditions, such as financing or the availability and quality of political programs, depend on the corresponding factors in the region where the respondent lives (e.g. the planning unit) and in the whole state. Some of these numerous factors can be influenced by public policy, others not, or only to a slight extent. Government policies and government programs can therefore obviously be controlled directly by politics. Personal entrepreneurial attitudes, on the other hand, are more difficult to influence and, in particular, cannot be influenced in the short term by political measures.

The most important recommendations for entrepreneurial promotional policy at the beginning of the new millennium can be drawn from the findings of the recent country reports Germany within the Global Entrepreneurship Monitor, which – in contrast to REM – has for many years now allowed comparative analyses on subjects including the impact of political programs (see Sternberg and Bergmann 2003 and Sternberg, Bergmann and Lückgen 2004).

Political measures should promote both start-ups in general and, explicitly, those with considerable growth prospects. Current empirical studies based on older start-up data (see Brixy/Grotz 2002) show that there is a negative correlation between the proportion of start-ups and the survival ratios at planning unit level. Many start-ups in highly entrepreneurial regions disappear from the market again comparatively rapidly. As this correlation varies from one industry to another, the political emphasis should be on setting sector-specific directions which should be oriented towards the prevailing conditions in the respective regions. Generally speaking, not every start-up has the same macro- and regional economic relevance – a fact that that has been known for a long time: The competitive situation, the general environment in the industry and also the individual goals of the entrepreneurs (not every entrepreneur has the expressed intention to grow) influence the economic success of the start-up, for example, and should therefore be taken into consideration in the implementation of political measures.

The report by the Hartz Commission builds upon some of these aspects. It makes sense to want to create "new jobs in economic regions through the establishment of clusters", as the Hartz report suggests. The GEM country report 2002 for Germany (Sternberg and Bergmann 2003), analyses of the 10 REM regions reported here as well as other research work based upon secondary data (cf. Otto 2004) show that start-ups are not evenly spread spatially in Germany. This is even truer of highly knowledge-intensive start-ups, which are not taken into explicit consideration here. Businesses operating within a cluster benefit from their spatial proximity to other start-ups, which means that appropriate political support would support the achievement of economic goals. In Germany, it can also be shown that entrepreneurial activities are more common in regions which demonstrate the characteristics of spatially sectoral clusters than in other regions. All things being equal, the probability that a person will start a firm within a certain region increases as a function of the number and size of incubator organizations within the region whose fertility is sufficient for the emergence of start-ups. The development of already existing start-ups also profits from a positive regional environment, which, in addition to the incubators (availability and attitude to spin-offs), hinges necessarily on an equally positive entrepreneurial climate. Within the scope of a self-augmenting process, e.g. via role model effects of successful start-ups, and their interregional networking (see Fornahl 2003), regional clusters of start-ups may form regions, in which the development of start-ups is economically more favourable than outside these clusters. This is a result of agglomeration economies and other positive external effects associated with spatial proximity. A potential entrepreneur's knowledge or even anticipation of the existence of advantages of this sort makes the decision to start a firm more probable – thus setting into motion a regionally caused, self-propelling cumulative process.

Public policy should therefore promote efforts to initiate intraregional networks of and for the benefit of entrepreneurs and the entrepreneurially inclined. Programs of the federal government such as Exist, as well as InnoRegio, are on the right track. Both regionally focused federal programs and programs run by individual federal states and the regions themselves can help; but they have to be well coordinated and tailored to fit in with each other. Here, too, it can be said: Germany does not need more of these kinds of programs; what it needs is resilience and stamina in their implementation.

Finally, new instruments such as the "*Ich-AG*" ("Me Inc.") and the "*Familien-AG*" ("Family Inc.") and the mini-jobs that these create should also be welcomed in principle. They can at least make a contribution to reducing the level of the macroeconomic cost of by people "working on the side" (i.e. without declaring their employment for tax purposes). At the same time they – at least the first two instruments mentioned – represent a legal stepping stone to partial, and later perhaps full, self-employment of people who were formerly unemployed. The GEM country report for Germany showed that the level of nascent entrepreneurs and the total entrepreneurial activity in Germany have, for the first time in years, not sunk further (Sternberg, Bergmann and Lückgen 2004). As the proportion of necessity entrepreneurship has continued to grow in relative terms (with considerable differences between the individual regions), there is much evidence to support the idea that the halt in the decline of start-up levels is attributable to the new instruments mentioned.

Hopes of considerable short-term effects on the labor market should, however, not be too high: The number of unemployed people will not be rapidly reduced by the fact that some entrepreneurs are launching firms, nor will the start-ups grow at a disproportionately high rate and generate additional employment. Nevertheless, the improvement of entrepreneurially oriented framework conditions by public policies at national and regional level can help the increase in the number of start-ups to have a positive effect on the level of employment. It will soon become apparent how sustained the effects on the labor market and on the number of start-ups will be when the future phases of the Hartz concept are implemented. The forthcoming GEM country reports for Germany will also analyze developments in this area.

REFERENCES

Ashcroft, B. and Love, J.H. (1996). "Firm Births and Employment Change in the British Counties with Special Reference, 1981-89." *Papers in Regional Science* 75: 483-500.

Backes-Gellner, U., Demirer, G. and Sternberg, R. (2002). „Individuelle und regionale Einflussfaktoren auf die Gründungsneigung von Hochschülern." In J. Schmude and J. Leiner (eds.), *Unternehmensgründungen. Interdisziplinäre Beiträge zum Entrepreneurship Research*. Heidelberg: Physica, 63-96.

Bergmann, H. (2002). *Entrepreneurial Attitudes and Start-up Attempts in Ten German Regions. An Empirical Analysis on the Basis of the Theory of Planned Behaviour*. University of Cologne, Department of Economic and Social Geography, Working Paper No. 2002-01 (February).

Bergmann, H. (2004). *Gründungsaktivitäten im regionalen Kontext. Gründer, Gründungseinstellungen und Rahmenbedingungen in zehn deutschen Regionen*. Köln: Kölner Forschungen zur Wirtschafts- und Sozialgeographie, 57).

Brixy, U. and Grotz, R., (2002). "Räumliche Differenzierungen von Betriebsgründungsintensität und Überlebenschancen in Westdeutschland 1983-1997." *Raumforschung und Raumordnung* 60: 100-122.

Carree, M.A. and Thurik, A.R. (2003). "The Impact of Entrepreneurship on Economic Growth." In D.B. Audretsch and Z..J. Acs (eds). *Handbook of Entrepreneurship Research*. Boston, Dordrecht: Kluwer Academic Publishers, 437-471.

Carree, M.A. et al. (2002). "Economic Development and Business Ownership: An Analysis Using Data of 23 OECD Countries in the Period 1976-1996." *Small Business Economics* 19: 271-290

Davidsson, P., Lindmark, L. and Olofsson, C. (1995). "Small Firms, Business Dynamics and Differential Development of Economic Well-Being." *Small Business Economics* 7: 301-315

Engel, D. and Licht, G. (2004). „Zur Rolle öffentlicher Förderprogramme zur Belebung von Venture Capital-Aktivitäten in Europa." In M. Fritsch and M. Niese (eds.). *Gründungsprozess und Gründungserfolg*, Heidelberg: Physica, 63-90.

Feldman, M.P, (2001). "The Entrepreneurial Event Revisited: Firm Formation in a Regional Context." *Industrial and Corporate Change* 10: 861–891.

Fornahl, D. (2003): "Entrepreneurial Activities in a Regional Context." In D. Fornahl and T. Brenner (eds). *Cooperation, Networks and Institutions in Regional Innovation Systems*, Cheltenham UK, Northampton MA: Edward Elgar, 38-57.

Japsen, A. (2002). *Regionaler Entrepreneurship Monitor (REM) 2001 – Methodenbericht*. University of Lüneburg, Faculty of Economics and Social Sciences, Arbeitsbericht Nr. 271 (September).

Klose, B. and Sternberg, R. (2001). *Evaluation des Programms zur finanziellen Absicherung von Unternehmensgründern aus Hochschulen (PFAU) des Ministeriums für Schule, Wissenschaft und Forschung des Landes Nordrhein-Westfalen*. Köln

Lückgen, I. and Oberschachtsiek, D. (2004). *Regionaler Entrepreneurship Monitor II (REM II 2003/04)*, Köln, Lüneburg.

Müller, C. and Sternberg, R. (2004). *Wissenschaftliche Begleitforschung zum Programm „Junge Innovatoren" des Ministeriums für Wissenschaft, Forschung und Kunst des Landes Baden-Württemberg.* Zwischenbericht. Köln.

Otto, A. (2004). „Regionale Strukturen von Gründungen und Stilllegungen in Deutschland." In M. Fritsch, M. and R. Grotz (eds.). *Empirische Analysen zum Gründungsgeschehen in Deutschland*, Heidelberg: Physica, 59-84.

Reynolds, P.D., Bygrave, W.D. and Autio, E. (2004). *Global Entrepreneurship Monitor (GEM) 2003 Global Report.* Babson Park, MA.

Stel, A.J. van and Storey, D.J. (2002). *The Relationship Between Firm Births and Job Creation: Did this Change in Britain in the 1990s?* EIM Scales Paper N200202, Zoetermeer: EIM Business and Policy Research.

Sternberg, R. (2004). „Entrepreneurship Research: The Relevance of the Region and Tasks Facing Economic Geography." *Geographische Zeitschrift* 92: 18-38.

Sternberg, R. (2003). „Das Konzept endogener Regionalentwicklung – Implikationen für Existenzgründungen und deren Förderung." In R. Sternberg (ed.). *Endogene Regionalentwicklung durch Existenzgründungen? Empirische Befunde aus Nordrhein-Westfalen*, Hannover: ARL, 4-19 (=Arbeitsmaterialien der ARL, 299).

Sternberg, R. (forthcoming). „Gründungsförderung in Deutschland und seinen Regionen - eine Bewertung auf Basis des Regional Entrepreneurship Monitor (REM)." In F. Welter (ed.). *Dynamik im Unternehmenssektor: Theorie, Empirie und Politik; Veröffentlichungen des Round Table Mittelstand*, Vol. VI, Duncker & Humblot.

Sternberg, R. et al. (1997). *Bilanz eines Booms – Wirkungsanalyse von Technologie- und Gründerzentren in Deutschland (2nd edition).* Dortmund: Dortmunder Vertrieb für Bau- und Planungsliteratur.

Sternberg, R., Bergmann, H. and Lückgen, I. (2004). *Global Entrepreneurship Monitor (GEM). Länderbericht Deutschland 2003.* Köln: University of Cologne, Department of Economic and Social Geography.

Sternberg, R., Wagner, J. (2004). "The Decison to Start a New Firm: Personal and Regional Determinants. Empirical Evidence from the Regional Entrepreneurship Monitor." In M. Fritsch u. M. Niese (eds.). *Gründungsprozess und Gründungserfolg – Interdisziplinäre Beiträge zum Entrepreneurship Research*, Heidelberg: Physica, 19-38.

Wagner, J. and Sternberg, R. (2004): Start-up Activities, Individual Characteristics, and the Regional Milieu: Lessons for Entrepreneurship Support Policies from German Micro Data. *Annals of Regional Science* 38: 219-240.

Wennekers, A.R.M. and Thurik, A.R. (1999): Linking Entrepreneurship and Economic Growth. *Small Business Economics* 13: 27–55.

Chapter 8:

ASSESSMENT OF ENTREPRENEURSHIP POLICIES ACROSS NATIONS AND REGIONS

Heike Grimm
Max Planck Institute for Research into Economic Systems, Jena, and The University of Erfurt

1. INTRODUCTION

Since 2002, when the Social Democratic Party in coalition with the Green Party won the federal election in Germany, the re-elected coalition has intensified the implementation of new entrepreneurship policies to induce economic growth. With a wide range of new programs and initiatives, policy-makers aim to improve the entrepreneurial environment for start-ups and small and medium-sized enterprises (SMEs). Numerous public programs for the promotion of start-ups were initiated and re-designed in order to improve the entrepreneurial environment after evidence had accumulated suggesting that national, regional, and urban growth is strongly correlated with a significant yearly increase in the number of new companies, and a significant turnover rate of old and new firms (Audretsch and Fritsch 1992; Sternberg, Otten and Tamásy 2000; Sternberg and Bergmann 2002; Reynolds et al 2001; Reynolds and Storey 1994).

In other words, the current German government has widely accepted the view that economic growth is interdependently correlated with a favorable entrepreneurial environment and sees it as a major task to implement new policies for the promotion of start-ups and entrepreneurs. Undoubtedly, these federal initiatives are a step in the right direction.

There has also been significant activity at a local level to improve the entrepreneurial environment for start-ups and SMEs. Local policies become more and more important in a global world in which cities and regions compete for investors, on the one hand, and consumers, on the other. The "strategic management of places" (Audretsch 2003: 20) is becoming a major task for local policy-makers who need to strongly promote their region or city. Local policy-makers know best how to promote their locality in the optimum fashion. Federal policies offer an important and useful framework for the promotion of start-ups and SMEs, but the main impetus for the promotion of economic growth – which has been proven to being a regional process – is expected to derive from local policies (Feldman 2001; Bonser and Audretsch 2001; Ohmae 1995; Taylor 2002).

According to recent research findings and data we know that local policies for the promotion of new firms are important growth issues. They are universally important (although the design and focus of such promotional policies might differ substantially across regions and nations), and they are assumed to be contributors to regional economic development (Audretsch 2002; Lall and Yilmaz 2001). In Germany, the *"Bundesländer"* (federal states), regions and urban areas have successfully worked out regional and local image-campaigns, strategies and policies for the promotion of start-ups and for new firms to compete inter-regionally and, in a global context, with regions and metropolitan areas around the world. The support of "local heroes" (meaning new, innovative, mostly small firms and self-employed individuals) has become an important growth issue. Local heroes have successfully created jobs, occupied innovative niches and adapted flexibly to a constantly changing, global environment.[1]

Although the role of local and regional policies for the promotion of a so-called entrepreneurially friendly environment has increased, the capacity of local policy-makers to shape the entrepreneurial environment with new entrepreneurship policies has decreased during the last years. According to recent criticism expressed by researchers and policy-makers alike, a gradual weakening of the German federal states has taken place during the last 15 years, mainly due to European integration and the German re-unification process. Both processes have identified several trends which hardly existed prior to 1990. Most importantly, it fostered the trend toward centralization by allocating more and more fiscal and economic responsibility to the federal government and institutions thereby diminishing the capacity to act politically and economically at the local level, mainly with respect to the federal states and German regions (Beyme 1993; Sturm 1997; Wagner 2004). Along with the re-unification process, five new federal states – formerly belonging to East Germany – were added to the federal state (currently comprising 16 federal states in total).[2] The federal government budgeted for a huge financial transfer to former East Germany in order to achieve equal living standards and similar public services within the five new federal states. Due to this transfer and process, the role of the federal government greatly increased, as did its centralist tendencies. These centralist developments within Germany took place contrary to a regionalization process within Europe that was accelerated by European integration (Burgess and Gagnon 1993).

In the following text, I aim to discuss whether the policy-makers from the German federal states, regions and urban areas have developed a successful policy approach for coping with the global challenges by taking into account the above mentioned centralist tendencies. In the following, I will present results from a cross-national survey and look specifically at local public start-up assistance and other public services for entrepreneurs in six comparable metropolitan areas in two countries, the U.S.A and Germany.[2] I will focus on three regions, defined as Chamber of Commerce districts, in Germany, and three greater metropolitan areas, in the U.S.A., and the policy framework conditions in these regions. The goal is to assess the focus, quality and influence of local public policies on the promotion of an entrepreneurial environment across regions. The findings will be compared with evidence in the U.S.A.

In a nutshell, I will focus on the question of whether policy-makers at a local level have the capacity to shape and implement entrepreneurship policies while taking into account the advanced centralization of public services and responsibilities at the federal level.

In chapter 2, I will introduce some of the new German federal and local entrepreneurship policies in order to give an indication what goals and intentions the new programs and initiatives will have. I will also provide a theoretical framework and provide explanation of why I have chosen the assessment of financial assistance programs and counseling services as the major focus of my comparative research. In chapter 3, I will introduce the qualitative-comparative small-N approach and the selected cases. In chapter 4, I will present a selection of findings before summarizing my research findings, in chapter 5.

2. THEORETICAL FRAMEWORK
2.1 New Entrepreneurship and SME Policies in Germany

The federal government initiated several programs and tried to improve the political framework conditions for entrepreneurs and for small and medium-sized enterprises (SMEs) in order to open up new employment opportunities and create additional entrepreneurial dynamism. It would be too much to introduce all of them;[4] nonetheless, it is useful to introduce a few in order to give an idea what content and perspectives these initiatives and policies are supposed to contain:

- The federal government intends, for example, to gradually remove unnecessary bureaucratic provisions and guidelines. The goal is to minimize bureaucratic obligations for small companies and individuals when setting up businesses. This will also ensure that loan conditions for small companies improve. At the same time, initiatives will be required in order to strengthen the equity capital base of these enterprises.
- All financial assistance programs for medium-sized companies – which used to be carried out separately by two German banks (the *"Deutsche Ausgleichsbank"* (DtA) and the so-called *"Kreditanstalt für Wiederaufbau"* (KfW)) – are carried out by the new *"KfW Mittelstandsbank des Bundes"*.

- With risk-related margins and greater relief from the burden of liability, the federal government is increasing the incentive for house banks to process the federal government's support loans.[5] This relief is, at least, a step in the right direction. Nevertheless, SMEs and start-ups still have to submit their applications for public funding with the local house banks. In other words, local house banks decide whether an entrepreneurs' business plan makes them eligible for public funding.
- A number of new programs were initiated which specifically promoted previously-unemployed entrepreneurs in order to improve the environmental framework. One example is the so-called "*Ich-AG*" ("Me Inc.").
- In order to support innovative companies, the federal government started an initiative called "Innovation and Future Technologies for Medium-sized Companies". With this initiative, the financing of young technology companies will be secured, while the network of research for small and medium-sized companies as well as technology transfer in the crafts industry will improve (Federal Ministry of Economics and Labor and Federal Ministry of Education and Research 2004).

Apart from the programs and policies implemented by the federal government (for example, by the Federal Ministry of Economics and Labor and the Federal Ministry of Education and Research), there are promotional policies developed by the European Union, the federal states, and the municipalities (Grimm forthcoming).[6] Programs developed by the European Union have a clear focus on the promotion of innovative start-ups.

EXIST is an example of such a program. It explicitly supports innovative entrepreneurs and is jointly financed by the federal and state governments. It improves the entrepreneurial climate at universities and increases the number of companies starting up from academic institutions. EXIST was run as German regional competition in 1998. More than 100 proposals where submitted by regional institutions; only five regions (Wuppertal, Karlsruhe, Stuttgart, Dresden and South Thuringia) were selected as winners receiving financial support from the federal government and the winning region's state government for a six-year-period. In Thuringia, the public institution GET UP was one of the five winners and started its operations in October 1998, with the aim of achieve the following goals: The permanent establishment of a "culture of entrepreneurship" in teaching, research, and administration; the consistent transfer of academic research into economic wealth creation; the encouragement of the great potential for business ideas potential and start-up personalities at universities; and a marked rise in the number of innovative start-ups.[7]

At the regional level, a variety of new programs were implemented to improve access to capital (loan AND equity capital) for potential entrepreneurs and SMEs.[8] One of the most prominent at the state level campaigns was launched in North-Rhine Westphalia in the mid-90s. With the "Go!" initiative, local policy-makers responsible for the promotion of start-ups and SMEs were linked to a region-wide network. A so-called one-stop-shop was implemented for providing customers with all the information they may need on business related issues. The "Go" initiative has greatly contributed to a better entrepreneurial environment – for example, in the Ruhr area – and has been groundbreaking for other regional entrepreneurship initiatives.[9]

2.1 Theoretical Framework and Research Focus

Public administrations counsel, assist, and promote entrepreneurs. Above all, they take into consideration the special features of their locality. Furthermore, public capital accumulation and access to public capital are important factors which contribute to variations in regional economic structures. The availability and quality of the above mentioned factors are likely to influence economic performance (Sternberg and Bergmann 2002; Flora, Flora and Sharp 1997). Button underlines in his research, that public investments can be viewed as external shocks or perturbances that stimulate regions – in particular, lagging regions – and that they bring about some degree of regional convergence. He also stresses the importance of infrastructure investments as a policy strategy, to improve the entrepreneurial environment (Button 1998; Gramlich 1994; Lall and Yilmaz 2001; Boarnet 1998).

Analysis of the drivers of national and regional economic growth has become very popular, and one of the most important research problems, in the social sciences and in economics. Whereas economists emphasize the role of macro and microeconomic forces, political scientists look at political, institutional and social factors that contribute to and explain economic performance (Olson 1982; North 1994; Barro 1998).

In my analysis, I focus on the second of the above-mentioned approaches. I will look closely at the focus, quality, content and locus of public start-up assistance programs for entrepreneurs in Germany, and public information and counseling services, specifically focusing on three German greater urban areas. Although a number of cross-national references to three U.S. metropolitan areas will be made, I will mainly refer to findings from German regions. The aim is, on the one hand, to introduce German policies for the promotion of start-ups, and to then compare them with the entrepreneurship policy approach in the U.S.A. at the federal, state, regional and local level. On the other hand, it will be discussed whether local policy-makers from the German federal states and regions have developed a successful policy approach by taking into account the above mentioned centralist tendencies. The analysis on entrepreneurial framework conditions will therefore be linked to the current reform debate on German federalism, by questioning whether the de-centralization of the design and implementation entrepreneurship policies is in keeping with the local and regional demand. My hypothesis is that German federalism needs to be reformed by strengthening local policy-makers, in order to successfully cope with the global challenges. Findings from this analysis will be compared with the U.S. federal system and entrepreneurship policy-making experience.

Before beginning any discussion regarding the role of public and entrepreneurship policies for regional economic growth, however, it is important to clarify what is meant by entrepreneurship, on the one hand, and public policy, on the other. The term "entrepreneur" is used in this study in as broad a sense as possible, always referring to people founding a full-time or part-time self-employed activity, and not referring to institutions. Every founder is defined as a person commencing a self-employed activity within the near future. But founders also include those who started up a new enterprise or took over and participated in existing enterprises, if this lead to self-employed activity on the part of the respondent (Lehnert 2003). Sternberg (REM) and Reynolds (GEM) provide a definition of the so-called "nascent entrepreneur" and "young entrepreneur", which I found useful for the purposes of our study. Both define a "nascent entrepreneur" as a person who alone, or with others, is actively involved in starting a new business that will (as a whole or in part) belong to her/him, and that did not pay full time wages or salaries for more than three months to anybody. Sternberg continues: "A "young entrepreneur" (different from the "nascent entrepreneur") is a person who is the owner of an already existing business and who has paid salaries and wages for more than three but less than 42 months." (Sternberg and Bergmann 2002: 11).

This study focuses specifically on public policies generating an entrepreneurial environment for the nascent and young entrepreneur. By "public policies", I am referring to taxpayers` benefits which are directly or indirectly targeted at supporting entrepreneurial private activities. With this definition, I exclude from this study any services or assistances provided by the private sector, banks, accountants and lawyers (Storey 2003).

The idea of concentrating specifically on an assessment of financial assistance programs and counseling services for entrepreneurs is ascribed to the following very interesting findings from the Regional and Global Entrepreneurship Monitor: In the 2000, the Regional Entrepreneurship Monitor (REM) Executive Report for Germany analyzed a set of entrepreneurial framework conditions including financial start-up assistance and government programs for start-ups. The researchers came to the conclusion that content and design of the public programs and financial subsidies were positively evaluated by the survey respondents. But when it came to public policies (as distinct from public programs geared to entrepreneurship) the respondents criticized the policy framework conditions for entrepreneurs in Germany, referring to the implementation of policy regulations such as building regulations, police law, taxes etc. and also to a deeper understanding of entrepreneurship of public officials (Sternberg and Bergmann 2002). According to the so-called "Policy Regulation Index" set up by the researchers in 2000, Germany held the poor position of seventeen in an index of twenty countries, and in 2002 it held the low rank of twenty out of thirty-four countries (Reynolds et al 2001). Particular criticism was directed towards a bureaucratic administration which lacks flexibility, transparency, and has a "civil servant mentality". Other points of criticism were bureaucratic rivalry, a lack of centralized information services (one-stop shops) within the German regions and lack of economics and business skills in public institutions.

Whereas public business development programs and financial subsidies were less positively evaluated in the U.S.A. (position nine compared to position three for Germany amongst the thirty-four countries in GEM comparison), in general, the U.S.A is among the leading nations in the world with respect to the implementation of innovative public policies aimed at promoting start-ups, deregulation, and with pro-entrepreneurship public institutions and public services. These findings can be summarized in a table below as follows:

Tab. 8.1: GEM ranking "entrepreneurial framework conditions" (2001)

	Government Policy[a]	Government Programs[b]
U.S.A.	4	9
Germany	20	3

Source: Adapted from Sternberg and Bergmann 2002: 49
[a] Referring to regulations, taxes etc.
[b] Referring to number, quality and quantity of public programs for the promotion of start-ups

3. METHODOLOGY
3.1 Research Objectives and Research Design

According to the above introduced REM and GEM findings I emphasized specific policy questions in my research: Which public policies specifically exist in a nation-state or region for the successful promotion of entrepreneurs? What is their specific design, their content, their goal? Who is implementing these public policies; the federal government, the (federal) state government, and/or a municipal institution?

These questions can best answered by comparing existing policies cross-nationally and cross-regionally. The goal of this research is to discover significant local public policy patterns and to generate further hypotheses for public policy research at a cross-national level.

At this exploratory stage, a quota sample as a form of purposive sample was chosen for the survey by dividing the population into geographic regions using the regional classifications of the metropolitan areas in the U.S.A. and the German Chamber of Commerce and Industry (CCI). The survey took place between December 2002 and June 2003. A questionnaire was designed containing 30 questions, some of them designed as open questions, some answered following a yes/no filter, and most of them followed a Likert scale (Likert scale ranged from 1 (yes), 2 (mostly), 3 (partly), 4 (rather not), 5 (no)).

A sample of ten public experts per region, responsible for counselling entrepreneurs and providing information on public assistance programs, were interviewed in a structured face-to-face interview. I decided to approach ten experts in each region with a quota sample because it turned out that there are currently no more than ten to fifteen public institutions per region which are consulting start-ups. Among these institutions and organizations are district and municipal economic development centers, Chambers of Industry and Commerce, Chambers of Handicrafts, City Chambers of Commerce, Small Business Administration offices, economic technology transfer institutions, associated entrepreneurship institutes at universities and research institutes, capital venture companies, business angels, initiatives for the promotion of entrepreneurship networks and women in business, and credit institutes.

In June 2003, we managed to personally interview 10 experts from each region selected for case study.[10] In Germany, we selected the CCI districts Munich and *"Oberbayern"*, Leipzig and the so-called *"Bergische Städtedreieck"*. In the U.S.A., we selected the metropolitan and greater urban areas of Atlanta, the Research Triangle and Baltimore as research objectives.[10]

3.2 Cross-National and Cross-Regional Approach

The study focused on three metropolitan regions in the U.S.A. and three greater urban areas in Germany:

- Munich and Upper Bavaria (CCI District in Bavaria) and Atlanta (metropolitan area in Georgia),
- the Leipzig region (CCI District in Saxony) and the Research Triangle (greater metropolitan areas of Durham, Raleigh, Chapel Hill in North Carolina),
- the so-called *"Bergische Städtedreieck"* comprising the cities of Solingen, Wuppertal, and Remscheid in North Rhine-Westphalia (CCI District) and the Baltimore metropolitan region (Maryland).

The study focused on six cases – in total, two highly developed regions (Munich and Atlanta), two regions which successfully coped with socio-economic problems, and two regions which are still trying to cope with socio-economic problems (*"Bergische Städtedreieck"* and Baltimore metropolitan area).

The selection of the German cases is also ascribed to three studies which were completed between 1996 and 2002 and which provide findings and data specifically relating to new entrepreneurship policies and the entrepreneurial environment for start-ups within the selected German regions: the *"Münchner Gründerstudie"* (Brüderl, Preisendörfer and Ziegler 1996 and 1992), the *"Leipziger Gründerstudie"* (Hinz 1998), and the Ruhr area with special focus on Dortmund and Essen (Jansen and Weber 2003) in North-Rhine Westphalia.

3.3 Socio-Economic Profile of the Cases

The study takes into account that specific regional socio-economic factors associate with regional economic growth (Ceh 2001):

Munich. Since the 1980s, Munich has held its position as a leading high technology region within Germany, having been listed continuously among the top five planning regions (Sternberg and Tamásy 1999). The Munich region is characterized by very broad specialization in the high-tech industries with special concentration in motor vehicles and engineering (e.g. headquarter of BMW), aerospace, electronic engineering (e.g. headquarter of Siemens), and fine mechanics/optical instruments.

Leipzig. After German re-unification Leipzig became one of the German major industrial, commercial, and transportation centers in Eastern Germany. Manufacturing includes textiles, electrical products, machine tools, and chemicals. Before re-unification, Leipzig harbored major industries in heavy construction and engineering. The economic policy of the former German Democratic Republic (GDR) strongly favored very large – though inflexible – companies with strong specializations. Leipzig managed to develop excellent entrepreneurial framework conditions after re-unification which essentially contributed to regional development. It managed to cope with steadily rising pressure on innovation, as a consequence of the economic transition process, and emerged as one of the most prominent locations for start-ups and larger companies (such as BMW) in the new German federal states.

Wuppertal-Solingen-Remscheid. The so-called *"Bergische Städtedreieck"* (Wuppertal-Solingen-Remscheid) is located in North-Rhine Westphalia. The city triangle tries hard to achieve an all-embracing socio-economic structural change from a region in decline (dominated formerly by the manufacturing and mining industries) to a modern, technologically advanced region. The traditional German *"Mittelstand"* dominated the region and regional economic development until technological change in the 1970s caused a downsizing effect which especially affected the traditional manufacturing sector.

Atlanta. During the last decade of the 20th century, Atlanta became one of the so-called "hot spots" in the U.S.A., attracting a high amount of direct foreign investment and venture capital, which contributed to high-tech business development, and the development of excellent location factors for firms and entrepreneurs.

Durham-Raleigh-Chapel Hill (Research Triangle). The region Durham-Raleigh-Chapel Hill has evolved from an agricultural and manufacturing economy to achieve world-class status in the areas of medicine, research and technology. The internationally known Research Triangle Park is home to more than 50 major research and development organizations. The region took off in 1958 when its three major universities launched an initiative to use the rich knowledge base in the region.[12]

Baltimore. Baltimore stood out as an industrial centre specialized in older industries, such as shipbuilding and transportation, during the 19th century. During the 20th century Baltimore faced many socio-economic problems. In the 1970s, the city tried to regain its economic strength. It encouraged a re-doubling of efforts from public, private and volunteer partnerships, and tapped into ambitious federal programs for urban renewal. In the late 1990s, Baltimore started to invest more than $1 billion in new urban development projects over the period up until 2002.[13]

4. SELECTION OF FINDINGS

In order to generate first-hand, detailed information about public policies in both countries across the selected regions, I began the interviews by addressing questions relating to the design and availability of, rather general information on, how to successfully start up a business, and on the design and availability of public subsidies for start-ups. In other words, the first questions were intended to generate information from the supply-side with regard to the kinds of information provided by local public institutions, and to the kinds of subsidies which are offered within a region for the financial support of start-ups. We addressed the following question to respondents: What kind of information does the public institution you work for provide? In the following, we have only tabled the answers "yes", "mostly", and "partly" incorporating them into one category (frequencies in total numbers per country), and we show the percentages per country for each value label (kind of information). It is worth noting that the provision of most public information is given similar emphasis in both countries. Interestingly, all consultants interviewed confirmed that they see it as a major task to provide general and/or specific information on public financial assistance programs to entrepreneurs. Nonetheless, some interesting (though not significant) differences exist, for example, regarding information about (f) the opportunities for joint ventures, (k) personnel, and personnel management, and (l) the regional conditions such as regulations, taxes etc. U.S. consultants more frequently provide information on these three topics. Only 53.3% of the German consultants interviewed, confirmed that they provide information on questions referring to personnel and personnel management. Only 66.7% stated that they provide access to information on regional conditions such as regulations, taxes etc.

Tab. 8.2: What kind of information do you offer? We provide information about...

	U.S.A. (N = 30)		Germany (N = 30)	
	Total No. /Country	% within Country	Total No. / Country	% within Country
(a) ... region, the state...	25	83.3%	23	76.7%
(b) ... legal form of an enterprise...	25	83.3%	21	70.0%
(c) ... business concept...	28	93.3%	27	90.0%
(d) ... market potentials of an idea...	27	90.0%	26	86.7%
(e) ... partners for regional co-operation...	26	89.7%	28	93.3%
(f) ... opportunities for a joint venture...	25	83.3%	19	63.3%
(g) ... public advisory bureaus...	25	83.3%	26	86.7%
(h) ... regional networks...	24	80.0%	29	96.7%
(I) ... public programs of financial assistance..	29	96.7%	29	96.7%
(j) ... venture capitalists, business angels...	24	80.0%	20	66.7%
(k) ... personnel and personnel management...	24	80.0%	16	53.3%
(l) ... regional conditions such as regulations, taxes...	26	86.7%	20	66.7%
(m) ... visa and residents permits...	6	20.0%	8	26.7%

After familiarizing the interviewees with the questionnaire by beginning with questions related to the supply-side ("Which information do you offer?"), we continued addressing questions to the demand-side ("What kind of counseling do you offer?").

Tab. 8.3: What kind of counseling do you offer?

	U.S.A. (N = 30)		Germany (N = 30)	
We offer...	Total No./ Country (a)	% within Country	Total No./ Country (a)	% within Country
... website (entrepreneurs receive all information online)...	27	90,0%	22	73,3%
... release of information ...	30	100,0%	29	96,7%
... individual counseling with appointment...	25	83,3%	30	100,0%
... specific consultation days open to the public without appointment (open days)...	15	50,0%	13	43,3%
... seminars for entrepreneurs...	29	96,7%	26	86,7%
... lectures on specific topics...	27	90,0%	25	83,3%
... road shows...	27	90,0%	27	90,0%
... participation in fairs...	26	86,7%	23	76,7%
... others...	2	--	4	--

a) Responses on a Likert scale: (1) yes/ (2) mostly/ (3) partly

In Germany, high emphasis is placed on individual counseling. In the U.S.A, strong emphasis is, on the other hand, placed on the release of information. Websites are a very prominent source of information for entrepreneurs, in the U.S.A. There seems to be some backlog of demand in Germany with regard to the availability of online and virtual information. Nonetheless, it is worth noting that most public information is provided with similar emphasis in both countries (see tab. 8.2), and that the forms of counseling and of access to information are quite similar, in the U.S.A and in Germany.

To collect further information on which kind of public programs are important and whether federal programs are rated as more or less important as (federal) state, regional, and/or municipal programs, we addressed the following question to the survey respondents: "Are the following public assistance programs of high importance to entrepreneurs?" The interviewees were asked to rate the importance of federal, (federal) state, regional, and municipal subsidies for the promotion of start-ups within their region, again using a Likert scale ranging from 1 (yes), 2 (mostly), 3 (partly), 4 (rather not), 5 (no).

In both the U.S. and German regions which were selected for this research, <u>federal</u> assistance programs play a very important role for the promotion of start-ups.

Tab. 8.4: Are federal programs of high importance to entrepreneurs?

			Federal Programs		
			Yes/ mostly/ partly	Rather not/ no	Total
	Germany	Total No. / Country	28	2	30
		% within Country	93.3%	6.7%	100.0%
	U.S.A.	Total No. / Country	28	2	30
		% within Country	93.3%	6.7%	100.0%
Total		Total No. / Country	56	4	60
		% within Country	93.3%	6.7%	100.0%

Furthermore, (federal) <u>state</u> programs play a crucial role in promoting start-ups in both countries; in Germany state programs are even of higher importance than in the U.S.A. (see tab. 8.5)

As demonstrated below, the role of <u>regional</u> subsidies was rated with different emphasis (see tab. 8.6). There is a strong demand for regional financial assistance programs – specifically in the U.S. regions. U.S. respondents stated that regional financial assistance programs are of "very", "rather" or "partly high" importance for the promotion of start-ups (twenty-five out of twenty-nine respondents). In contrast, only sixteen out of thirty German respondents stated that regional subsidies for start-ups are of "very", "rather" or "partly high" importance to entrepreneurs. To summarize these findings for the U.S.A., regional financial assistance programs are of high importance for the promotion of start-ups and for regional economic development. In Germany, it is federal and state programs that play the major role.

Tab. 8.5: Are state programs of high importance to entrepreneurs?

			Federal Programs		
			Yes/ mostly/ partly	Rather not/ no	Total
	Germany	Total No. / Country	29	1	30
		% within Country	96.7%	3.3%	100.0%
	U.S.A.	Total No. / Country	26	3	29[a]
		% within Country	93.3%	6.7%	100.0%
Total		Total No. / Country	55	4	59[a]
		% within Country	93.3%	6.7%	100.0%

a) One missing value

Tab. 8.6: Are regional programs of high importance to entrepreneurs?

			Regional Programs		
			Yes/ mostly/ partly	Rather not/ no	Total
	Germany	Total No. / Country	16	14	30
		% within Country	53.3%	46.7%	100.0%
	U.S.A.	Total No. / Country	25	4	29[a]
		% within Country	86.2%	13.8%	100.0%
Total		Total No. / Country	41	18	59[a]
		% within Country	69.5%	30.5%	100.0%

a) One missing value

Local public policies for the promotion of entrepreneurs and entrepreneurial companies are rated with far more importance in the U.S.A. than in Germany. Although competition among regions is continuously increasing due to the challenges of a global economy, the strong focus on federal and state subsidies and the apparent absence of emphasis on regional and municipal programs come as a surprise.

Tab. 8.7: Are municipal programs of high importance to entrepreneurs (a)?

			Municipal Programs		
			Yes/ mostly/ partly	Rather not/ no	Total
	Germany	Total No. / Country	8	22	30
		% within Country	26.7%	73.3%	100.0%
	U.S.A.	Total No. / Country	23	6	29[a]
		% within Country	79.3%	20.7%	100.0%
Total		Total No. / Country	31	28	59[a]
		% within Country	52.5%	47.5%	100.0%

a) One missing value

Table 8.8: Are municipal programs of high importance to entrepreneurs (b)?

			Municipal Programs		
			Yes/ mostly/ partly	Rather not/ no	Total
Region	Atlanta	Total No. / Country	8	1	9[a]
		% within Region	88.9%	11.1%	100.0%
	Triangle Region	Total No. / Country	6	4	10
		% within Region	60.0%	40.0%	100.0%
	Baltimore	Total No. / Country	9	1	10
		% within Region	90.0%	10.0%	100.0%
	Munich and Upper Bavaria	Total No. / Country	3	7	10
		% within Region	30.0%	70.0%	100.0%
	Leipzig	Total No. / Country	5	5	10
		% within Region	50.0%	50.0%	100.0%
	„Berg. Städtedreieck"	Total No. / Country	0	10	10
		% within Region	.0%	100.0%	100.0%
Total		Total No. / Countries	31	28	59[a]
		% within Region	52.5%	47.5%	100.0%

a) One missing value

Moreover, the majority of German interviewees confirmed that there is a lack of municipal financial assistance programs. Municipal programs are still non-existent in their region. Twenty-two out of thirty German respondents (76.9%) stated that municipal programs play no or relatively little role for entrepreneurs in their region. On the contrary, twenty-three out of twenty-nine U.S. experts stressed the high, rather or partly high importance of municipal financial assistance programs. Only eight out of thirty German public consultants came to the same conclusion.

Above all (and particularly in the region which I focused in this study that clearly has to cope with socio-economic challenges – the "*Bergisches Städtedreieck*" in North-Rhine Westphalia), municipal programs do not (or almost not) play any significant role in the promotion of start-ups (see tab. 8.8). On the contrary, an American region which is facing similar challenges (the Baltimore metropolitan region) sees municipal financial assistance programs as a major prerequisite of a prosperous entrepreneurial environment and for contributing to a rising number of start-ups.

After assessing the locus of financial assistance programs in Germany versus the U.S.A, we continued assessing which specific programs play in particular a major role in the promotion of start-ups. The respondents were asked to name all those financial assistance programs which – in their opinion – contribute very successfully and sustainable to the entrepreneurial environment. Below you will find the respondents' answers:

Box 1: Atlanta
- SBA loans, ACCION
- SBA funding, government agencies (like NASA) for high-tech arena
- SBA guarantee programs, Atlanta Business Development Initiative (government sourced low-interest financing), Individual Development Account (IDA) programs
- SBA loan guarantee programs, micro-loans, local economic development funds funded through banks and large companies (in Georgia)
- SBA
- 7a loan programs
- SBA Loan guarantee programs 7a, micro-loan programs
- Micro-loan programs (GRASP enterprises) SBA programs, ACCION capital (international loan program)

Box 2: Research Triangle Region
- "Most technology start-ups don't really use these types of programs."
- North Carolina Biotechnology Center's low interest loans, SBIR program
- SBA programs, Biotech Center loans, seed venture funds, MCMS
- SBA guarantee loan program

Box 3: Baltimore

- SBA guarantee program, Low Doc and Contract financing, 504 for real estate, state sponsored direct funding program in MD, MD Competitive Advantage Financing Fund (MCAFF)
- SBA guarantee low doc, loans offered by private banks, MD Small Business Development Financing Authority (public funds managed by a private corporation (MMG ventures, L.P.) Development Credit Fund (DCF) (public "dollars" managed by a private company")
- Venture Capital Funds (private and public), direct grants and/or low interest loans from local and state governments, loan guarantee programs
- SBA 504 loan guarantee program
- State Department of Business and Economic Development MD, programs similar to SBA programs
- DBED Maryland Department of Economic Development, TEDCO MD Technology Economic Development Corporation, SBIR Small Business Innovation and Research Grants, private investors, angels, venture capital

Box 4: Munich and Upper Bavaria

- "*Überbrückungsgeld*"
- Micro-credits
- Munich Fund ("*Münchenfonds*"): A co-operation between the city of Munich and the "*Stadtsparkasse München*". Financial start-up programs of the "*Landesförderbank Bayern*" (LfA), specifically the "LfA-*Mittelstandskreditprogramm*" and "LfA-*Ergänzungsdarlehen*"
- "*Überbrückungsgeld*", "*Ich-AG*" („Me Inc."), "*LfA-Mittelstandskreditprogramm*", "*DtA-Startgeld*"
- BayTou, BayTP, "*Bayern Kapital*", Fbg = BTU, EKH, "*Bayern MkP*", ERP, "*Flügge*" (Bavaria)
- "*Flügge*"
- "*Mittelstandskreditprogramm*", "*Ergänzungsdarlehen*"

Box 5: Leipzig

- URBAN-II, "*DtA-Startgeld*", "*BSB Sachsen*", URBAN-II
- "*Überbrückungsgeld*", "*Eingliederungszuschüsse*", ESF, "*Kleinstdarlehen*", Microcredits, "*DtA-Startgeld*", "*Gründungshilfe des AA Leipzig nach §10SGBB*","*Frauenförderung*" (regional),"*Ich-AG*"
- ESF, "*AA (Personalförderung)*", "*Start-Geld*", "*Existenzgründungsförderung in Sachsen*", "*GuW*" ("*Gründung und Wachstum*")
- "*DtA-Eigenkapitalhilfeprogramm*", "*Zuschüsse GA-Bürgschaftsprogramme*", "*KfW – Mittelstandsprogramm*", Microcredits, "*Investitionszulage*"
- "*GA-Förderung*"
- in first place "*Existenzgründungszuschuss*", "*Ich-AG*", "*Überbrückungsgeld*", ESF, "*Frauen in ländlichen Räumen*" (regional program); in second place microcredits, "*DtA-Startgeld*", "*DtA-Eigenkapitalhilfeprogramm*"
- "*DtA-Microdarlehen*", "*Überbrückungsgeld*", "*AA*", "*Ich-AG*", ESF, "*Frauen in ländlichen Regionen*" (Saxony)
- DtA-programs, "*SAB*", "*Bürgschafts- und Garantieprogramme*", "*BBS*", KfW-programs

Assessment of Entrepreneurship Policies

Box 6: *"Bergisches Städtedreieck"*

- *"DtA-Startkapital"*, DtA-microcredits, GuW *"Gründungs- und Wachstumsprogramm"*, *"DtA-Existenzgründung"*, no specific regional prrograms
- *"DtA Startgeld"*, *"GuW Gründung und Wachstum"*, *"EKH Eigenkapitalhilfeprogramm"*
- *"DtA-Startgeld"*, microcredits, *"ERP-Existenzgründerdarlehen"*
- *"DtA Startgeld*, Microdarlehen, *"KfW Mittelstandsprogramm"*, *"DtA Arbeitsplatz"*, *"GuW"*
- *"Überbrückungsgeld"*, *"Existenzgründerbeihilfe"* (ESF), *"Beratungsprogramm Wirtschaft (Förderung einer Unternehmensberatung durch das Land)"*
- EXIST Seed, *"PFAU"*, *"Personaltransfer"*, *"TiP"*, *"DtA-Darlehen"*, *"Überbrückungsgeld"*, *"Technologieprogramm Wirtschaft"*, *"PRO INNO"*
- *"DtA-Darlehen"*, KfW-programs, *"Beratungsprogramm Wirtschaft"*, ESF-programs, *"TiP"*, *"Landesinitiative Energie Investitionskostenzuschüsse"*
- *"DtA-Startgeld"*
- *"PFAU"*, *"EXIST"*

At first sight, the above listed answers do not provide a clear picture of which programs play a major role within a region for the financial promotion of start-ups. In the following table we have, therefore, listed all those programs which were mentioned at least twice by all respondents within a region, and which supposedly play a major role in the promotion of start-ups. All those programs and subsidies which have only been mentioned once by the respondents have been listed as "others".

The programs which have been mentioned most often are listed at the top of each region's listing. In other words, the subsidies which have the highest impact in the region are listed first, followed by other programs in decreasing order. The total number of programs mentioned by the respondents is added in brackets. Not all experts answered this question. In Atlanta, seven respondents expressed their opinion, in Baltimore we counted four cases, and in the Research Triangle, six cases. In Munich, four respondents answered the question. From Leipzig we realized 9 cases and from the *"Bergisches Städtedreieck"*, a total of ten cases.

The first impression is that the results from the U.S. regions can be more easily assessed. In Atlanta, the "SBA Loan Guarantee Program" plays a major role in the promotion of start-ups within the region. Public experts underline the great contribution that this program makes to the entrepreneurial environment. Likewise, the so-called "federal/state funds managed on a local level" (and among others, the program "GRASP") are of high importance to start-ups. Experts agreed on the importance of these two explicitly mentioned programs.

In Baltimore, interest was focused on the "SBA Loan Guarantee Program" and the so-called "state sponsored direct funding programs in Maryland managed by private companies" – for example, provided and promoted by the Maryland "Small Business Development Financing Authority".

Tab. 8.9: Diversity of public financial assistance programs for start-ups across regions

Atlanta (7 cases)	Research Triangle Region (4 cases)	Baltimore (6 cases)
SBA loan guarantee programs (7) (7(a) Loan Guarantee Program)	SBA programs (2)	State sponsored direct funding programs in MD managed by private companies 6) (MD Small Bus. Development Financing Authority)
Federal /State funds managed on a local level (7) (GRASP Enterprises Micro-loan Program, individual Development Account)	NC Biotechnology Center's loans (2)	SBA loan guarantee programs (5) (SBA *LowDoc* loan program, 504 Loan Program)
		Venture Capital Funds (2)
Others:[a] 1	Others: 3	Others: 2
Munich and Upper Bavaria (4 cases)	Leipzig (9 cases)	"*Bergisches Städtedreieck*" (10 cases)
LfA-programs (5) ("*LfA-Mittelstandskreditprogramm*", "*LfA- Ergänzungsdarlehen*")	DtA-programs (7) ("*DtA-Startgeld*", "*DtA-Eigenkapitalhilfeprogramm*")	DtA-programs (10) ("*DtA-Startgeld*", "*DtA-Mikrodarlehen*")
	ESF-microcredits (4)	GuW ("*Gründung und Wachstum*") (3)
	"*Überbrückungsgeld*", "*Ich-AG*", "*Frauenförderung*" (3)	"*Überbrückungsgeld*", ESF-program ("*Existenzgründerbeihilfe*") Beratungsprogramm Wirtschaft "*PFAU*", "*TiP*" (2)
	URBAN-II, "*BBS Sachsen*", "*GuW*" (2)	
Others: 11	Others: 7	Others: 10

a) Programs mentioned only once by the interviewees.

(Grimm 2004: 45)

There were only four responses from the Research Triangle. The result should, therefore, not be over-weighted. Two experts pointed out that the "SBA programs" command a high priority within the region; two other experts referred to the loans provided by the North Carolina Biotechnology Centre as a very prominent and successful example of the promotion of start-ups.

The result for the German regions was, on the contrary, very diffuse and not transparent. While the experts in Munich unanimously referred to the financial start-up programs provided by the *"Landesförderbank Bayern"* (LfA), there was no consensus among the public policy experts in Leipzig and within the „*Bergische Städtedreieck*" in North-Rhine Westphalia whose programs specifically play a major role in the promotion of start-ups. In both regions, the programs provided by the *"Deutsche Ausgleichsbank"* (in the meantime, provided by the new *"KfW Mittelstandsbank des Bundes"*), have had a major impact on the entrepreneurial environment. In addition, a variety of other programs were listed more than once by the experts. In Leipzig, the subsidies provided by the *"Europäischer Sozialfonds"* (ESF), *"Überbrückungsgeld"* (provided to unemployed persons who start up a business or become self-employed), *"Ich-AG"* ("Me-Inc."), special subsidies for female entrepreneurs, the programs URBAN-II (which is the Community Initiative of the European Regional Development Fund (ERDF) for sustainable development in the troubled urban districts of the European Union), the *"Bürgschaftsbank Sachsen"* (BBS Sachsen) and *"GuW"* (an ERP Innovation program) are listed. In the *"Bergische Städtedreieck"*, subsidies provided by the *"Europäischer Sozialfonds"* (ESF) and the so-called *"Überbrückungsgeld"* (provided for unemployed persons who start up a business or become self-employed), the *"Beratungsprogramm Wirtschaft"*, *"PFAU"* (specifically designed for university start-ups) and a program called *"TiP"* are specifically mentioned.

Another striking result was the high number of programs and subsidies which have been mentioned by the experts only once: in Munich and in the *"Bergische Städtedreieck"*, a total of 11 other programs were listed; in Leipzig a total number of seven. Contrary to this, the U.S. respondents named a very few number of other financial assistance programs which play particularly a crucial role for the promotion of start-ups only once.

In a nutshell, the American loan and support program for entrepreneurs is transparent and easy to understand for any entrepreneur who is looking for public subsidies. There is a "few-programs-fit-the-region" approach which makes it easy for potential entrepreneurs to look and apply for public financial assistance. For German entrepreneurs the situation is different. The loan and support program is very complex, confusing and lacks transparency. The public institutions in Leipzig and the *"Bergische Städtedreieck"* refer to very different programs when asked what programs they would recommend as a prominent example to an entrepreneur. The numerous programs are directed at different target groups. The application procedures are different from program to program and are mostly difficult to fathom. For one program (*"TiP"*), there is no available information online. This, no doubt, leads to some confusion and to the discouragement of potential entrepreneurs who may be interested in public financial assistance; this policy does not contribute to the entrepreneurial environment.

On the other hand, it can be argued that there might be a higher demand for financial assistance for entrepreneurs in Germany than in the U.S.A. In addition, the importance of public subsidies might be evaluated higher in a country which has the characteristics of an "ordoliberal" market economy (Broyer 1996; Rieter and Schmolz 1993; Müller-Armack 1948).[14] In this context, we asked the respondents *"Is the number of public assistance programs for start-ups adequate with regard to the demand in your region?"* We wanted to also know whether public promotional programs play an important role, in general, for start-ups in the regions.

Tab. 8.10: Is the number of public assistance programs for start-ups adequate with regard to the demand in your region?

		Yes	Mostly	Partly	Rather not	No	Total
Region	Atlanta	2	2	2	2	2	10
	Triangle	1	1	3	3	2	10
	Baltimore	2	-	1	-	6	9[a]
	Munich	8	-	1	1	-	10
	Leipzig	2	3	2	1	2	10
	Solingen	2	3	1	1	3	10
Total		17	9	10	8	15	59[a]

a) One missing value

In fact, the majority of German respondents stated that the number of programs is adequate with regard to the demand. In semi-structured interviews the respondents rather criticized the variety of public programs on a federal, state and the regional level with respect to negative influences on the entrepreneurial environment.

On the contrary, U.S. experts rather underlined the need for more public financial assistance programs. In other words, public support is definitely needed for the promotion of local heroes. More public programs are necessary to meet the demand, particularly in the Baltimore region, but also within the Research Triangle and in Atlanta.

Public financial assistance programs matter within both nations and in all regions. The majority of U.S. and German respondents clearly affirmed the high importance of public subsidies for the promotion of start-ups and self-employed persons.

This is clearly not an astounding result, but one which disproves a common myth which exists in both Germany and Europe, that public financial assistance plays no major role in the U.S.A. In the following table, the results are presented by region.

Tab. 8.11: *Do public assistance programs play an important role for start-ups within your regions?*

		Yes	Mostly	Partly	Rather not	No	Total
Region	Atlanta	9	-	-	-	1	10
	Triangle	5	-	2	1	2	10
	Baltimore	8	2	-	-	-	10
	Munich	7	1	2	-	-	10
	Leipzig	8	1	-	-	1	10
	Solingen	7	2	-	1	-	10
Total		44	6	4	2	4	60

5. SUMMARY

In both the U.S.A. and Germany, there is a high demand for financial assistance programs promoting entrepreneurship. Experts in both countries rated them as a very important driving force for the promotion of regional economic development. This appears interesting from the point of view that state and public interference in business affairs is more appreciated than criticized in the U.S.A. (as in Germany), although economic policy in the U.S.A. is rooted in classical liberalism, which implies strong self-restriction by the state. In addition, the focus and quality of information and counseling provided to (potential) entrepreneurs does not differ greatly in the U.S.A. vs. Germany. The majority of German respondents stated that the number of programs is adequate with regard to the demand, and that there is no need for new programs. In the U.S.A., the public policy experts express a higher demand for public financial assistance programs.

In summary, the findings of the cross-nation and cross-regional qualitative small-N study show that the focus and quality of financial assistance programs are quite similar in the U.S.A. and in Germany. But the locus of entrepreneurship policies and the number of public subsidies for the promotion of entrepreneurship are very different at a comparative level. Whereas the U.S. approach to facing the challenges of globalization seems to result in a strong promotion of regional and local public policies for entrepreneurship, the German approach is still to favor state and federal financial assistance programs and public policies. In Germany, the gradual trend toward centralization by allocating more and more political and economic responsibility to the federal government, and thus diminishing its capacity to act politically and economically at the local level, is also affecting the implementation of entrepreneurship policies. With the above presented findings I have established that the locus of financial assistance programs is anything but local, in Germany. There are, as yet, no municipal programs in existence which are specifically designed for the promotion of local heroes. Although economic development is mainly derived from local entrepreneurial activity, and although the promotion of a favorable entrepreneurial environment at the local level is of high importance in a global world, policy-makers have not yet achieved the appropriate leverage for the implementation of local entrepreneurship policies (in this context specifically meaning financial assistance programs for the promotion of start-ups).

The aim of policy-makers to improve the entrepreneurial environment in Germany resulted in the design and implementation of a huge variety of new loan and support programs for potential entrepreneurs during recent years. The number of financial assistance programs for start-ups has grown significantly, with the result that a net of very elaborate and complex loan and support programs for potential entrepreneurs has been woven. One needs to question whether the policy approach has contributed to a more favorable entrepreneurial environment. The result from the above introduced small-N survey rather suggests that current loan programs are too complex, non-transparent and differ greatly from region to region. Further policy analysis needs to be focused on the question of whether this is not merely a different (however, also less successful) policy approach to improve the entrepreneurial environment, in Germany.

NOTES

[1] In 2002, for example, newly established firms provided on average three new jobs (including that of the founder), in Germany. See Lehnert 2003.

[2] Germany is a federation of 16 states called *"Länder"* (singular *"Land"*) or *"Bundesländer"* (singular *"Bundesland"*, German *federal state*). Each *Land* is represented at the federal level in the *"Bundesrat"*. In the following, we will use the term *federal states* when referring to the German *Bundesländer*.

[3] This project is funded by the German Ministry of Economics and Labor. I am grateful to the funding body for supporting this project with the title "Local Heroes in the Global Village. Coping Strategies for Small Start-ups in a Global Economy. – A Comparison Between the U.S.A. and Germany."

[4] The Ministry of Economics and Labor set up the so-called *"Förderdatenbank"* online. This search engine provides the user with information about all promotional programs existent at the European, federal, regional and municipal level, in Germany. The search engine may be accessed via http://db.bmwa.bund.de.

[5] See Sternberg: 128/129 in this book.

[6] The so-called *"Hausbank"* ("house bank" or "main bank") is responsible for making entrepreneurs' business plans eligible for public funding, in Germany. Although the funding body might be either the federal government or the federal state the entrepreneur is requested to contact his local bank branch to re-view his or her business plan and for handling his or her application.

[7] I would like to thank Ralph T. Kersten, Project Manager with GET UP Thuringia, for his comments and information.

[8] Particularly in the new German federal states, there is a huge equity gap which makes it very difficult for potential entrepreneurs to start-up a business and for SMEs to overcome financial crises.

[9] See www.go-online.nrw.de.

[10] A comprehensive list of the institutions we selected for our survey and the names and affiliations of the interviewees is provided in Grimm 2004: 12-14.

[11] The author would like to recognize the many important contributions to this research from her colleague Iris Beckmann of the "Entrepreneurship, Growth and Public Policy Group" at the Max-Planck Institute for Research into Economic Systems in Jena, Germany.

[12] For further information see http://www.kansasinc.org/pubs/kcspu01/appendix_c.pdf.

[13] For more information see, for example, http://www.goodjobsfirst.org/pdf/balt.pdf.

[14] See Chapter 1 of this book for further discussion of this issue.

REFERENCES

Audretsch, D.B. (2002). "Understanding Entrepreneurship Across Countries and Over Time." In D.B. Audretsch and C. Bonser (eds.). *Entrepreneurship: Determinants and Policy in a European-US Comparison*, Boston, Mass., Kluwer Academic Publisher, 1-20.

Audretsch, D.B. (2003). "Entrepreneurship Policy and the Strategic Management of Places." In D.M. Hart (ed.). *The Emergence of Entrepreneurship Policy. Governance, Start-ups, and Growth in the U.S. Knowledge Economy*, Cambridge, Cambridge University Press, 20-38.

Audretsch, D.B. and Fritsch, M. (1992). *Market Dynamics and Regional Development in the Federal Republic of Germany*. WZB discussion paper FS IV 92-6, Wissenschaftszentrum Berlin für Sozialforschung, Berlin.

Barro, R.J. (1998). *Determinants of Economic Growth. A Cross-Country Empirical Study*. MIT Press.

Beyme, K. von (1993). *Das Politische System der Bundesrepublik Deutschland nach der Vereinigung*. München und Zürich: Piper.

Boarnet, M. (1998) "Spillovers and the Location Effects of Public Infrastructure." *Journal of Regional Science* 38 (3): 381-400.

Broyer, S. (1996). *The Social Market Economy: Birth of an Economic Style*. WZB discussion paper FS I 96 – 318, Wissenschaftszentrum Berlin für Sozialforschung, Berlin.

Brüderl, J., Preisendörfer, P. and Ziegler, R. (1996). *Der Erfolg neugegründeter Betriebe. Eine empirische Studie zu den Chancen und Risiken von Betriebsgründungen*. Berlin: Duncker & Humblot.

Brüderl, J., Preisendörfer. P. and Ziegler, R. (1992). "Survival chances of newly founded business organizations." *American Sociological Review*, 57: 227-242.

Burgess, M. and Gagnon, A.G. (eds.) (1993). *Comparative Federalism and Federation: Competing Traditions and Future Directions*. Harvester Wheatsheaf: Hempel Hampstead.

Button, K.J. (1998). "Infrastructure investment, endogenous growth, and economic convergence." *Annals of Regional Science*, 32: 145-162.

Ceh, B. (2001). "Regional Innovation Potential in the United States: Evidence of Spatial Transformation." *Regional Science 80* (3): 297-315.

Feldman, M.P, (2001). "The Entrepreneurial Event Revisited: Firm Formation in a Regional Context." *Industrial and Corporate Change* 10: 861–891.

Federal Ministry of Economics and Labor and Federal Ministry of Education and Research (2004). *Innovation and Future Technologies in the SME Sector. – High-Tech Master Plan*. February 2004.

Gramlich, E.M. (1994). "Infrastructure Investment: A Review Essay." *Journal of Economic Literature* 32: 1176-1196.

Grimm, H. (forthcoming). "Do Public Information and Subsidies Contribute to the Entrepreneurial Environment? An Exploratory Transatlantic Study with Local-Global Perspectives." *International Journal of Public Administration*.

Grimm, H. (2004). *Abschlußbericht des Forschungsprojektes „Local Heroes in a Global Village. Globalization and New Entrepreneurship Policies"*. Bundesministerium für Wirtschaft und Arbeit, ERP-Transatlantik Programm, Erfurt, March 2004.

Hinz, T. (1998). *Betriebsgruendungen in Ostdeutschland*. Berlin: Edition sigma.

Jansen, D. and Weber, M. (2003). *Survival. Erfolgsbedingungen Neu Gegründeter Betriebe im Ruhrgebiet*. Forschungsinstitut für Öffentliche Verwaltung bei der Deutschen Hochschule für Verwaltungswissenschaften Speyer.

Lall S.V. and Yilmaz, S. (2001) "Regional Economic Convergence: Do Policy Instruments Make a Difference?" *The Annals of Regional Science* 35: 153-166.

Lehnert, N. (2003). *Ergebnisse des DtA-Gründungsmomitors 2002. Schwerpunktthema: Gründer im Voll- und Nebenerwerb*. Frankfurt a.M.: DtA Die Mittelstandsbank.

Müller-Armack, A. (1948). „Die Wirtschaftspolitik sozial gesehen". In W. Eucken and F. Böhm (eds.). *Ordo Jahrbuch für die Ordnung der Wirtschaft und Gesellschaft*, 1: 125-154.

National Academy of Sciences (ed.) (2001). *Global Networks and Local Values. A Comparative Look at Germany and the United States*. Washington, D.C.: National Academy Press.

North, D.C. (1994). Institutionen, institutioneller Wandel und Wirtschaftsleistung. Tübingen.

Ohmae, K. (1995). *The End of the Nation State: The Rise of Regional Economies*. New York: Free Press.

Olson, M. (1982). *The Rise and Decline of Nations*. New Haven: Yale University Press.

Reynolds, P., Hay, M., Bygrave, W.D., Camp, S.M. and Autio, E. (2001). *Global Entrepreneurship Monitor. 2001 Executive Report*. Kansas City: Kauffman Center for Entrepreneurial Leadership at the Ewing Marion Kauffman Foundation.

Reynolds, P., Hay, M., Bygrave, W.D., Camp, S.M. and Autio, E. (2002). *Global Entrepreneurship Monitor. 2002 Executive Report*. Kansas City: Kauffman Center for Entrepreneurial Leadership at the Ewing Marion Kauffman Foundation.

Reynolds, P. and Storey, D. (1994). *Regional Characteristics Affecting Small Business Formation: A Cross-National Comparison*. OECD Working Papers 2 (8).

Rieter, H. and Schmolz, M. (1993). "The ideas of German Ordoliberalism 1938-45: pointing the way to a new economic order". *The European Journal of the History of the Economic Thought* 1 (1): 87-114.

Sternberg, R. and Bergmann, B. (2002). *Regionaler Entrepreneurship Monitor (REM): Gründungsaktivitäten und Rahmenbedingungen in zehn deutschen Regionen*. Köln: Univ.

Sternberg, R., Otten, C. and Tamásy, C. (2000). *Regionaler Entrepreneurship M (REM): Gründungsaktivitäten und Rahmenbedingungen in zehn deutschen Regionen*. Köln: Univ.

Sternberg, R. and Tamásy, C. (1999). "Munich as Germany's No. 1 High Technology Region: Empirical Evidence, Theoretical Explanations and the Role of Small Firm -- Large Firm Relationships." *Regional Studies* 4: 367-377.

Storey, D.J. (2003). "Entrepreneurship, Small and Medium Sized Enterprises and Public Policy." In Z.J. Acs and D.B. Audretsch (eds.). *International Handbook of Entrepreneurship Research*, Dordrecht: Kluwer Academic.

Sturm, R. (1997). "Föderalismus in Deutschland und in den USA – Tendenzen der Angleichung? *Zeitschrift für Parlamentsfragen* 28: 335-345.

Taylor, F.B. (2002). *Capitalism's Forces of Creative Destruction Unleash Opportunities for Investors*. Paper published for the U.S. Trust, 4.09.2002.

Wagner, G. (2004). *Eichel braucht Mut*. In Die Tageszeitung (*taz*) 8 May 2004.

PART FOUR

IMPLICATIONS AND RECOMMENDATIONS

Chapter 9:

THE GLOBAL ENTREPRENEURSHIP MONITOR: IMPLICATIONS FOR EUROPE

Paul Reynolds
Florida International University

The following contribution is an excerpt of Dr. Paul Reynolds speech held at the Conference "Local Heroes in the Global Village" on 4 September 2003.

1. INTRODUCTION: WHAT IS GEM?

"(...) We have teams all over the world, including a very fine team in Germany, probably our best, headed by Rolf Sternberg; he will be speaking next. There are over 30 of them. Each national team has to raise between $50.000 and $100.000 a year to participate and some have not managed to do that every year. We have had some loss for 2003 but the 37 countries participating in 2002 represent 92% of the world GDP and 62% of the world population. So it is easy to say this looks like a global project.

What are we doing? There are four project objectives. We started these objectives in 1998 when we started the project and they have served us well. The first one is: Can we find a way to measure differences in entrepreneurial activity across countries? Now it may seem like a simple objective but I can assure you it is technically very complicated and there is no other cross-national measure of entrepreneurial behavior in existence. Even in the European Union with all the effort and all the "smarts" at Eurostat, they have not been able to figure out how much entrepreneurship is in Germany versus France versus Belgium versus Sweden. This is because the individual national data sets for the various EU countries use quite different criteria when it comes to identifying new firm registrations; they each pick up new firms at different stages in the start-up process. You can not even compare the U.S. and Canada. So, the first GEM objective is to provide cross-national comparisons of entrepreneurial activity. If we fail on that, the project is useless. I will go into this in more detail in a few minutes.

The second question is: Is this level of activity related to economic growth? Because if the answer to that is no, who cares? These national teams can not raise $100.000 a year to participate in the project if we can find no relationship to economic growth.

The third question, and of course this is the reason why I am here today, is: Why are some countries more entrepreneurial than others? Why do some countries have higher levels of entrepreneurial activity than others?

And finally, the fourth issue: What can you do about it? What can governments do if they choose to increase the level of entrepreneurship? I will tell you that is a tough one. They are not going to do a lot in a hurry. I will get to this later on.

The meaning of "entrepreneurship" is a major issue; and here we have a disconnection between the previous presentations. This conference has been organized around a focus on high-tech, high-growth, basic manufacturing start-ups. I will be talking about anyone who is involved in starting a business. The GEM definition is as broad as we can make, including, for example, someone who is doing part-time childcare or driving a truck on the week-end. It means someone who is starting a new law firm, a new dentist, a new plumber, or a new software company. We have even someone who is trying to start a regional airline in our sample. It is the broadest possible range of start-up business activity.

Our working model is presented in Figure 9.1. The top part of this model was borrowed from the World Economic Forum Global Competitiveness Reports and it reflects the dominant view toward economic policy and economic growth following World War II. That is the view that the large, multi-nationals in the world markets drive national growth.

The top part of this model was borrowed from the World Economic Forum Global Competitiveness Reports and it reflects the dominant view toward economic policy and economic growth following World War II. That is the view that the large, multi-nationals in the world markets drive national growth.

It was about 25 years ago that David Birch began to look at this issue more carefully in the U.S. He discovered that new and small firms, as he defined them, were having a big impact; they turned out to be the only source of job creation. The question and the answers, however, were misspecified. For about 20 years the focus became one of small versus large firms. I can tell you right now that this was a mistake. It has now become quite clear that the issue is new versus old. It is critical. In the United States virtually all net job growth comes from new businesses. It was mis-specified because most small businesses are old and most old businesses are small. But it is the new creation of businesses establishments—a stand-alone business or a new subsidiary or branch (for example, a new manufacturing plant)—that creates new jobs. The focus has shifted to new, not small, firms.

The bottom part of fig. 9.1 represents a very rough summary of the mechanisms linking entrepreneurial framework conditions to new firm creation. The entrepreneurship sector is seen as having two components: one is the presence of opportunities and the other is an adult population with the skill and the motivation to take advantage of these opportunities. If you have the happy event of those occurring together, then you will presumably get new firm creation.

Fig. 9.1: GEM Conceptual Model

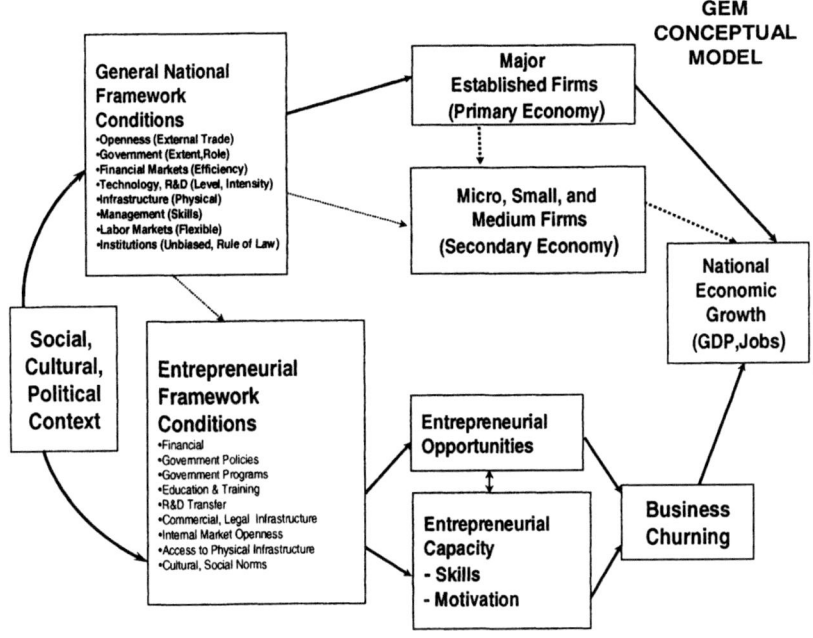

Source: GEM 2000 Executive Report: 7/8

New firm creation, however, is one aspect of the most critical part of this model and that is business churning, business volatility, or business turbulence; it is business churning and turbulence that is correlated with economic growth. This is the dark side of entrepreneurship. Firm birthrates and firm death rates are highly correlated (about 0.7). You can not have new firm births without existing firms disappearing; this is the part politicians do not like because it is the people with existing firms that complain when they go out of business. So, this is a major problem in trying to decide how to adapt public policy to foster new firm creation.

In terms of data collection, GEM teams all over the world are doing the same four things. One is sponsoring adult population surveys completed in each country by commercial research firms. Each GEM team interviews national experts with a one-hour face-to-face interview; they then complete a questionnaire. This questionnaire provides a lot of nice, reliable multi-item scales. The GEM coordination team assembles all of the standardized data from the IMF and the World Bank and the United Nations and the OECD and the U.S. Census etc. All the teams use the same harmonized data for analysis.

2. GEM DEFINITION OF "ENTREPRENEURSHIP"

What do we mean when we say "entrepreneurship" in this project? We pay for surveys of representative samples of all adults living in an each country. These are done by market research firms because we can afford them and they are fast with the results. They go through an interview and they ask somebody what kind of breakfast food do you eat? What kind of car are you thinking of buying? Are you going to do on vacation? Somewhere in this they ask them, "Are you starting a business?" If they say yes, we ask them a couple of questions to find out if they are seriously involved in a business start. First, have they done anything in the last year to put the business in place? We do not want cocktail party entrepreneurs. We want people who are actually doing it. Second, will they own part of the business? And third, have they had salaries or wage payments for more than three months? Because if they have had salaries and wage payments for more than three months, we say, "This is very interesting. You are not a start-up. You are a new business." So we are tracking people before they reach the point where they actually have a going business in place.

We also measure people who have a going business that is from 3 to 42 months old—a new business. We add those numbers together to create what we call the total entrepreneurial activity [TEA] index. So if you appear to qualify for being in the start-up phase, you get a count of one. If you qualify for having a new or baby business, you get a count of one. The 6% that qualify for both still get a count of one. So, we have an underestimate of the number of business activities but a more accurate estimate of the percentage of people involved. What does that mean when you start looking at the data? This is a comparison of 37 countries and it shows you the number of people per hundred in the population from 18 to 64 years old involved in trying to start a business or that has a new business. We call it the TEA index.

2.1 The TEA Index

We have deliberately conveyed to you our uncertainty about the estimates by keeping the confidence intervals in the chart (Figure 9.2); the vertical bar is the 95% confidence interval or the margin of error. That represents the imprecision of our estimate because our samples are small, about 2,000 for most countries. If you look at the middle of the chart, you will see a very narrow bar for the U.K. and Germany. That is because both had samples of 15.000 and that reduces the confidence interval.

There are several things to say about the patterns in Figure 9.2. One, there is quite a bit of range. You go from the low end which is Japan and that is about 3 per 100 adults to the high end which is Thailand, close to 20 per 100 adults. Among adjacent countries, however, most are not statistically significantly different. So, there is no real difference between Thailand, India, and Chile at the high end. One cannot say that Japan, Russia, Belgium, France, Hong Kong, Croatia, and Sweden are really statistically significantly different. They are all low and about equal in terms of entrepreneurial activity.

In terms of what this means, all you have to do is just invert these numbers: Two per hundred means one out of fifty adults. One out of fifty people in Japan are involved in starting a business. If you live in a country where one out of fifty people are doing something entrepreneurial, you are very unlikely to know anyone who is doing it and it is a very rare phenomenon. But suppose you are at the other end; in a in a country like Thailand where it is one out of five are involved in business start-ups. That means that everyone probably knows someone who is involved in this activity and it is not a strange, mysterious sort of "unnatural" experience. Everyone has an understanding of what is involved because everyone knows someone who is doing it—if not themselves.

Fig.9.2: Total Entrepreneurial Activity (TEA) per Country

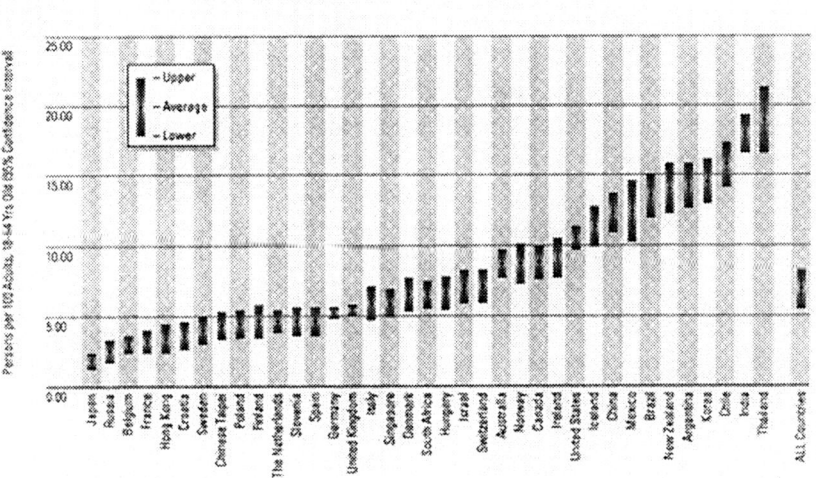

Source: GEM 2002 Executive Report: 9

Let us move along here. It is useful to sort these countries into six groups to get a better sense of what kind of major differences might be present. The four countries at the bottom—very much at the bottom with 4 per 100 adults active—include Taiwan, Hong Kong, and Singapore, along with Japan. We call them Asian developed. The countries at the very top are countries like India and China, Thailand, and South Korea. We call them Asian developing. Ironically countries from the same part of the world represent the top and the bottom of the scale. Moving up from the bottom you have Central and Eastern Europe: Russia, Poland, Slovenia, Croatia, and Hungary, with about 4.5 per 100 adults active. The next group, where the average is between 5 and 6 per 100 adults, we call the European Union plus four. We have almost all the European Union in the project [not yet Austria or Greece] but we also include Switzerland, Iceland, Norway, and Israel.

Then we have a group we call, for lack of a better label, the former British Empire-Anglo countries: New Zealand, Canada, the U.S., Australia, and, not knowing where to put it, South Africa, although it may not belong there. There you see the average level of activity is twice that of Europe, about 10 per 100 adults 18 to 64 years old. Then, we have the Latin America group, at about 14 per 100 and which is remarkable for the homogeneity. There is no statistically significant difference among Mexico, Brazil, Chile, and Argentina. Finally, we have these four Asian developing countries at the high end, at about 16 per 100.

How many people are represented by the TEA index? We estimate that among our 37 GEM countries, there are 286 million people involved in trying to start businesses. If you go to the whole population, from the 62% of the world in this sample to the whole world; the estimate grows to about 460 million people. As there is an average of two people involved in each business start-up you cut these estimates in half to count the number of business entities. For example, 460 million people are trying to start 230 million businesses. There are about a hundred million each in India and China, about 18 million in the U.S., a little less than 12 million in the E.U. plus four, of which 2.8 million are in Germany. So for 2002, there are 2.8 million Germans trying to start 1.4 million businesses.

It is useful to contrast these magnitudes with the stories from government officials who will tell you about all their programs to help people start a business. This is the same in every country I have been. The program officials come and basically say, "We have a wonderful program. We talked to 150 people and we got 20 business plans. Or 20.000 called a business start-up hotline. And we say, "Well that is very nice. But what about the hundreds of thousands—or millions—of other people who are trying to start a business. Who is helping these people? Why government programs have such low counts is discussed later.

If you look at the global location of those starting businesses, the vast majority—over 75%—are in Asia.

I have been living in the U.K. and paying taxes to the E.U. and everybody else for about five years now. And I can tell you that in the U.K., when they are not worried about the U.S., they are worried about Germany. What is going on in Germany? How can we keep up with the Germans? And, of course, we are here now in Germany because of worries about how to keep up with the U.S. But in two generations this will be irrelevant. China and India are taking the lead. There are ten to twenty times as many people in developing Asia trying to start businesses as in Europe.

2.2 Opportunity versus Necessity Entrepreneurs

One of the things that struck us when we did the GEM 2000 survey is: why is the U.S. not higher? Why is Brazil higher than the U.S.? Why is South Korea higher than the U.S.? We started thinking about this and we decided to separate people on the basis of their motivation. So, we added one a simple question. We asked everyone involved in businesses "Why are you doing this? Because of an opportunity or because you have no better choices for work?" This question was very carefully developed so we would not insult them. Basically, we are asking people, are you a willing volunteer or are you a "draftee"? Have you been driven into entrepreneurial activity because you cannot find any other way to participate in the economy? And this works like gangbusters as a single social science item in an interview. I will not go into the technical details but we never conceived a single item could be so successful or unambiguous. We can classify 97% of our respondents on this simple question.

What difference does it make? Figure 9.3 shows the TEA rate for people who are doing it to take advantage of a business opportunity; it looks very much like the previous Figure 9.2.

Fig. 9.3: Opportunity-Based Entrepreneurial Activity by Country

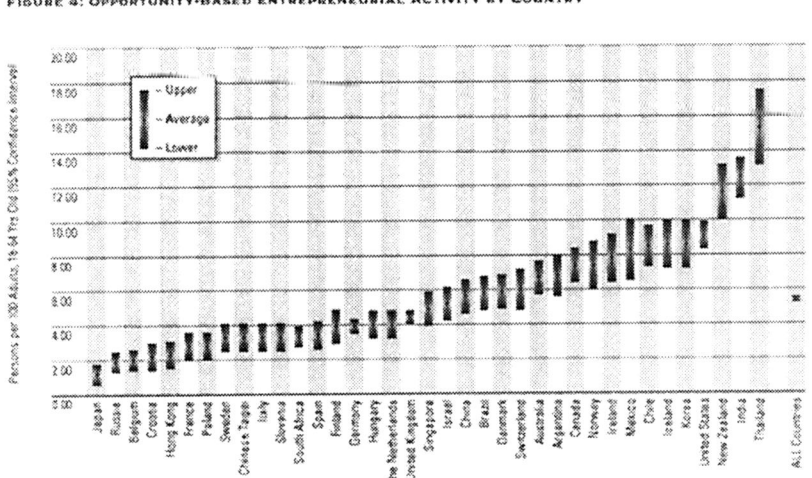

Source: GEM 2002 Executive Report: 15

The rank order is about the same. The level is lower because we have lost a third of the respondents, those active out of necessity. The U.S. rank is slightly higher.

If you look at the necessity entrepreneurs in Figure 9.4, you really get some new information. There are a large number of countries where there is virtually no one involved out of necessity. If you read up from the bottom the countries are France, Spain, Belgium, Finland, Denmark, Norway, and Italy. Does that sound familiar? Many are neighbors of Germany. In fact, you have to get almost halfway past the middle before you get above 1 in 100. The U.S. and Germany are in the middle of the list and identical at about 1 per 100.

Fig 9.4: Necessity-Based Entrepreneurial Activity by Country

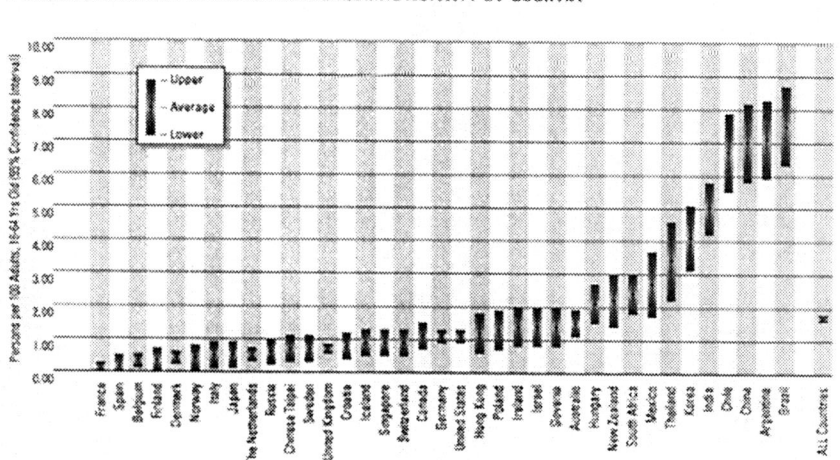

Source: GEM 2002 Executive Report: 16

But look at the high end where necessity entrepreneurship is 7 to 8 per 100. This makes clear which the rates are so high in developing countries, such as Brazil, Argentina, and India. People are involved because there is no other way they can participate in the economy. They are driven into trying to start businesses because they have no other choices. I can tell you who they are, too. The typical necessity entrepreneur is an unemployed, uneducated young man with few options. Either they go out and try to start a business or they turn to a life of crime and start kidnapping wealthy visitors for ransom. Trying to start a new business would seem a better choice.

I should say that almost all the theories about entrepreneurship have been developed by people living and working and studying in all the countries that are on the left side of Figure 9.4; countries in Europe and North America. They have totally missed necessity entrepreneurship because it has not been present where they live.

3. ENTREPRENEURSHIP AND ECONOMIC GROWTH

Now what about economic growth? Related to that was a desire to determine if those with new firms were creating innovative businesses. And innovation is quite relevant to any discussion on economic growth. We asked three questions to get a measure of innovation. First, do the customers know what you are selling them? Second, do you have competition? Third, is the technology more than a year old? If the customer understands the product, if there is a lot of competition and the technology is more than a year old, then we can assume this is an established product or service. It is replicating what is already on the market. On the other hand, if the customers have no idea what you are selling them, if you have no competition, and it is brand new technology, you can assume that the firm is doing something new and maybe this will expand the market. We can assume the effort is creating a new product or service that has not been available before.

The surveys provide data on potential firms in the start-up phase before the salaries and wages are paid; new firms that are from are 3 to 42 months old, and established firms that are over 42 months old. The percentage of these firms that are in the market creation categories goes from 14% to 8% to 5%; the more advanced the firms are in the business life course, the smaller the percent that are creating new markets. This measure of market creation is consistent with most ideas about firm innovation; it is more prevalent among new firms and less prevalent among older, established firms.

This suggests that the measure of market innovation can be used to compare the six groups of countries in terms of the firms in the TEA measure. This is provided in Figure 9.5. The prevalence of market innovation TEA businesses is about o.5% for Developed Asian countries, about 0.3% for central European countries, a little over 0.5% for the EU countries, and about 1% for the Former Anglo, Latin American, and Developing Asian countries. There then, clear differences in the level of innovative businesses in these six groups of countries.

These levels may appear to be low; but the absolute amounts can be substantial. For example, in India a one percent of a hundred million people are involved in innovative start-ups, but that is a million people trying to start businesses that will provide new innovations, new goods and services in the market. While there are a lot of new restaurants and local service business in this mass, there are also a substantial number of high-tech, sophisticated new ventures.

Fig 9.5: TEA Entities–Replication versus Market Expansion by Global Type

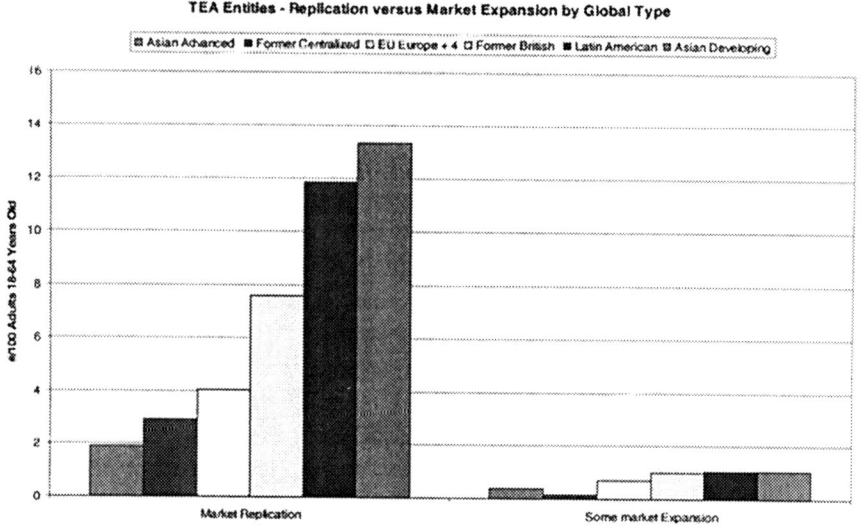

Source: http://www.gruenderkonferenz.de/en/rede_reynolds.html

What about economic growth? This is where all my colleagues say "Go easy, Reynolds." And I agree; it is hard to make strong causal statements with the data available to this point, we have measures of association, not definitive measures of causality. However, when we consider the measures of association between the overall, opportunity and necessity TEA rates and the percentage growth of GDP in the same year, inflation adjusted using the national currencies, and pool the data for three years, the correlations are 0.19, 0.20, and 0.23; none are statistically significant. If we add a one year lag between the TEA measures and economic growth, the correlations go up to 0.22, 0.22, and 0.35, highest and significant for necessity entrepreneurship. With a two year lag they increase further, to 0.42, 0.26, and 0.49, again highest and statistically significant for necessity entrepreneurship.

We have discovered that, as you probably know; poor countries are growing faster than rich countries. We also have evidence that entrepreneurship is high in poor countries, due to necessity entrepreneurship. It is hard to escape the conclusion that some of these "draftees" may be contributing to the national economic growth of the poor countries. The people who are involuntarily participating in the economic adaptation may be making a substantial contribution to economic growth.

The scatter diagram for the relationship between TEA overall and growth with a two year lag is provided in Figure 9.6. Note there are some countries in the lower right quadrant. Those are countries that have pretty good growth rates but not much entrepreneurial activity. I can tell you who those are. There are countries with a very high level of imports and exports compared to their GDP such as Singapore, Belgium, and the Netherlands. But what is missing, are countries in the upper left-hand corner. There are almost no countries in the quadrant with high levels of entrepreneurship and low levels of economic growth. In fact, the one data point that is up there is Brazil, in 2000.

Fig 9.6: TEA Overall and National Economic Growth: 2 Yr Lag

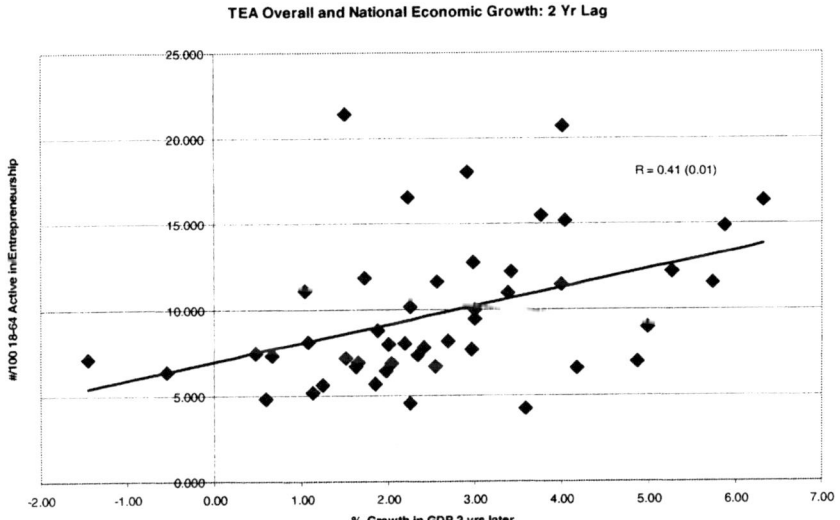

Source: http://www.gruenderkonferenz.de/en/rede_reynolds.html

This suggests that if a policymaker asked if promoting entrepreneurship likely to pay off in providing growth, I would have to say that it seems to in almost all cases where we have data. We cannot find many examples where more entrepreneurship has NOT been followed by more economic growth.

4. MATERIALISM VERSUS POST-MATERIALISM

There is a periodic cross-national survey of peoples' values coordinated through the University of Michigan's Institute of Survey Research. One major focus is to determine whether or not the adult populations in different countries value materialism or what is called post-materialism. People who favor materialism would consider it important to have order in the nation, to fight rising prices, have a strong national defense, a stable economy and so forth. People who favor post-materialism will give preference to allowing citizens more say in government decisions, protection for freedom of speech, people having more influence in decisions at work, more beautiful cities and countryside, a friendly society, and what have you.

Figure 9.6 is one of one of about 20 prepared to provide comparisons of these six groups of countries on a number of dimensions. There are 6 comparisons in Figure 9.6. The first one is purchasing power which shows you the relative wealth in the countries; it is lowest in the developing countries and central Europe. The second and third provide measures of income disparity and indicates that Developed Asian and Europe plus four countries have the lowest income disparity of any of these six groups. It is a little bit higher in central Europe. It is a little higher still among the former Anglo and is the highest by far among the Latin American countries. .

Fig 9.7: TEA Overall and National Economic Growth: 2 Yr Lag

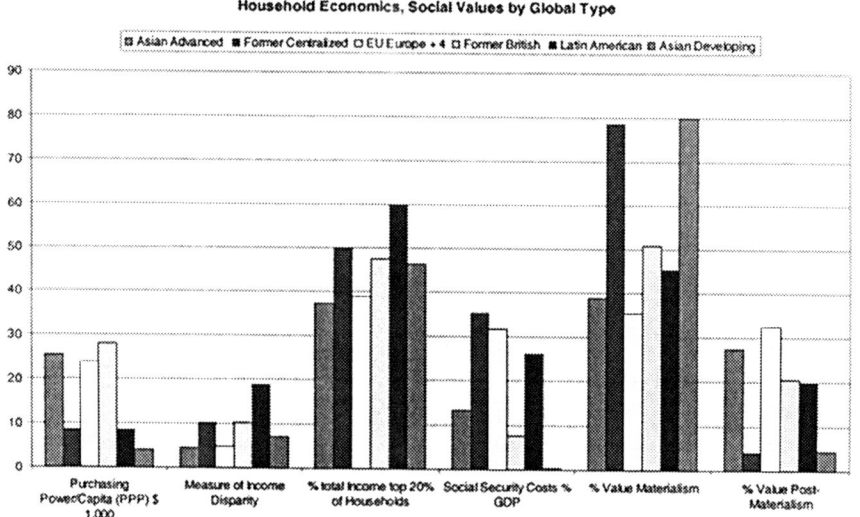

Source: http://www.gruenderkonferenz.de/en/rede_reynolds.html

The forth comparison shows the social security cost as a percentage of GDP; this is by far the highest in central Europe and the Europe plus four countries. The next highest group is Latin American but if we took Brazil out of Latin America, it would drop down substantially. It is much lower in the former Anglo and Developed Asian and almost zero in the Developing Asian—there are no safety nets in China and India.

Essentially there is low income disparity and a high level of social and economic security payments as a percentage of GDP occurring in the European countries. They are also the countries with the lowest emphasis on materialistic values and the highest acceptance of post-materialism. By far, the largest percentage of the population valuing post-materialism occurs in developing Asian and Europe plus four countries.

Does this help understand the relationship between levels of entrepreneurship and cultural differences? This is pretty strong evidence that several related national features occur together. One of the critical issues is the causal relationship. My guess is that economic prosperity lead to a high value placed on post-materialism that led to a very high level of social and economic security expenditures in the Asian Developed and European plus four countries.

5. IMPLICATIONS FOR EUROPE

What is special about the European Union plus four? In our survey we ask about fear of failure. There tends to be a relatively high fear of failure, low income disparity, high social security cost, and strong post-materialism values. The public sector has a massive presence; a very large percentage of the GDP and a large percentage of the employment are funneled through the government. It is as high as 40% in some Scandinavian countries. If the government is controlling 40% of the economic activity, that just reduces the scope for entrepreneurship. If nothing else, the government has got a monopoly in those sectors. This can have a real impact on reducing opportunities for entrepreneurship.

The former "British Empire Anglo countries" are characterized by less income disparity, lower social security costs, and lower support for post-materialism. The public sector is smaller in scope but rated as reasonably effective. A major, largely unrecognized competitive advantage of North America (Canada and the U.S.) is the extremely high percentage of people that attend some sort of post-secondary educational activity. This cuts across the board. It is everything from people being diesel mechanics to becoming software programmers to becoming lawyers and dentists and physicians and scientists; it reflects huge investments that these countries have made in the institution to do this training and the research infrastructure present in these organizations.

Why is there so much entrepreneurial activity in the U.S.? It is useful to turn the question around. It is not because there is more equity debt available for start-ups, certainly not through the venture capital system. Remember, there are roughly five million new ventures being put in place in the U.S. each year. At the height, venture capitalist provided support for 2,000 of them. Over 99% get no money from venture capital sources.

It is not because U.S. start-ups get a lot of direct help from government programs. We have had a lot of interesting examples but 75% of start-ups make no contact with any kind of government helping program or agency. There is a plethora of these programs in the U.S. We did a study in Wisconsin five years ago. There were 700 programs in the state of Wisconsin, a state of five million, to help people start businesses, two hundred just for financing support. There is an enormous range of them. But those starting businesses do not know about them; they are not marketed well. Nascent entrepreneurs are off doing it by themselves on their own.

It is not because there are not government regulations in paperwork. When you start a business, for example, in Denver, you have to deal with the city, the county, the state, and the "feds" in terms of paperwork. You have four levels of government to satisfy. There is no shortage of paperwork in North America.

It is not because entrepreneurs are cultural heroes. You would be amazed at how many people in the U.S. do not want to be called "entrepreneurs". They do not want people to see them as some sort of scam artists. There are unsavory connotations associated with the word "entrepreneur." A lot of people actually resist that label.

In the U.K., by the way, they do not have entrepreneurship policy. They do not have entrepreneurship programs. They are not going to make the U.K. a leading country for entrepreneurship. The UK is promoted as the leading enterprise country by promoting enterprise programs. That is how the Brits feel about the word entrepreneur.

The US is not active in entrepreneurship because every child gets intensive training on entrepreneurship in high school. There are almost no programs in high school in entrepreneurship. They are not that many in the colleges. There are a lot more in colleges but they are mostly in the business schools. They are not provided to those getting serious technical and substantive training.

So, why is there so much activity in the U.S.? I think—and I am trying to be diplomatic about this—that in the U.S. most people assume they have the prime responsibility for their own economic well-being; they expect to take care of themselves.

In addition, trying to start a business is no big deal. If you have to shut one down, that is no big deal. Entrepreneurship is just one career option. There is so much of it around everyone knows the basics about what is involved. If you do not, you can go talk to a friend, you can go talk to your mother and she will send you to Uncle Harry who started a business. Uncle Harry knows how to apply for a bank loan.

If the start-up works out, that is great. Everyone says fine and you can still come to the family Christmas parties and they will still talk to you. If it does not work out, that is fine. They will say "I know somebody over here that is looking for somebody with your skills" to help you find a job. It is remarkable how entrepreneurship is seen as just an ordinary part of life.

The institutions—government, financial—operate under the assumption that there is going to be business churning. Businesses will start and shut down and the whole system assumes that businesses will eventually terminate. By the way, all businesses fail. Period. The only question is when and under what conditions. The idea that the SME [small, medium enterprise] sector will consist of a lot of permanent SMEs and permanent jobs, and everyone can have stability in their work life is just not going to happen. Most of the churning does not involve bankruptcy. Less than 5% of business terminations in the U.S. involve any loss to creditors. Most of it is the normal transition in the business population. The owners realize the business is no longer profitable; they shut it down, and go off and do something else.

Choices for Europe seem limited. The major focus has been to maintain past institutions, value systems, emphasize the allocation of economic wealth, emphasize structural stability, work and train people for career predictability (one training, one career), and centralize economic decision-making. Or European countries can try to adapt to an enterprise economy, using the U.K. phrase here, and emphasize growth of the total social wealth; emphasize structural adaptation; educate, train for work career flexibility and adaptability; and decentralize economic decision-making.

Ordinary people starting new businesses are the ultimate decentralization of the decisions about the future structure of the economy. When ordinary members of the work force make these decisions, they know the industries, they know the cost structures, they know the customers, they know the competition, and they are the ones deciding the time is right to start a business. The only way to have an economy that can keep up with the current high speed global transformations is to decentralize these structural decisions that down to the people who know the most about the different market segments.

I do not think there is a big choice for Europe. European countries will adapt or stagnate. There are many positive fundamentals in Europe: highly educated people in good health; excellent physical infrastructure; quality educational systems, and comprehensive healthcare at a decent cost. There is a global orientation. The EU is adapting to incorporate central Europe. There is an effort, with some success, to harmonizing the intellectual, legal, and financial structure and allow diversity in individual cultures; perhaps English is becoming the standard language, but only as a second language for most.

Europe is trying to create the kind of advantage you have in the U.S. that if you have a product in Florida, you can sell it anywhere to 300 million people. There has been some clear success in this regard.

The major adjustment, however, is going to require a fundamental change in the social contract – the contract between the people and their governments. People are going to have to accept the greater role in economic decision-making, accept more risk, and be entitled to more rewards when they are successful. The government needs to focus on providing the training, perhaps shrink the safety nets, but help ease the costs of transitions. The transition costs are substantial when you have an industry that goes out of business and you have the whole region that is suddenly devastated. It is appropriate that governments reduce the individual costs of the transitions. But they generally fail when they try to prevent structural change. This adaptation will not be fast nor cheap nor smooth. It is going to take real cultural leadership, real political leadership, and it is going to have to be uniform across Europe—or some countries will lag while others prosper.

I think conferences like this are of great value because they transmit the message, one more time, that political and government leaders have discovered that Europeans have to take more responsibility for their economic change and their economic well-being. That has to be driven home on every front; these discussions have a major role to play. Europe is poised to decentralize economic adaptation through increased entrepreneurship-- opportunity to the people.

INDEX

Acs, Z.J. 25, 40, 43, 85, 88, 143
Advanced Research Program 37
Advanced Technology
  Centers 37
  Program (ATP) 70, 88, 89
Aeronautics 6, 51, 52, 69
Aldrich, H.E. 98, 104, 111
America (United States of)
  and American Dream 14, 15
  and American way of life 11, 13
  and Puritans 11
  antitrust policy 6, 57, 59
  competitiveness 35
  corporations 31
  economic and social system 10
  economic development 11
  economic model 14
  economic policy 15
  economy 10, 16, 31
  history 12
  identity 11
  ideology 12
  immigration policy 6, 17, 57, 63
  innovation system 67, 72, 76
  North America 24-30, 34, 180, 185
  political economy 8
  society 10, 11
Applied research 51, 54, 70
Argentina 178, 180
Arkansas 38
Asian 66, 97, 177, 178, 181, 183, 184
Asian developed 177
  developing 177, 178
Association of University
  Research Parks 61

Atlanta 16, 153, 154, 160, 162, 163, 167
Atomic Energy Commission 64
ATP (see Advanced Technology Program)
Audretsch, D.B. 3, 4, 6, 10, 18, 21, 22, 25, 26, 30, 31, 40-43, 85, 86, 88, 143, 145, 146, 171
Auerswald, P.E. 69, 77, 78, 85, 86, 88
Austin 16, 37
Australia 36, 178
Austria 177
Baltimore 153, 154, 160-163, 167
Bavaria 12, 103, 128, 153
Bayh Dole 59, 66, 86, 89
  Bayh-Dole Act 58, 60, 61, 86, 88, 89
Belgium 173, 176, 179, 183
Birch, D.L. 85, 88, 175
Branscomb, L.M. 69, 77, 78, 85, 86, 88
Brazil 178, 180, 183, 184
Brock, W.A. 25, 40
Brown, C. 24, 40, 58, 87, 89
Broyer, S. 8, 18, 166, 171
Bush, G.W. 57, 58, 66, 70
California 13, 16, 43, 60
Calvinist 12
Canada 31, 36, 173, 178, 185
Carlsson, B. 37, 40
Carré, M.A. 115
Cecchini, P. 31
Chamber of Commerce 147, 152
Chandler, A. 26, 41
Chapel Hill 38, 42, 153, 154
Chile 176, 178
China 177, 178

Clinton, W.J. 12, 16
Clusters 23, 32, 33, 36, 37, 40, 58, 63, 141
Cologne 113, 115, 119, 121, 122, 131, 143, 144
Commercialization 21, 35, 38, 60, 61, 62, 64, 69-71, 75, 79, 82, 83, 86
Companies
  large 9, 10, 63, 160
  small 9, 61, 76, 79, 80, 148
Comparative advantage 21, 26, 29, 30, 34, 39
Competitive advantage 10, 77, 185
Competitiveness
  in global markets 9, 35, 70
  international 35, 38, 50
  in traditional industries 27
  loss of 26
  of a particular region 38
  of a region 30
  of firms 30, 39
  of firms and regions 30
  of locations 39
  of corporations 30
  of the U.S.A. 6
Cooperative Research and Development Agreement (CRADA) 61
Corporate Downsizing 27-29, 39
Corporations
  large 22, 27, 29, 30, 34
CRADA (see Cooperative Research and Development Agreement)
Crain, W.M. 69, 88
Creative deconstruction 9
  destruction 22
  people 3, 5, 9, 12, 14, 17
  spirit 14
Croatia 176, 177
Cross-national approach 6
Cross-regional approach 153

Decision-making 22, 32, 99, 104, 105, 106, 186
  decision-making process 32, 105, 106
Defense Advanced Research Projects Agency 64
Denmark 179
Denver 185
Department of Defense (DoD) 62, 64, 74, 79, 86, 88
Department of Energy 59, 64, 74
Detroit 30
Deutsche Forschungsgemeinschaft 115
DoD (see Department of Defense)
Dresden 39, 49, 127, 149
Durham 42, 153, 154
Durham-Raleigh-Chapel Hill 154
Early-stage financial support 82, 87
East Germany 146
East vs. West European comparison 6
Eastern Enlargement of the EU 49
EBN (see European Business Incubator Network)
Econometric theories 3
Economic
  activity 21, 26, 27, 29, 30, 185
  and social development 10, 24
  change 9, 187
  decision-making 186, 187
  development 5, 9, 11, 18, 42, 62, 109, 116, 146, 152, 154, 158, 160, 167, 168
  differences 7
  efficiency 24, 52, 55
  environment 5, 105
  growth 3-6, 8, 9, 12, 22, 39, 53, 67, 68, 74, 79, 81, 115, 116, 118, 145, 146, 150, 153, 173, 175, 180, 182, 184
  knowledge 21

liberalism 7
opportunities 22
perspective 22
policy 7, 15, 39, 50, 154, 168, 174
value 12, 33, 74
Ecosystem 6, 68, 70, 77, 80, 83, 84
Edison BioTechnology Center 37
Edison Centers 38
  Program 38
  Technology Program 37
Employment downsizing 39
Emscher-Lippe 119, 131
Engineering 27, 48, 51, 63, 64, 65, 69, 74, 153, 154
Entrepreneurial
  activity 6, 10, 21, 22, 23, 26, 33, 34, 39, 97, 114-117, 119, 121-129, 137-142, 168, 173-176, 179, 180, 183
  attitudes 114-117, 123, 126, 135, 140
  behavior 32, 94, 95, 97, 99, 100-110
  culture 38
  economy 3-5, 9, 10
  enterprises 26
  environment 5-9, 145-153, 160-168
  firm 21, 33, 34, 113
  opportunities 96, 122, 123
  patterns 6, 109
  propensity 128, 140
Entrepreneurs
  nascent 98, 117, 121, 128-136, 142, 150
  young 102, 117, 121
Entrepreneurship
  civic 83, 87
  concept 23
  definition 8, 22, 23
  features 23
  policies (*see policy*)

policy 4-7, 31-34, 38, 114, 147, 150, 168, 185
  new entrepreneurship policies 4, 6, 17, 145, 146, 153
  promotion 32, 39, 167, 183
  Re-emergence of 4, 10, 25, 26
  traditions
    Austrian 22
    Chicago 22
    Schumpeterian 22
  value of 23
Environments
  fragile 94, 100, 105
  global 50, 146
  political 105, 106
  social 9, 140
  unfamiliar 98, 105
ERA (see European Research Area)
Erfurt 3, 5, 47, 48, 145, 171
Eucken, W. 8, 18, 172
Europe
  Eastern Europe 49, 53-55, 64, 94, 177
  Central Europe 177, 181, 183, 184, 187
  Western Europe 24, 30, 55
European
  Airbus 52
  and American firms 27
  approach 51, 57
  Community 53, 54, 114
  cooperation 51, 52
  countries 25, 49, 52, 54-55, 72, 184
  economies 84
  history 49
  immigrants 11
  integration 6, 31, 49, 53, 146
  policies 50
  research 6, 49, 54, 72
  research policy 6, 49

European Business Incubator Network (EBN) 127
European Research Area (ERA) 50, 52, 89
European unification 49
European Union
  countries 173
  enlargement 54
  policies 51
Evans 25, 40
EXIST 38, 127, 142, 149, 162
Family business 102, 103, 104
Federal
  agencies 37, 79
  assistance programs 157
  government 3, 6, 58, 59, 64, 65, 77, 113, 114, 127, 142-149, 152, 168, 170
  laboratories 6, 57, 59, 61, 62
  research 58, 66
Federal Ministry of Economics and Labor 127, 148, 171
Federal Ministry of Education and Research 148, 171
Federal Republic of Germany (GDR) 127, 171
Feller, I. 37, 41, 81, 88
Financial assistance programs 147, 148, 151, 155, 157, 160, 163, 165, 167, 168
  entrepreneurship promotion programs 35, 126, 185
Finland 179
Firm
  large-scale 24, 26, 28, 69, 72, 85
  new and small 10, 21, 24, 26, 35-37, 41, 69, 73, 74, 85, 95, 99, 100-109, 114, 117, 146, 175
Florida, R. 3, 6, 16, 17, 18, 173, 187
Flügge 128, 161
Framework
  conditions 113-129, 137-142, 147, 150-154, 175
  programs 50, 51, 53
France 30, 36, 49, 173, 176, 179
Free market economy 8
Freiburg School 8
FUTOUR 2000 127
Gates, B. 14, 19, 73
GDP (see Gross Domestic Product)
GDR (see Federal Republic of Germany)
GEM (see Global Entrepreneurship Monitor)
Georgia 16, 153, 160
German 14
  companies 27
  culture 15
  tradition 21
  unification 53
Germany 3-19, 25-31, 37-39, 47-49, 67, 68, 81-84, 95, 96, 100-179
GET UP 39, 149, 170
Gilbert, B.A. 4, 18
Global Entrepreneurship Monitor (GEM) 7, 43, 97, 112-117, 122, 126, 140- 144, 150-152, 172-180
Global
  economy 9, 34, 158
  market 26, 67, 72
  village 5, 68
Globalization 4-9, 21, 25, 26, 29, 30, 39, 52, 54, 168, 171
Goldstein, H. 38, 42
Government
  agency 31, 32
  intervention 37
  regulations 15, 74, 129, 185
Government-sponsored technology policies 37
Great Britain 37
Greece 122, 177

Grimm, H. 3, 6, 7, 145, 149, 164, 170, 171
Gross Domestic Product (GDP) 25, 72, 73, 173, 182, 183, 184, 185
Hartz
  Commission 141
  concept 142
  report 141
Hebert, R.S. 21, 22, 41
Henrekson, M. 72, 88
Herberg, W. 11, 18
High-wage countries 21, 26, 30
Hong Kong 176, 177
Hopkins, T.D. 69, 88
Horst, T. 26, 41
Hungary 177
Immigration 6, 13, 17, 32, 57, 63, 65
Incremental mode 107
India 176-182
Indiana University 3, 21, 41, 47
Innovation
  center 37, 118, 128
  process 67, 69, 70-72, 84, 85
Innovation Relay Centres (IRC) 127
Innovative
  activity 22, 24, 29
  change 23
  elite 10, 12, 15, 16
  entrepreneurs 67, 98, 149
  ideas 6, 23, 63
  Institutional
  changes 105, 110
  framework 4, 68
  competition 50, 58
IRC (see Innovation Relay Centers)
Italy 25, 36, 179
Japan 36, 37, 176, 177
Jena 3, 18, 21, 48, 49, 112, 145, 170
Joint research 57, 61, 62, 115

Karlsruhe 39, 127, 149
Karlsson, T. 97, 98, 111
Keilbach, M. 10, 18
Kerry, J. F. 66
Knight, J. 22, 94, 111
Knowledge
  activities 33, 38
  creation and commercialization 34
  spillovers 33
  -based activities 33
  -based entrepreneurship 39
  -based firm 33
Krugman, P. 9, 18, 42
Latin America 178, 182, 183, 184
Leadership 58, 67, 81, 187
Leipold, H. 14, 18
Leipzig 122, 123, 153, 154, 161-167
Lerner, J. 35, 36, 42, 76, 85, 86, 89
Link, A.N. 21, 22, 38, 41, 42, 86, 89
Local heroes 5, 7, 67, 68, 77, 84, 146, 167, 168
Love, J.H. 115, 143
Loveman, G. 25, 42
Lucas, R.E. 9, 18
Lugar, M. 38, 42
Lundstrom, A. 32, 42
Macroeconomics 58
Market
  economies (see economy)
  economy 3, 4, 7, 23, 95, 100, 102, 106, 107, 166
  failure 33, 34, 39
Massachusetts 11
Mathur, V.K. 4, 18
McDougall, P.P. 4, 18
Mexico 178
Mississippi 38
Munich 49, 81, 115, 119-122, 126, 129, 130, 153, 161-167, 172

Nanotechnology 6, 51, 69
National Institutes of Health (NIH) 59, 64, 79, 86
Netherlands 25, 31, 36, 183
Networks 5, 23,19, 32- 34, 41, 43, 52-55, 102, 112, 114, 118, 125, 128, 141, 143, 148, 149,172
New entrepreneurship policies 4, 6, 17, 145, 146, 153
New Jersey 37
New York 13, 16-19, 42, 89, 172
New Zealand 178
Night 16
NIH (see National Institutes of Health)
NorCom Information Technology AG 15
Nordbakk, L. 15
North Carolina 38, 42, 153, 160, 165
North Rhine-Westphalia 153
Norway 177, 179
Oak Ridge National Laboratory (ORNL) 59
OECD 22, 23, 32, 37, 39, 41, 42, 86, 89, 143, 172, 175
countries 32, 37, 39, 41
Ohio 37, 40
Ohmae, K. 9, 18, 146, 172
Oligopolistic market 24
Olofsson, C. 115, 143
Ordnungspolitik 7, 8
ORNL (see Oak Ridge National Laboratory)
Ownership 25, 30, 34, 41, 60, 61, 79, 117
Partnership 58, 77, 107, 108
Pennsylvania 58, 81
Pioneers 9, 12, 13, 14, 15
Pittsburgh 30, 64, 81
Poland 177
Policies (see Policy)
Policy

approach 3, 30, 34, 147, 150, 168
changes 6, 57, 58
entrepreneurial 39
innovative 4, 5, 67, 68
instruments 3, 31, 32, 34, 114
laboratory 61
new policies 3, 145
Policy-makers 3-7, 21, 67, 68, 72, 145-150, 168
Porter, M.E. 33, 42
Portugal 25, 36
Post-materialism 183, 184
Post-war
economies 24
era 24, 30
period 24, 25
Privatization 26, 34, 37
Public policies 3-5, 8, 67, 76, 114, 128, 129, 142, 147, 151, 152, 155, 158, 168
policy 3, 21, 31, 24, 30-39, 69, 114, 115, 126, 128, 131, 134, 140, 141, 150, 152, 165, 168, 175
Putnam, R. 4, 19
R&D (see Research & Development)
Regional Entrepreneurship Monitor (REM) 7, 113, 115-144, 150-152, 172
Relationship 5, 24, 49, 82, 110, 116, 129, 173, 184
REM (see Regional Entrepreneurship Monitor)
Remscheid 153, 154
Research & Development (R&D) 9, 10, 24, 34, 35, 36, 40, 41, 67-89, 126, 139
Research and Technological Development (RTD) 50
RTD (see Research and Technological Development)
Research

institutes 37, 54, 152
parks 38
Research Triangle 21, 38, 42, 153, 154, 160-167
Reynolds, P. 7, 43, 97, 112, 116, 144, 145, 150, 151, 172, 173, 182
Rhein-Ruhr region 39
Rieter, H. 8, 19, 166, 172
Romer, P. 9, 19
Rosenberg, N. 72, 88
Ruhr area 149, 153
Russia 111, 112, 176, 177
San Francisco 13, 18
SBIR (see Small Business Innovation Research)
Schipanski, D. 6, 47
Schmolz, M. 8, 19, 166, 172
Schumpeter, J.A. 8, 9, 19, 22, 43
Scientific community 49, 50, 55
Scott, J.T. 38, 42, 94-99, 105, 106, 111, 112
Sengenberger, W. 25, 42
Servan-Schreiber, J.J. 31, 43
Shivakumar, S.J. 68, 85, 89
Silicon Valley 15, 16, 21, 43, 63
Simon, C. 4, 19
Singapore 177, 183
Slovenia 177
Small and medium-sized enterprises (SMEs) 10, 16, 24, 25, 26, 31, 32, 35, 36, 38, 41, 100, 111, 113, 145, 147, 148, 149, 170, 171, 186
Small business 24, 26, 31, 35, 36, 41, 60, 61, 68, 78, 87, 175
Small Business Act 31
Small Business Administration 31, 69, 86, 88, 89, 152
Small Business Innovation Research (SBIR) 34-37, 41-43, 68, 77-89, 87, 160, 161

Small Business Research and Development Enhancement Act 35
Smith, A. 7, 86, 88
Social Market Economy 7, 18, 171
Solingen 153, 154, 167
South Africa 178
South Korea 177, 178
Space technology 6, 52
Stanford 60, 81, 86, 89
Start-ups 5, 10, 33, 34, 37, 38, 49, 113-115, 118, 125-132, 135, 137-142, 145-155, 157, 160-163, 165-168, 174, 185
companies 61
Sternberg, R. 6, 37, 43, 113-115, 122, 124-131, 140, 141-145, 149, 150-153, 170, 172, 173
Stevenson-Wydler Act 22, 32, 42, 61, 62
Storey, D.J. 4, 34, 36, 43, 115, 144, 145, 151, 172
Strategic management 3, 21, 29, 30, 39, 145
Strauss, I. 12, 13
Stuttgart 18, 19, 28, 29, 39, 119, 122, 125, 127, 149
Sweden 30, 36, 40, 72, 88, 94, 173, 176
T index 176, 178
T indices 182
T rate 179, 181
Taiwan 177
Technology
advancement 8, 12
advances 14
change 25, 154
development 37, 53, 69, 70, 75, 77, 78, 86
immigration 64
innovation 16
industries 29, 64
Texas 16, 37

Thailand 176, 177
The T Index 176
Theorie der wirtschaftlichen Entwicklungen (Theory of Economic Development) 22
Thuenen, J. H. von 21
Thurik, R. 3, 4, 18, 19, 26, 30, 31, 40, 41, 115, 143, 144
Thuringia 5, 47, 48, 49, 127, 149, 170
Tocqueville, A. de 15, 19
Total Entrepreneurial Activity rate 117, 121
Transatlantic conference 5
Transformation process 53, 54, 106
Turner, J. 6, 41, 57, 87, 89
U.K. 176, 178, 185, 186
University of Michigan's Institute of Survey Research 183
Upper Bavaria 115, 153, 161, 163
Vernon, J.E. 26, 86
Weber, M. 11, 12, 19
Weiss, L.W. 24, 43
Welter, F. 6, 94, 95, 96, 100-108, 112, 113, 144
Wennekers, S. 4, 19, 40, 41, 115, 144
Wessner, C.W. 6, 35, 42, 43, 67, 68, 85, 86-89
Western Saxony 119, 122, 125, 129, 130
Williamson, O.E. 30, 43, 98, 99, 113
Wisconsin 60, 185
Wolfsburg 30
Wuppertal 127, 149, 153, 154
61, 62

Printed in the United States
82636LV00002B/269/A